membership essentials

Recruitment, Retention, Roles, Responsibilities, and Resources

DEVELOPED BY THE
**ASAE & THE CENTER
MEMBERSHIP SECTION COUNCIL**

EDITED BY
SHERI JACOBS, CAE
AND **CARYLANN ASSANTE**

asae & the center™
for association leadership

WASHINGTON, DC

The authors have worked to ensure that all information in this book is accurate as of the time of publication and consistent with standards of good practice in the general management community. As research and practice advance, however, standards may change. For this reason, it is recommended that readers evaluate the applicability of any recommendation in light of particular situations and changing standards.

ASAE & The Center for Association Leadership
1575 I Street, NW
Washington, DC 20005-1103
Phone: (202) 626-2723; (888) 950-2723 outside the metropolitan Washington, DC area
Fax: (202) 408-9633
Email: books@asaecenter.org
We connect great ideas and great people to inspire leadership and achievement in the association community.

Keith C. Skillman, CAE, Vice President of Publications, ASAE & The Center for Association
    Leadership
Baron Williams, Director of Book Publishing, ASAE & The Center for Association
    Leadership

Cover design by Beth Lower
Interior design by Cimarron Design

This book is available at a special discount when ordered in bulk quantities. For information, contact the ASAE & The Center for Association Leadership Member Service Center at (202) 371-0940.

A complete catalog of titles is available on the ASAE & The Center for Association Leadership web site at www.asaecenter.org/bookstore.

Contents

Preface v
Sheri Jacobs, CAE, and Carylann Assante

1 The Context for Our Work 1
Gregory J. Fine, CAE, Lori A. Ropa, CAE, and Jay Younger

2 What is Your Value Proposition? 7
Jay L. Karen, CAE, and Ben Martin, CAE

3 An Overview of Membership Research 25
Dean A. West

4 Organizing the Membership Function to Deliver Value 45
Sheri Jacobs, CAE, and Sara Miller, CAE

5 The Membership Department Working With Others to Accomplish Goals 65
Sheri Jacobs, CAE, and Sara Miller, CAE

6 Membership Categories and Dues Structures 73
Michael Connor and Jay Younger

7 Dues Structures, Increases, and Restructuring 83
Michael Connor and Jay Younger

8 Association Database Management Systems 97
Wes Trochlil, Sherry Budziak, and Don Dea

9 Collecting, Managing, and Using Membership Data 107
Don Dea and Carolyn Hook

10 A CEO's Perspective on Membership Data and Its Use 121
Tom Hood, CPA

11 Web Sites and Membership Directories: Their Key Roles in Membership 131
Don Dea

12 New Member Contact, Renewal, and Communication Processes 139
Katie Jones and Don Dea

13 Financial Management and Budgeting 145
Susanne Connors Bowman and Lori Gusdorf, CAE

14 Financial Metrics for the Membership Professional 157
Susanne Connors Bowman and Lori Gusdorf, CAE

15 Recruitment Strategies 171
Tony Rossell

16 Retention 181
Tony Rossell

17 Membership Communications 189
Christy Jones, CAE

18 Engagement 205
Stuart K. Meyer

19 Member-to-Member Recruitment 231
Lori A. Ropa, CAE

CD-ROM Contents 239

Index 241

Preface

By Sheri Jacobs, CAE, and Carylann Assante

MORE THAN ONE MILLION associations are active in the United States alone, and while those organizations vary significantly in size, member demographics, and resources, they share a common mission: To advance their respective industries and enable their members to succeed by providing the best possible benefits and services. On a fundamental level, associations would not exist without the members they serve.

Like your peers in the association community, you understand that members are critical to your organization's mission and that membership must be an organizational priority if it is to succeed in fulfilling its vision and purpose. Yet, if you are like most membership professionals, you did not follow a career path that began with a goal to become a "membership professional." In fact, if you ask 10 colleagues to describe their background including their academic and professional experience, you will most likely receive 10 different answers. As a result, many association professionals, regardless of their position or title, learn the essentials of membership "on the job" or through interactions with their peers.

This realization became crystal clear a few years ago when the ASAE & The Center for Association Leadership Membership Section Council reviewed the existing print materials and educational offerings for membership professionals at all levels. Although various elements of a membership professional's job are addressed in other publications and programs, the opportunity to bolster the body of knowledge to successfully manage and maintain a membership department was apparent.

This handbook, written by membership professionals and other experts, is for membership professionals and anyone else responsible for the membership function in a membership organization. This publication covers the essential elements and responsibilities of the membership department, or function, in a membership organization. Our goal was to create a reference to be used by early careerists and seasoned professionals alike. From internal operations to external communication, this book offers practical guidance, tips, and examples on topics such as recruitment, retention, dues (categories and structures), research, databases, budgeting, and marketing.

This book is a compilation of the expertise of numerous authors and editors. We would like to thank each one for his or her commitment, patience, and hard work in helping turn our goal into a reality. In addition, special thanks and appreciation goes to Sara Miller, CAE, director of membership and customer services at the Humane Society of the United States, who generously guided the process at the beginning.

Sheri Jacobs, CAE, is managing director of McKinley Marketing, Inc., with offices in Washington, DC, and Chicago. In 2006-2007 she chaired the ASAE & The Center for Association Leadership Membership Section Council. Email: sjacobs@mckinleymarketing.com.

Carylann Assante is vice president, development, ASAE & The Center for Association Leadership, and previously served the organizations as senior director, membership. Email: cassante@asaecenter.org.

The Context for Our Work

By Gregory J. Fine, CAE, Lori A. Ropa, CAE, and Jay Younger

IN THIS CHAPTER:

- Core purpose, motivation, and the relevant member offer
- Association type, scope, and tax status
- The evolving role of the membership professional
- Change in value and face of membership organizations today

T HE MORE THINGS REMAIN the same, the more they change. That flip of phrase really fits membership organizations, whose origins date to at least the medieval merchant and craft guilds. Today, still, associations and other membership organizations reflect an unchanged, fundamental reason for being that was present even in the 13th century: to serve as a gathering place for people with common interests and goals. Seemingly everything else—the environment in which members operate, the technologies at their and our disposal, constituents' expectations—shifts or changes altogether and with sometimes alarming frequency.

Tuning into this dichotomy of constant and change is of vital importance to professionals such as yourself, who are on the front lines of extending value propositions and offerings to prospective and existing members whom you'd like to keep as members. You might think of your organization's fundamental reason for being as a grounding point, or touchstone, for what your organization is about and your constituents' ever-evolving reality as impetus for continually shaping, communicating, and executing an offer of value and benefits that is not only true to purpose but relevant today.

Equally important, we membership professionals must understand some additional context to be effective: Who are our members? What is our organization type? What is our geographic scope? What is our tax status and its implications? Why does all this matter? We will get to all of that in the balance of this chapter.

Core Purpose and Motivation

Understanding an organization's core purpose and the primary motivations of its members and prospects is at the heart of crafting and conveying a membership appeal. Here is an example of a membership organization that remains both true to its core purpose as envisioned more than 200 years ago and every bit as vital today. According to a history published on the web site www.nycp.org, the New York Chamber of Commerce, one of the oldest extant associations in the United States, formed in 1768 to "encourage business and industry, develop dependable commercial arbitration procedures, defend sound money, and maintain standards of fair trade like common units of measurement." With some of the most prominent businesspeople of the day as members, the chamber was instrumental in shaping New York City, supporting efforts such as building the Erie Canal in 1820, laying the Transatlantic Cable in 1866, and consolidating the city in 1898 (From "City Lore: The Art of the Deal Guilded Age Style," *The New York Times*, December 26, 2004).

From its formation through today, the chamber's primary purpose has not changed. In 1979 David Rockefeller, whose family has a several-generation history with the organization, formed the New York City Partnership and affiliated the chambers of commerce with it. The partnership, which expanded the chamber's scope but never abandoned its original purpose, has enabled business and civic groups to work more closely with the government to resolve economic and social problems. In 2002, the group became known as the Partnership for New York City, and although "chamber" no longer appears in the name, its members continue to do important work set out in its original charter.

Likewise, your organization's core purpose has probably remained constant, or relatively so, even as you have adapted benefits and services to fit the specific needs of contemporary members. Associations, generally, contribute to society in several key ways, by

- **Marshalling a collective voice.** Association members use their collective strength to change and improve workplace practices, public policies, and governmental positions.

- **Creating standards of quality.** Many associations are the standard-bearers for quality work in a specific industry or profession. Members wish to play a part in the development of these standards to ensure that they are effective and

Organization Type

Most nonprofit organizations exist to support their members, advance a cause, or both. The distinguishing characteristic of membership organizations, of course, is that they have members. While there certainly are other types of member-focused organizations (such as unions), the four primary types of member-focused associations are

- **Professional (also known as societies or individual membership organizations).** Composed of individual members, these associations draw their membership from specific professional disciplines. They can be extremely broad, as is the American Medical Association, or narrowly focused to a specialty within a larger profession. Generally, professional associations seek to advance the entire profession and tend to focus on education, training, certification, and other activities designed to increase the ability of the members to practice their craft.

- **Trade.** Composed of company members, these associations draw members from a specific industry and exist to advance the industry, not the professionals in it. Examples of trade associations are the American Petroleum Institute, Aerospace Industries Association, and National Homebuilders Association. Generally, these associations focus on big issues affecting their member companies and often devote significant resources to lobbying and advocacy.

- **Combination.** A combination association has both individual and company members and often focuses on both advancing a profession and an industry at the same time. An example of a combination association is InfoComm International, the international trade association of the professional audiovisual and information communications industries. The organization has both company members and individual members. Like a professional association, combination associations provide professional training and certification for individuals, and like a trade, they advance the industry through trade shows, advocacy, and research on industry trends.

- **Federation.** A federation is an association composed of other associations. Often, a federation is created by a group of professional associations to advocate or advance a specific cause or industry related to their respective members. The American Association of Engineering Societies is a good example. AAES was created to be the advocate of the engineering profession's common viewpoints on issues important to the nation and the profession, according to its web site, www.aaes.org. By creating a separate, independent organization, AAES members can pool their resources and increase their impact. Another benefit of organizing as a federation is that the federation will often have a tax status that allows active lobbying, when the member associations do not.

A major portion of the nonprofit sector is composed of another type of organization, and that's the caused-based organization, often identified as a philanthropic group or foundation. These types of organizations typically do not have members but do have donors and constituencies that they serve. These organizations' primary mission is to raise and distribute money for a specific cause. Prominent examples are the American Heart Association, American Diabetes Association, American Lung Association, and the American Association of University Women (AAUW) Educational Foundation. All of these groups solicit donations and then fund various activities in support of their respective missions.

Many professional and trade associations create related foundations of their own. These organizations are separate but related nonprofit organizations that hold their own tax-exempt status. There are two primary reasons for doing this. The first is to collect and pool contributions from an association's members in support of a cause. The second is to provide an avenue for the organization to receive tax-deductible charitable contributions. Most often the funds raised by these foundations are used to conduct research, provide educational scholarships, and perform other altruistic activities that complement and enhance the underlying mission of the "parent" organization.

reasonable, and often to preempt regulatory involvement. High standards of quality protect the public from harm.

- **Facilitating peer-to-peer connections.** Association members work with one another to solve shared problems, innovate, and create a social network of empathetic colleagues. These connections are invaluable to members.

- **Providing education and professional growth.** Not unlike the early associations that provided apprenticeships, today's associations provide countless educational programs each year that enable members to be more effective in their jobs and enhance professional growth.

Very likely, one or more of those areas of contribution underlie your organization's benefits, products, and services, and forms the fundamental draw your members and prospects feel to affiliate with the group. That brings us to motivation. Members' basic reason for belonging to associations and other membership organizations remains the same today as ever. Our need to connect with others with whom we can identify is built into our psyches, and the desire to exchange knowledge and collectively achieve shared goals is as old as, well, the guilds.

Understanding what actually triggers a person's decision to join and participate is a good deal more complex, influenced as it is by a host of demographic, attitudinal and other factors. We know from research by ASAE & The Center for Association Leadership, for example, that the decision is not strictly a cost-benefit analysis but takes into account an assessment of the value generated among the community of interests in which the individual contemplates membership. In other words, concern for the "good of the order" enters into the equation. The research, published by ASAE & The Center in August 2007 and based on 16,944 responses from members and nonmembers, really is essential reading and is an invaluable resource for anyone involved in crafting membership strategy and appeal. The book, *The*

Geographic Scope

Regardless of their membership base, most associations in the United States have a defined geographical area of focus: local, state, regional, national, or international.

- A local organization limits its membership and activities to a specific local area, usually a town or county. City Realtor associations and chambers of commerce are good examples. Often a local organization may be part of or affiliated with a larger organization.

- A state association draws members from a specific state and usually limits its activities to that state. The Florida Automobile Dealers Association and Montana Bar Association are two examples. Like a local organization, a state association is often part of or affiliated with a larger organization. A state association can be quite large, as in the case of the California Dental Association,

which has more than 20,000 members and a staff and budget larger than many national associations.

- A regional association comprises more than one state. The Western Governors Association is an example. A regional association is often formed to deal with issues that affect several states but not the entire nation.

- A national association draws its membership from the entire nation and usually focuses on issues affecting the entire nation. Many national associations use chapters or components to serve the state and local level or they affiliate with a state or local partner.

- An international association's members come from multiple countries, and the organization's focus and intent extends across borders.

Tax-Exempt Status

Another lens through which we can view associations is tax status. Most associations are tax exempt under a section of the Internal Revenue Code. While there are many others, the two primary tax-exemptions for associations are 501(c)(3) and 501(c)(6). Though many issues an association faces are guided and determined by the organization's tax status, the one most relevant to membership professionals is the deductibility of membership dues.

Most trade and professional associations fall under the 501(c)(6) section of the tax code. Membership dues paid to a (c)(6) are not charitable and may only be claimed as a business expense by the member. Further, 501(c)(6) associations must include language on dues invoices advising members that dues are not a charitable contribution. The association may add language advising members of the business expense deduction but certainly should also include a statement that emphasizes that members should seek a tax professional's advice in determining whether they may deduct dues as a business expense.

Donations to philanthropic organizations or foundations exempt under Section 501(c)(3) may be claimed as tax deductible as a charitable contribution. However, dues paid to a professional association that is tax exempt under Section 501(c)(3) are not considered charitable contributions and therefore are not deductible as such.

Again, though, membership dues are generally deductible as a business expense.

The impact of lobbying on dues deductibility

Strict rules govern what a 501(c)(3) can do in the lobbying arena. If you are working for a (c)(3), you should be aware of these rules. To learn more, consult the *Association Law Handbook, Fourth Edition; Professional Practices in Association Management, Second Edition;* and *Principles of Association Management,* all published by ASAE & The Center for Association Leadership and available via www.asaecenter.org/bookstore.

Generally, 501(c)(6) organizations may lobby. However, you must keep track of the percentage of dues revenue that supports these activities. This percentage becomes non-deductible as a business expense for the members and must be reported to the membership.

As a membership professional, in the most general of terms, remember that 501(c)(3) means no lobbying and a 501(c)(6) means lobbying impacts dues deductibility. And by all means, consult the *Association Law Handbook* and the other resources mentioned earlier for additional information about the impact of tax status on an organization's activities and vice versa, as well as for information on other legal issues affecting membership organizations.

Decision to Join: How Individuals Determine Value and Why They Choose to Belong, available via www.asaecenter.org/bookstore, creates a great deal more understanding around the motivation to affiliate.

The More They Change

Were they here today, the merchants and craftspeople who inhabited the guilds of medieval times, and the founders of organizations like the New York Chamber of Commerce, could no doubt relate to the core purposes of contemporary membership organizations and the basic motivation of the people and organizations that populate them. Perhaps little else would look the same. The availability of information in an instant, global competitive pressures, and changes in the workforce are but some of the factors that color an evolving environment—and the member's reality.

Likewise, that member's reality colors the challenging work of all professionals charged with the membership function of our organizations—in fact creating an opportunity to appeal with an offering that helps our constituents sort through the intensity of their profession or trade and a proposition of value that forever bonds them to the organization and its mission. It's hardly an easy task, however. Gone are the days of association membership as a matter of only duty, pride, and loyalty. Today's members want to know why they should join, and they expect both a return on investment and a positive impact on the "good of the order."

Perhaps 25 years ago typical membership departments printed membership applications, sent them to people who inquired about joining, and managed the renewal notice mailings. Today's membership professionals must focus on developing recruitment and renewal strategies and tactics. They must be able to identify the value of membership and be able to communicate it well. They must learn to position their organization's appeal against that of competitors including other associations, for-profit companies, and the web. They must put together convincing arguments for the resources it takes to achieve their goals—and show a return on that investment. Membership professionals must also be able to work with their board members, other volunteers, and staff to continually improve the products and services offered by their association. And they need to avail themselves of every tool in their toolbox to serve constituents in the manner they demand.

The power of associations relies on members. To get and keep members, associations need to assure constituents that they will receive value for their membership dollar. If associations cannot meet those needs, other organizations can and will, and members will not hesitate to go where their needs will be met. As a professional charged with the membership function, you are at the front line of translating the dichotomy of rock-solid purpose and swirling environment into offerings that fit their picture of today.

Gregory J. Fine, CAE, is director, communications and marketing, at the Association Forum of Chicagoland, and the 2007–2008 chair of ASAE & The Center's Membership Section Council. Email: fine@associationforum.org.

Lori A. Ropa, CAE, is director, affiliate operations at the National Foundation of Dentistry for the Handicapped, Denver. Among her many voluntary positions, she has served as the lead subject matter expert for ASAE & The Center's Membership Boot Camp Course. Email: lropa@nfdh.org.

Jay Younger is managing partner and chief consultant at McKinley Marketing, Inc., with offices in Washington, DC, and Chicago. An ASAE & The Center Fellow, he also chaired the organization's Membership Section Council in 2004–2005. Email: jyounger@ mckinleymarketing.com.

What is Your Value Proposition?

By Jay L. Karen, CAE, and Ben Martin, CAE

2

IN THIS CHAPTER:
- Determining what you want to be to members
- Understanding and articulating the value proposition
- Quantifying value and members' ROI
- Defining mission-critical benefits
- Auditing your programs and identifying gaps
- Creating and segmenting new benefits
- Fostering communities with technology
- Evaluating affinity programs

WHO ARE YOU TO your members and who do you want to be? This vital assessment should drive your association's benefit and services packages. Determining who you are to your members is among the most important things you can do as a membership professional, whether you're a staff of one or direct 20 others. In fact, it's probably even more important that your board and staff determine what the association is to the entire membership and other audiences as part of strategic planning and mission building.

Your decisions about what benefits and services to offer will come from not only your ability to understand your members but also from a keen awareness of what you are capable of doing and what you should or should not be doing. If you look at any association's membership offering, you will likely see some critically important programs and services, and you may also see some fluff programs and services—programs that sound good and look good and that someone may have thought would be good for members and the association but that don't address critical needs of your members and may have little to do with the mission of your organization.

Because the success of an association depends on membership performance, the entire staff is affected by the membership function. Similarly, membership professionals depend closely on other departments that may produce and administer programs that are essential elements of the membership package. You cannot work in a vacuum. In addition to other staff, you will work with members at large, the board, and the executive team to evaluate and communicate your association's value proposition to potential members.

Determining What You Want to Be to Members

Think about your membership offering—the complete package of benefits and services available to your members—and now a look at the figure below. In which quadrant do you think your membership offering and your membership support is or should be focused?

Figure 1. What is Your Association Trying to Be?

Some things to all people	**All things to all people**
Some things to some people	**All things to some people**

In association management, there is a natural tendency to try to be all things to all people. After all, whenever a member calls or emails with a problem, you want to do whatever you can to solve it—even if you can't! That natural desire to help your members is good. It's what drives you to provide great customer service and develop relevant, useful benefits. But that desire to help your members solve any of their problems can get you into some troubling circumstances as well. For instance, you may have an influential, involved member who has a pet project or issue that is not related to your association's mission and strategic plan. You may have to tactfully turn down the member's efforts to include his issue in the association's agenda.

Consider the implications of aligning your membership efforts with each of the four quadrants in the grid. You cannot be all things to all people, so you shouldn't try, but even if you try to be some things to all people, you're not going to succeed. You represent a particular group of people—your membership. But can you really be all things to them? You want to project yourself as a solutions provider, but you should not market your membership services as covering all of their possible needs. The only reasonable strategy is to provide membership benefits and services limited in scope and aimed at your defined constituencies—you can be some things to some people.

You might become enamored with some out-of-the-box program ideas for your members or new nondues revenue ideas, but if they don't pass the litmus test of meeting the critical needs of your members within the context of your association's vision or strategic plan, you should think hard about moving in that direction. And limited in scope doesn't necessarily mean offering few things to your members. It just means identifying what you should do for your members and doing only those things—at least until the day the association widens its scope or changes its mission.

Why is this exercise important? Because you need to be clear about what your role is with members, ensuring that, as a membership department/function, you know what the association realistically offers and to whom, so that the membership messaging can be on target. You need to be acutely aware of your association's mission, strategic plan, objectives, or any other formal documentation that defines who the association is or who the association wants to be to your membership.

Later in this chapter, you'll see Figure 2, an illustration that should help you think about how mission-critical some of your programs might be.

Understanding and Articulating the Value Proposition

Is your association's membership directory a benefit of membership? Are networking events a benefit of membership? What about a salary survey? The answer to all three questions is no. All three are features. When describing the benefits of membership, it's crucial to put yourself into the shoes of the prospect or member. When communicating about any program, the benefit is more powerful than the feature because it defines the actual value or outcome for the user or participant.

Table 1. Comparing Features and Benefits

Feature	Benefit
Membership Directory	Locate peers in your profession with whom you can solve problems, discuss issues, or capitalize on opportunities.
Networking Events	Develop and strengthen contacts to help you advance in your career. Enjoy the fellowship of your peers.
Salary Survey	Make informed compensation decisions and requests based on the latest research. Hire better employees by remaining competitive in the marketplace.

It's essential to be able to describe the benefits, rather than the features, of membership if you're responsible for talking or writing about the value of membership. Teasing the benefit out of a feature can be a difficult task for anyone who doesn't regularly use the association's programs, including the association's own membership professionals. For this reason, members are often the best resource for uncovering the benefit wrapped up in a feature. Ask several members what value they get from your association's magazine, educational events, or research. Their answers will help you define the benefits.

Sometimes, benefits are more difficult for members to understand than features. As you can see in Table 1 above, the definitions of benefits are often longer and more complex statements than a feature's description. You must strike an appropriate balance between brevity, clarity, and articulating the value. Your audience's

Benefit Semantics

Throughout this book, and even within this chapter, you'll see the term benefit used to describe a feature of membership. Don't get hung up on it. In a marketing context, benefit has a stricter definition than it does in a membership context.

Marketing Definition for Benefit	Membership Definition for Benefit
The value derived by the user, participant, or buyer.	Any product, program, discount, or service to which a member is entitled upon joining the association.

demographic characteristics will be a significant factor in how you communicate benefits. (See Chapter 17: Membership Communications.)

New Definitions of Value. Traditionally, associations' reasons for being have been to advance a mission such as enhancing the success of the trade, profession, industry, or cause that they represent. Years ago, belonging to one's professional or trade association was routine and membership dues were often paid without questioning the benefit. Association membership was viewed as a way to support the profession or defend the industry and that was seen as valuable enough to justify a lifetime of membership.

Over the years, however, consumers have come to develop higher expectations of membership organizations. For most members, it is no longer acceptable for the association to simply advance a cause or defeat forces that negatively affect its constituents. Today's members expect a quantifiable return on their investment of dues dollars in addition to the association's delivering on the mission. For every dollar they spend in dues, they demand at least a dollar's worth of value in return. Membership dues have become a type of investment for today's consumers, and the investments that yield lower returns are scrutinized or withdrawn entirely.

To respond to this trend, associations must continually demonstrate the value they return to their members and communicate that value consistently.

Your Association's Value Proposition. Every membership professional must understand the association's value proposition and know how to communicate about it effectively. The association's value proposition is composed of all the discrete programs that are given to members when they join.

Associations exist primarily to advance a mission or tax-exempt purpose. However, associations are permitted to offer programs that don't necessarily advance their purpose, and many associations do. Whether a program helps advance the association's mission or not, it also usually provides a tangible or intangible benefit to the member. From a value standpoint, all association programs can be processed through these two filters:

• Does the program provide a tangible or intangible benefit to the member?
• Is the program related to the mission of the organization, or unrelated to the mission of the organization?

Table 2 shows how common association activities are normally perceived by members.

Figure 2. Programs in Relation to Mission

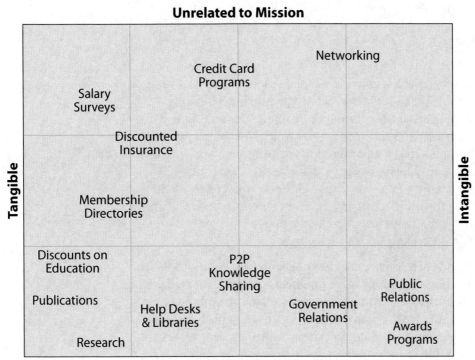

Programs closer to the left are more tangible than those farther to the right. They are easier to explain and comprehend. They're also usually things that members have to read, attend, purchase, or participate in to realize the benefit. Members and prospects are likely to be more compelled by the benefits conveyed through programs grouped towards the bottom.

Programs closer to the bottom are more central to the association's tax-exempt purpose, or mission. Successfully delivering on tangible programs on the left side of the chart usually means the association is fulfilling its mission. Keep in mind that members usually consider the association's successful pursuit of its purpose to be a benefit as well.

The membership professional's job is easier when most benefits cluster near the bottom of this graph. The benefits of membership are straightforward and easily grasped. From a CEO's standpoint, the more benefits the members think belong in the bottom left quadrant, the better. This is the benefits sweet spot: The association is delivering on its tax-exempt purpose, and members are getting direct and real benefits that are easily understood. But don't assume that programs in the upper right of this chart are less valuable than those closer to the left or bottom. The value of those programs in the upper right may be far higher than the others, but they are simply unrelated to the purpose and require more explanation.

Quantifying Value and Members' ROI

Discounts, products, and services that are included in the cost of membership are easily communicated to prospects and members alike in terms of dollars and cents. When describing the value of tangible benefits, you might say: The value of membership really adds up. From a $200 discount on our annual convention, to a free subscription to our monthly magazine ($45 value), to your complimentary listing in our industry guide (normally $149), it's easy to see how your $299 dues investment pays for itself.

Intangible benefits aren't necessarily less convincing than tangible benefits. But describing them does require more thought and creativity, and understanding them takes more effort on the part of the member or prospect. Consider how you might describe the value delivered to your members by your association's role in helping convince a senator to pass legislation that protects your members' interests. If possible, try to assign a dollar value to intangible benefits. In the case of your association's role in getting the senator to pass legislation, you could quantify the benefit by determining how much a member might have spent independently to lobby for the bill. Or if the bill ultimately resulted in a savings of time or resources for your members, estimate the dollar value of the savings.

How do you measure the value of a contact made at a networking reception? What value do your members receive when your association helps portray their trade or profession in a favorable light though the media or trade press? Can you assign a dollar figure to increased knowledge that your members gain through all association programs? These are more difficult, but don't shy away from talking about them. Underestimating the ability of your members and prospects to comprehend

---

Examples for Computing and Communicating ROI

- Number of discounted attendees at trade show 12 $\times$ $99 = $1188
- Number of discounted seminar attendees 5 $\times$ $125 = $625
- Number of included publications shipped to employees 25 $\times$ $57 (3 @ $19 each) = $1425
- Number of included magazine subscriptions 25 $\times$ $49 = $1225
- Number of help desk calls fielded from member 3 $\times$ $29 = $87
- Discount on benchmarking study purchase 1 $\times$ $99 = $99
- Discount on general liability insurance through affinity partner = $171
- Defeated S.B. 223, which would have required HQ and each branch to pay a new tax of $250 per location. 3 locations $\times$ $250 = $750
- Rebate from market share reporting program = $544
- Negotiated agreement with U.S. Surface Transportation Board to avert new regulations on shipping widgets across state lines. Annual cost passed along to distributors from new regulations could have cost an estimated $1900.
- What your company might have spent independently to lobby these issues = $7,000
- Public relations campaign to raise awareness of the value of widget distributors. New survey shows that 18 percent of widget end users have decided to start buying through distributors and have stopped buying direct as a result of this campaign. The value to your firm = (This figure can depend on the dollar amount calculated for media exposure.)

intangible benefits can weaken your value proposition. We all understand that everything in life can't be counted in dollars and cents, and you can play up the fact that some things your association does are priceless. When describing the value of intangible benefits, you might say: Through our public service campaigns and the 40 million media impressions that followed, we helped increase public awareness of the important role you play in the business world. How can you put a dollar figure on that?

See Chapter 15: Recruitment Strategies and Chapter 16: Retention for more information on communicating about the benefits of membership to prospects and members. Effectively communicating intangible benefits is a mix of science and art. Read *Selling the Invisible* by Harry Beckwith[1] for more information on this topic.

Defining Mission-Critical Benefits

How do you determine if a program or benefit is mission-critical and if you should risk adding it to your package of membership services? Many times you will find yourself putting on your member's hat to determine if something might be useful, but that kind of decision-making process is obviously limited. Have you consulted your association's strategic plan or stated objectives? That is your litmus test. If you can pinpoint which part of your strategic plan justifies the benefit you are considering for you membership, you are halfway toward acceptance by your board and/or justification for continuing an existing program.

For example, your strategic plan may say, "To offer the most relevant educational opportunities for our members." Your idea might be to begin a series of web seminars that also offer continuing education points for your members. You'll need to work with your colleagues in charge of education and IT to develop a proposal, but it's easy to see how this new offering could help advance the strategic plan; it's a new way to deliver education to your membership.

But suppose a former board member approaches you about promoting a credit card service. Your organization aims to advance the career of a particular profession and this credit card promotion is not mission-critical. You need to decide if your members will find this program relevant and vital to the advancement of their careers. As a membership professional, you should focus on only those programs that keep your association relevant in the minds of your members.

Auditing Your Programs and Identifying Gaps

Too seldom do we make a close examination of our total membership offerings. It's likely you have some programs that should have been eliminated years ago and others that should never have gotten off the ground. And, of course, you have some relevant offerings or you wouldn't have members.

Decisions about adding or deleting programs don't have to fall on your shoulders alone. Many of the programs that comprise the organization's membership offering are not administered by the membership function. Your association may have staff working on meetings and trade show planning, publications, public relations, and the web. All these individuals will have insights into what is working well and what is waning in popularity. You might have an advisory committee of members that can be tapped to give you input. Surveying your members is another reliable way to determine what a sampling of your members think about your programs and services. When consulting with members or a special committee that advises your staff about membership programs, be sure to craft questions in the right way. If you simply ask, "Would you like for us to offer $\times$ program?" the response will more than likely be yes. After all, sometimes your own members want you to be all things to all people. If you ask it in the following way, you might get a different and more valid response: "Do you think the X program would help advance your career and support your profession?"

Another surefire way to determine what should go to the chopping block is to examine member participation. Obviously, if a high percentage of your members participate in a particular program or buy certain products you sell on an ongoing basis, you probably should keep those programs and products. The operative words in the previous sentence are "on an ongoing basis." You might be able to run a report from your database and show 2,000 members purchased a particular book, but what if 75 percent of those transactions occurred between 2000 and 2004? That kind of discovery is found by close examination. It may be time to shelve that book or come out with a newer edition. If you've been marketing a program or book for two years and have experienced minimal response, you might want to consider eliminating the item.

Ask your members regularly if they find your inventory of programs relevant. Many associations send surveys with membership invoices or renewal kits. In such surveys, you should ask members how useful they find each of your programs. Don't just ask them what they would like for the association to provide, but seek their feedback on your existing portfolio. When developing or auditing your membership benefits portfolio, you also should ask which benefits target your entire membership and which ones appeal to certain segments of your members.

To create an asset audit, list every program or service offered by your organization. Under each topic, identify the membership categories that benefit from each item. This exercise will give you a better understanding of your existing strengths and weaknesses. For example, when the Association Forum of Chicagoland completed this activity, it was discovered that the majority of the organization's products, programs and services were geared toward mid-level and senior-level association professionals. (See Table 2, Asset Audit.) Therefore, if the Forum wanted to expand its reach to entry-level executives, it would need to reconsider its current member benefits.

To identify shortcomings or gaps, put your strategic plan or association objectives next to your list of benefits and services. Match each benefit or service with one of your association's objectives. Surely you will find that most have a perfect match. But you may discover two interesting things. First, you may find that some of your programs don't have a match with any particular association objective. Secondly, you may also find that some of your objectives don't have any corresponding benefits. Congratulations! You just completed a gap analysis.

When you've identified the fact that one or more strategic objectives have no corresponding program or service, then you have identified an opportunity. At some

Table 2. Asset Audit

Asset	CEO (old)	CEO (new)	Senior ME	Junior ME	Entry Level	SP	Distance
CEOnly web site		●					●
CEOnly e-newsletter		●					●
Online Career Center	●	●	●	●	●		●
Career counseling	●	●	●	●	●		
Forum web site	●	●	●	●	●	●	●
Listservers	●	●	●	●	●		●
Online salary calculator	●	●	●	●	●		●
This Week	●	●	●	●	●	●	●
Compensation Survey	●	●					
FORUM magazine print	●	●	●	●	●	●	●
FORUM articles online	●	●	●	●	●	●	●
Associationjobs.org	●	●	●				
Membership Directory print	●	●	●	●	●	●	●
Membership Directory online	●	●	●	●	●	●	●
Buyers Guide	●	●	●	●	●		●
Peer Consulting Directory	●	●	●	●	●		
Info Resource Center	●	●	●	●	●		
Thirty on Thursday						●	
CEO SIGs	●	●					
Governance SIG		●					
SIGs	●	●	●	●	●	●	
CAE Study Groups	●	●	●	●			
Cmt, volunteer opportunities	●	●	●	●			
Wine Tasting Event	●	●	●	●	●	●	
Scholarships				●	●		
Chef's table	●	●					
SP Resource Exchange						●	
Educational Programs							
CEOnly Event: 4 Breakfasts		●					
Masters Series		●	●				
Holiday Showcase	●	●	●	●	●	●	
Annual Meeting	●	●	●	●		●	
CEOnly session at Annual		●					
Association 101				●	●		
ENCORE	●	●	●	●			
Brown Bag Lunches			●	●			
E-Learning Boot Camp			●	●			
Audio-conferences			●	●			●
Speed Learning				●	●	●	

Source: Association Forum of Chicagoland

time, stakeholders developed the list of objectives with the hope the association would advance them. As a membership professional, you should consider it your duty to investigate how to introduce an initiative that advances the objective.

Creating and Segmenting New Benefits

Suppose that after using a gap analysis to figure out what new benefits would be useful and valued highly by your membership, validating your idea with member research, and consulting with other staff who may be involved in producing or administering the new program, you decide a new program or service would be mission-critical and fill a need. The first question you will likely be asked is, "What's the budget for this project?"

If the prospective benefit is a book, a new research product, a web seminar or even an attempt to influence public policy important to your members—whatever it might be—you need to work with your staff colleagues or appropriate outsourcers to complete a cost-benefit analysis. What will the costs be to print and produce a book, conduct and report on research, or write curriculum for a course and develop a web page for it? How much staff time will be invested? Can you secure any sponsors for the project? What will it cost to market? And what will your return be? How many copies do you expect to sell or how many participants will sign up at what rate?

If you cannot clearly estimate these numbers, you will have a difficult time getting the new benefit approved. Worse yet, if you happen to get it approved without a clear analysis of the resources needed and return expected, it means you have no solid plan and no expectations. You might spend a lot more than necessary in money and staff time, and with no goals for sales or participation, how could you claim success? You will be in good favor with financial and executive staff if your budget has more dollars coming in than going out for any project.

Of course, associations provide many benefits as a part of membership that do not yield their own revenue streams. An unsponsored listserver is a good example. Sometimes leadership will view such programs as loss leaders or elements that advance the strategic plan without the need to produce income. If there is no revenue stream associated with a new program and you plan to offer it as a basic membership benefit, the assumption is that the return will come in the form of strong retention or a spike in recruitment results.

Just as you have diverse segments within your membership, you should have benefits that address different needs. All associations have some degree of heterogeneity within the membership, even if it is only age or gender of members. Some of the

Golden Handcuffs

Golden handcuffs are benefits associations have developed that keep members "handcuffed" to the association indefinitely, perhaps because that benefit is not available from any other source and it is indispensable to the profession or trade. Examples include the multiple listing service (MLS) system provided by National Association of Realtors and sub-specialty certification of physicians by medical associations. Every membership director who doesn't have such benefit programs dreams of discovering or inventing them. But conversely, every membership director who has golden handcuffs dreads the day when the handcuffs may be cut loose.

The danger you run as custodian of a golden handcuff benefit is over-reliance on the benefit to meet all needs of your members. What if that benefit suddenly becomes obsolete or less valuable or the marketplace changes dramatically? The opening of the MLS to consumer use illustrates such a change. What if another association or private-sector entity finds a way to market the same or similar program? Just like any good investment portfolio, it's wise to have a diverse set of benefits and services. Many associations that have such indispensable benefits spend time trying to protect their status as "handcuff-providers." In some cases, one would not be allowed to practice a certain profession without membership and/or certification by an association.

diversity is formalized, as in categories of members, tenure or status, and sections of membership based on some delineating line, such as geography or profession. Chapter 7: Dues Structures, Increases, and Restructuring discusses some of the formalized categories of membership. Here are examples of segments of membership:

- The American Association of University Professors (AAUP) has a category of membership for full-time professors and another for part-time professors.

- The National Association of Newspapers has a membership category for school newspaper advisors and faculty and another for the newspapers themselves.

- The Professional Association of Innkeepers International has categories for active, aspiring, and retired innkeepers.

- The National Automobile Dealers Association has dues categories for U.S auto and light truck dealers, U.S heavy and medium duty truck dealers, and international dealers, including dues structures separating Canada and Mexico from other international members.

In addition to the formal segmentation, and perhaps just as important, are the informal groups and categories of members. These informal segments might be based on interest in certain aspects of your association or the content you are addressing. Today you will find greater success by getting inside the heads of your members and determining their needs, interests, and "pain points." This kind of categorization enables you to do niche marketing and create niche benefits. For example, an association of acting professionals might segment their members based on interest in performing on stage, television, or film. An association of healthcare professionals might determine which of their members are having serious problems with malpractice insurance coverage, track those members in the database, and create information, publications, or services specifically focused on issues regarding practice standards, problem situations, and sources for insurance.

In most cases, benefits and programs are designed with a wide net in mind. It makes sense because you'd expect to maximize the return on your investment of time and money in the benefit when more members participate. But programs designed for and marketed to all your members might have higher marketing and sales costs, and suppose you discover only 20 percent of your members actually participate. If you take the rifle approach instead, identifying a segment of your membership (either formal or informal) and developing a benefit or program just for that audience, you may be able to lower your marketing and sales costs yet realize the same or even better results than from the shotgun approach. In your membership of 2,000, you might have identified a subset of 800 having a particular interest. By marketing to 800, you could realize an increase in retention or involvement from the members in this niche market because you have demonstrated that you are keenly aware of their particular needs and have responded with something valuable. Any time you make an investment in a benefit or program, you are taking a calculated risk that your members will reciprocate by investing their time or money in the program, so the more personally relevant a program can be, the better your chances for returns.

A caveat about developing and marketing niche benefits for niche markets: A possible backlash of niche marketing is that some members who are not part of a particular group may think their association dollars are being spent on alternative issues and a minority of members. But in today's business environment, most people understand the concept and need of segmentation. Just be prepared for when that one member calls to complain.

Fostering Communities with Technology

Membership professionals want a thriving community of members, and who can blame them? An association's ability to sustain a community can be a significant competitive advantage. The fellowship of like-minded members can be viewed as a gold-plated handcuff. Members who understand the value of peer-to-peer learning will be more likely to continue their affiliation with an association.

Traditionally, association members are often grouped in two ways. When members are grouped geographically, the communities may be called chapters or regions. When members are grouped according to their interests, the communities are called interest groups, sections, or professional interest areas. Chapters and regions historically have had a distinct advantage over interest groups because they could more easily accrue a critical mass of members in a single geographic location where information and experience can be swapped. However, interest groups can offer a more specialized focus for members, and now many tools are available for these members to collaborate electronically. Both chapter components and electronic groups are valuable ways to build community and add to your value proposition.

The challenges of getting members to engage in peer-to-peer learning and connecting people with narrowly drawn commonalities is now far easier than it was even five years ago. Several technologies enable this phenomenon, and they can be broadly grouped into two categories: asynchronous and synchronous.

Asynchronous Technologies

Technologies in this category allow participants to engage in the community whenever they choose. In an always-on professional environment, this is an extremely convenient way for members to participate at their leisure.

- **Electronic mailing lists.** An electronic mailing list is an email distribution group (commonly referred to as a listserv, which is a copyrighted term, or listserver, the term ASAE & The Center use) that enables groups of members to have conversations via email. Most association electronic mailing lists are for members only. To enable community, many electronic mailing lists are set up as discussion groups, meaning anyone who has joined the group can contribute to it. Because email is so pervasive and because they are so simple to set up and administer, electronic mailing lists are popular to enable members to engage in online community. Electronic mailing lists are also among the most limiting means of cultivating online community. Today more sophisticated solutions, such as threaded bulletin boards, offer customizable social networking platforms and facilitate online community.

- **Bulletin boards.** Also known as online forums, bulletin boards allow participants to post new topics and responses to existing ones. The conversations are sorted in threads, with responses appearing under the entries to which they were made. Few associations use bulletin boards anymore, perhaps because most bulletin boards require participants to go to the site to view them and don't offer a push technology to let users know that new content has been posted. Bulletin boards can be placed behind a member firewall, but it is more common to find bulletin boards that allow anyone to read but only members to contribute.

- **Blogs.** Web logs, or blogs, are generally single-author online journals that enable contributors to easily post content to a web page. Some blogs are authored by multiple people, but usually fewer than 10. Each entry to the blog gets a dedicated page known as a *permalink*. The entries are also posted to the blog's main page and sorted by date, with the most recent posts at the top. Most allow users to comment on posts made to the blog. In addition to being viewable via a web page, many blogs are accessible via Really Simple Syndication (RSS), a type of Internet communication protocol similar in many ways to email. Blogs can be used to communicate informally about professional issues, such as standards and regulations, or about association activities, such as a convention or annual meeting. You could supplement your association's magazine with blogged content. Most blogs are publicly available but can be placed behind a members-only firewall.

- **Wikis.** Wikis are web pages that anyone can edit. A user can update data that has become stale, correct erroneous information, supplement a definition, add images, and otherwise enhance the entry or create a new entry. Wikis are ideal for documenting changes in standards, developing evolving definitions, and capturing user-generated data about a given topic. An encyclopedia containing more than 2 million English-language entries (as of November 2007) has been created at www.wikipedia.org. Wikis don't have to be developed or even maintained by associations. Many associations could simply use the existing platform at Wikipedia to document a body of knowledge for their field or industry. They create community by allowing members to opt into a collaborative effort to build and distribute knowledge. Research has shown the veracity of wikipedia articles comes close to that of Encyclopedia Britannica.[2] Still, associations should relentlessly monitor and verify entries on wikis that aim to catalog a field or industry's body of knowledge.

- **Podcasts.** Apple's iPod and similar personal media players that can play multimedia files are among the hottest electronic devices on the market. A podcast is a type of multimedia file that can be downloaded into personal media players. Often the downloading is done automatically by subscription. Podcasts are similar to radio and television shows and can be audio or video. Because people can subscribe to podcasts and blogs using the same RSS (really simple syndication) technology, many podcasts integrate a blog and invite feedback about the content through comments. This sort of interactivity is encouraged and cultivates community. One association is offering software tips by video podcast; another is offering continuing education; still another is offering updates from its annual leadership conference. Your association could produce a series of interviews with industry experts or a podcast of committee conference calls to keep the profession in the loop about emerging issues.

Synchronous Technologies

Technologies in this category allow members to communicate in real time. Although the number of participants you can expect to participate in any given program likely will be low relative to asynchronous programs, the members' experience can be much richer.

- **Chat rooms.** Chat rooms offer yet another way for members to interact, build community, and engage in discourse about issues that matter to them. Generally speaking, online chats should be organized for a given day, time, and topic. There are few things sadder than a persistent chat room with nobody in it and no unifying conversation.

- **Conference calls.** Associations commonly use conference calling services to conduct distance learning programs and idea-sharing sessions. Don't forget to record (and then podcast) these conversations for people who couldn't participate at the appointed hour.

Combined technologies

Some full-service online community portals available on the Internet strive to make many of the above technologies available through a single application suite. Offering libraries of user-uploaded documents, on demand chat rooms, message boards, community directories, and more, these portals provide a comprehensive array of services that enable members to learn from their peers and develop community virtually. Examples of full-service online community portals are Ning and Collective X.

Evaluating Affinity Programs

Tangible benefits are easily communicated by association staff and easily understood by current members and prospects alike. A temptation for many membership professionals is to build a large cache of tangible benefits by bringing on numerous affinity programs.

Affinity programs are usually discounts on products and services sponsored by companies that want to sell to your membership base. Some of the most common affinity programs are discounts on car rentals, office supplies, cell phone service, and customized or branded credit cards. In return for access to your association's membership list and use of its logo, the company will usually offer a royalty payment to the association. Once you enter into an agreement with a company to offer an affinity program, the company is commonly referred to as an affinity partner.

As associations strive to diversify their income sources and provide additional benefits to members, they have started engaging many types of affinity programs. One unique, out-of-the-box affinity program is the American Speech-Language Hearing Association's partnership with Subaru auto. (See ASHA's web site for information: www.asha.org/about/membership-certification/subarufaqs.htm.) Affinity programs that are only tangentially related to the association's mission or only tangentially relevant to the membership's demographic will ultimately dilute your overall value proposition. Here are some guidelines about affinity relationships:

What should I look for in an affinity partner? In short, don't be a "sell out." Consider only programs that have at least some overlap with your association's tax-exempt purpose or programs that have a significant appeal to your members' demographic. If you work for an association of in-home tutors, for example, you would do well to pass on a program offering discounts on luxury cars; however, an affinity program for teaching aids would probably be a good fit. It can be tempting to pursue partnerships that promise great financial rewards for only a little work by your staff. Use discretion and approach all offers with critical eye and your mission in mind.

Remember that people offering affinity programs may have little understanding of your association's mission. Some will be persistent, offering lucrative scenarios under which your association would earn significant royalties, and won't understand how you could justify turning away easy money. But as an association executive, your ultimate responsibility is to advance the organization's mission, not make a profit.

If the affinity program seems like a good fit, what do I do next? Negotiate and sign a contract and give serious consideration to an up-front investment from the affinity partner. If they're serious about the relationship, they'll be willing to invest in the partnership and value they will get from their association with you. This investment could be counted toward future royalty payments. Setting up affinity programs always requires a good deal of staff time, and an upfront investment will help offset that expenditure of time.

My predecessor picked a bad affinity partner. What should I do? Don't be afraid to cut loose underperforming affinity partners, even if members are using the programs. Perhaps you are new to your job and have inherited some affinity partners with little relevance to your association's profession, trade, or cause. Evaluate affinity programs annually to ensure they are meeting expectations. Maintaining affinity programs also costs staff time, so unless the association is earning significant royalties or the partnerships have high levels of overlap with the mission, you should give serious consideration to cutting them.

Is there anything else I should know? Affinity partnerships can be complex arrangements and should never be entered into lightly. This is only a brief overview of how affinity programs affect the member benefits package, and many more factors, including tax and legal issues, must be considered when evaluating them. You may want to ask an attorney to review all your association's new and existing affinity partner contracts. See *Professional Practices in Association Management* (ASAE & The Center, 2007) for a more thorough treatment of the subject.

So, what is the sum of your value proposition? Although associations hold some things in common, the answer to this question will be different for each association. The membership professional, working for other staff, must continually evaluate the association's value proposition and its alignment with the association's mission, while judging new benefit opportunities against the same touchstone. Creating and communicating the value proposition is one of the priorities of the membership function.

References

1. Harry Beckwith. *Selling the Invisible: A Field Guide to Modern Marketing.* (Warner Books, 1997)

2. Jim Giles. Internet Encyclopedias Go Head to Head. *Nature.* December 14, 2005; 438:900-901.

Jay Karen, CAE, is president and CEO of the Professional Association of Innkeepers International, representing owners of bed and breakfasts and country inns throughout North America. Prior to his role at PAII, he was director of membership with the National Golf Course Owners Association. He has been a speaker at ASAE & The Center annual conferences and served on the ASAE & The Center's Membership Section Council. Email: jay@paii.org.

Ben Martin, CAE, is director of communications and new media at the Virginia Association of Realtors, Glen Allen, Virginia. He is a frequent author, speaker, and volunteer for ASAE & The Center. Email: bkmcae@gmail.com.

An Overview of Membership Research

By Dean A. West

3

IN THIS CHAPTER:

- Why membership research is important
- Establishing a research management strategy
- Areas of inquiry for membership research
- Research methodologies for associations
- Survey deployment and analysis
- Engaging a research consultant

I N 2004, ED SALEK, executive director of the Society for Tribologists and Lubrication Engineers (STLE) faced a difficult situation. The association was struggling because of industry changes and external factors beyond the association's control. Decisions at the association were based on home grown research and it was difficult for staff and volunteers to come together on what strategies were necessary for success.

In 2005, STLE conducted its first membership needs assessment in more than 10 years. This online survey provided information about its membership audience, members' participation with the association, environmental forces affecting member companies, and the relationship of other organizations that directly and indirectly competed with STLE.

The board and staff reviewed the analysis of this information, internalized it, and used it to guide decisions.

To internalize this information, several tactics were implemented. The information was presented to their board by an external research consultant who also met with their executive committee to discuss the findings. These initial discussions created a common understanding of the information and agreement on its meaning. During the succeeding months, staff met to discuss how the information applied to each department and program within the association. In addition, the information was presented to various membership groups and committees.

This communication ensured that decision-makers were aware of how best to use the information and members understood that their input was being used to improve membership value.

By 2007, the STLE had achieved the following outcomes:

- Increased the association's net worth by over 20 percent
- Increased the association's revenue by approximately 30 percent

"The research made us more confident in our decision making, less risk averse. Our staff and volunteers had a feeling that we understood the market and were not being pushed and pulled by forces we did not understand," Salek says.

While the research was not the only factor contributing to this success, Salek believes the research was a "catalyst" that provided the first key to the decisions necessary for this growth. He is "certain that the research gave us a foundation for success."

The STLE experience is a good example of how an association can use membership research to effectively guide decision making and how better decisions lead to improved performance. Unfortunately, STLE's success is too often the exception, not the rule. Many associations continue to struggle with the decision to use research, the effective implementation of research, or the use of research information in decision making.

This chapter provides an overview of the membership research process, guidance on the use of membership research, and examples of how associations use membership research to improve decision making. While by no means a comprehensive treatise on research, it provides association executives with the basic insights necessary to establish a methodical and effective membership research process for their associations.

Why Membership Research Is Important

Membership research is defined in this chapter as the planning, collection, and analysis of data relevant to membership decision making and the communication of the results of this analysis to staff and volunteer leaders. The association can study many different constituencies to address a wide range of potential issues. Membership research often takes priority for the following reasons:

- Members represent the primary market of the association.
- Members represent a sample of the potential market of the association.
- Members represent an accessible, definable audience for research activities.
- Decisions affecting members have the greatest potential return on investment for the association.

The ongoing collection, analysis, and use of membership information are critical for sustainable association growth and success, and the ability to manage this process is a fundamental competency of the membership executive.

What decisions do you want to make? When determining which decisions you want to make, it is helpful to identify what outcomes you hope to achieve by making better decisions. For example, the following are common membership outcomes:

- We want to increase the number of members.
- We want to increase the number of attendees at our annual meeting.
- We want to improve our retention rate of members.
- We want to improve the satisfaction of our members.

If you have a clear understanding of the outcomes you hope to achieve, you can identify the areas of inquiry important for a research process to address. You can also evaluate the return on investment of your research activities.

Key questions membership research can address. Common membership outcomes generate a series of key questions that are often answered through membership research.

- Whom do we represent and how is the membership divided into different markets and constituencies?
- What are the programs and services that provide the most value to our members?
- What are the issues and problems with the greatest impact on our members?
- How can we improve the marketing and implementation of our programs and services?
- What competitive influences have the most impact on our members?
- What opportunities exist for our association and how do we take advantage of these opportunities?

Establishing a Research Management Strategy

By developing an ongoing process to answer these questions, the association creates a research management strategy providing decision makers with the information and insight necessary for the association to create long-term, sustainable growth. When establishing the association's ongoing research process, consider the following questions:

Who is going to use the research results? Associations often serve many different audiences. As a result, research activities are often designed to serve a wide variety of decision makers.

In 2007, the Association Forum of Chicagoland conducted a comprehensive membership needs assessment and used the information collected through it to provide:

- Guidance to the board for strategic planning
- Guidance to individual staff department heads on program improvement
- Guidance to volunteer leaders of special interest groups to improve programming and members' access to function-specific special interest group meetings

• Guidance to the association's Content Committee on the identification and prioritization of educational topics

This example represents only a portion of the decisions that were supported by this membership research project.

The Association Forum has established an annual process for collecting membership information and both staff and volunteer leaders habitually use this information to guide decisions ranging from the tactical to the strategic.

Different groups within the association have different roles and responsibilities. Each group needs information for different types of decisions. By understanding who will be using your information, you can make sure that the information collected addresses their needs.

What is the venue(s) for decision making? There are three main venues for decision making within the association. The needs of decision makers within each venue should guide research efforts of:

• Volunteer leadership groups (e.g., board of directors)
• Staff/volunteer leader combinations (e.g., membership committee)
• Staff groups (e.g., staff meeting or budget committee meeting)

Information at its most strategic level regarding the association's membership and the member environment is necessary to support board-level decisions about organizational strategy. For staff/volunteer groups, information must help these groups make decisions within their areas of influence, such as chapter development, conference education, or member marketing activities. Staff-directed groups need tactical information to guide execution of programs and services by improving the configuration and marketing of these efforts.

Although information collected through the research process should be reconfigured to meet the needs of decision makers within each venue, information used in each venue is not mutually exclusive. Volunteer groups may also need tactical information and staff groups will also need strategic information.

What is the time frame of the decision? Some decisions are made on an immediate basis, while others are considered over a long time frame. For planning purposes, three general timeframes may be used.

• Long term—greater than 1 year. Long-term decisions relate to the ongoing assessment of the member market and the evolution of the association over time to serve members within this market. Decision makers must anticipate how factors will affect members three to five years in the future and prepare accordingly. Environmental scanning information to guide strategic planning is an example of information supporting long-term decisions.

• Annual—Annual decisions relate to the annual planning and implementation of the association's programs and services, for example budget development and approval. These decisions are predictable and important to effective allocation of resources. For example, an annual satisfaction study could provide insight into which programs or services are expanded, reduced, or modified.

• Short term—less than 1 year. Short-term decisions may take place at a committee or staff meeting and guide the direct implementation of association programs and services. Staff needs specific information relevant to these decisions. An example might be insight into how to improve the rate of renewals during the membership renewal process.

By understanding the time frame of decisions, you can establish specific tactics for data collection and analysis to ensure that information is available when the decisions are being made.

What is the impact of the decisions being researched? The value of research is in the application of data, not the collection of data. If the association is not going to use research, then conducting research is a waste of time and resources. Depending on the impact of a decision, the association executive can determine the relative worth of a research process supporting a decision.

STLE, cited earlier, had a budget of approximately $2.3 million in 2005. Their investment in a unique research study was approximately $15,000. Decisions based on the research and the improved decision-making environment initiated by the use of research eventually helped produce an increase in net revenue of approximately 30 percent.

In this instance, the staff's use of the information justified the investment because they made decisions that had a direct impact on the business results, and these results greatly exceeded the direct costs of the research.

The association executive should consider not only the beneficial outcomes of better decision making but also the opportunity costs of continuing activities based on incorrect assumptions or knowledge. Consider the following simple analysis for a sample association.

The association has a budget of $1.5 million and represents 3,000 members with a dues amount of $200 per person. The association's retention rate has been a steady 80 percent for many years.

Each year the association conducts a fall and spring new member campaign, mailing 1,000 membership brochures to prospective members. The brochure outlines the key membership value proposition and member benefits and the two mailings cost a total of $6,000 (excluding staff time).

Unfortunately, since the brochure is based on the wrong member value proposition, the performance of the promotion is not as effective as it could be. Instead of getting 100 new members each year from this campaign, the association acquires only 50. Table 1 highlights the costs of this reduced performance.

The total costs for this decision error are $63,000 over three years. In addition, this example demonstrates that the costs increase for each year the association fails to correct its mistake. Finally, in this example, we've only considered a single promotion. Since the fundamental understanding of the member value proposition is incorrect, every new member promotion is flawed, so the total cost of this mistake is amplified.

This is a simple example but it illustrates how using membership research effectively can have substantial short- and long-term benefits that must be considered when making decisions about the annual research investment of the association.

Table 1. Performance, Expenses, and Lost Revenue

Year 1 Lost Revenue	Year 2 Lost Revenue	Year 3 Lost Revenue
50 new members @ $200 = $10,000	40 retained members @ $200 = $8,000	40 retained members @ $200 = $8,000
	50 new members @ $200 = $10,000	40 retained members @ $200 = $8,000
		50 new members @ $200 = $10,000
Lost revenue = $10,000	Lost revenue = $18,000	Lost revenue = $26,000

Year 1 Direct Expense	Year 2 Direct Expense	Year 3 Direct Expense
Campaign Costs = $3,000 (1/2 are wasted)	Campaign Costs = $3,000	Campaign Costs = $3,000
Total Cost $13,000	Total Cost $21,000	Total Cost $29,000

Saving $15,000 in the direct costs of a quality research study fails to take into account the opportunity costs and direct impact of decisions based on a flawed understanding of the market. As the potential opportunity costs of making the wrong decision increase, the justified investment in research also increases. If in doubt about the decision to conduct research, simply ask yourself if you can afford to be wrong. The more strongly you answer no, the more important research to support your decision becomes.

Areas of Inquiry for Membership Research

Research can be as simple or as complex as your budget and time frame allow. Based on the assumption that the association does not currently have a robust research program, there are four key areas of inquiry that represent common areas of inquiry for membership research. The following diagram identifies these four areas of inquiry and their relationship to membership marketing strategy.

By collecting information in each of these areas, the association creates a comprehensive picture of the membership and the factors with the greatest impact on membership strategy. The identified four areas of inquiry should not limit the association's exploration of potential research topics but should begin providing the necessary context about which areas might be most useful to study, given limited resources and the association's distinct research goals.

Market Identification. Who do we represent? A key step in membership analysis is to create a membership profile identifying the individual and organizational characteristics of your membership that are important to decision making. Individual characteristics are demographics related to the person, for example age or gender.

Organizational characteristics are demographics related to the employing organization within which the person may operate, such as the number of employees or gross revenue. The purpose for creating an audience profile is to clearly identify primary audiences for service, their unique characteristics, and similarities and differences between audiences.

Understanding the characteristics of an audience is essential to customizing the association's service to these audiences. In addition, this audience definition helps leadership prioritize between audiences so that resource allocation decisions can be made openly and objectively given the strategic priorities of the association.

Figure 1. Areas of Inquiry for Membership Marketing Strategy

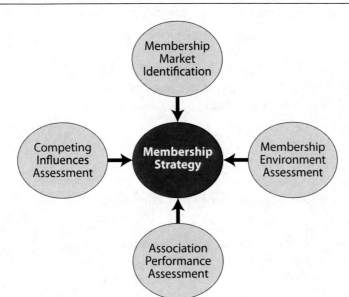

Membership Environment Assessment. What is the environment in which members operate? The impact of the environment on your members will shape their relationship to the association. The purpose for researching this area is to collect the evidence necessary to identify the concerns and challenges facing or anticipated by the association's members. By understanding the problems of the target audience; your association can produce, modify, or expand programs that address these problems.

Association Forum of Chicagoland Market Identification

Beginning in 2005, the Association Forum of Chicagoland (Forum) implemented a wide variety of changes in programming and instituted several new membership initiatives. Because of these changes, a goal of the 2007 membership study was to profile the audience of the association to provide more detailed information about the constituencies of the association and how these constituencies were related.

The Forum identified a link between age, title, and work responsibilities. By understanding this link, the Forum was able to identify how the career progression of a young professional—from a young executive through chief staff officer—affected his or her participation with the association.

Environmental analysis can range from macro-factors, such as immigration or changes in technology, to micro-factors specific to the individual, such as a personal desire to limit business travel. Five distinct areas should be considered for analysis:

1. External environmental factors. External factors are defined as issues completely outside the member's industry but with an impact on their company or profession. An example of these factors from the PCMA study (See sidebar.) was dealing with new competition to meetings, conventions or exhibitions enabled by new technology.

2. Industry factors. Industry factors are defined as issues within the industry in which your members operate. An example of industry factors from the PCMA study was building overcapacity for meeting venues, meeting space, hotels, etc.

3. Company factors. Company factors are defined as issues within the employing organization of your members. An example of a company factor from the PCMA study was recruiting new staff who have the attitudes and ability to meet the service expectations of meeting attendees.

4. Professional factors. Professional factors are defined as issues within the profession represented by your members. An example from the PCMA study was improving the credibility of professional meeting, convention or exhibition management as a desirable career.

5. Personal factors. Personal factors are defined as issues which directly impact the individual. An example from the PCMA study was developing greater personal competence in general business management or leadership skills.

By creating a comprehensive understanding of the environment within which your members operate, you can identify what changes or threats might represent opportunities for the association.

Association Performance Assessment. What is the relationship of members to the association and how is this relationship reflected in their use of association programs, products, or other association initiatives?

Members join an association to receive some determined value. How they receive this value is reflected in their choices for participation with the association.

Avenues of participation can be as complex as volunteering for a committee or as simple as purchasing a book. The goal when researching this area is to identify patterns of behavior and assess the level to which the association is successfully serving members through its existing portfolio of programs, services, or initiatives. Key factors to assess within this area include factors with the greatest impact on the decision to join and the decision to retain membership. Which factors have the greatest influence on membership value and how do these factors differ for each audience?

In addition, information can be collected on the awareness of, use of, satisfaction with, and perceived value or perceived importance of individual association programs. This information provides a framework for assessing your association's current performance and for modifying existing programs and services to deliver improved value to your members. This area of research focuses on understanding the relationship between the member and the association. Also important to assess, separately from the distinct programs and services, is the role of the association in the life of the member and how this role is reflected in the emotional connection between the association and the member.

Competing Influence Assessment. What other organizations compete with the association and what is the impact of these organizations? No association operates in a vacuum. This area of inquiry identifies primary competitive influences and the criteria members use to make decisions relative to these competitors.

Michael Porter is considered the leading expert on competitive analysis. His seminal work identified Porter's Five Forces (below) that are important to the understanding of the competitive environment and the use of this information in decision making.[1]

• Jockeying among current providers. This area relates to the current competition between existing providers within a market. For example, two different associations may be attempting to serve the same market with education programs delivered through a conference.

• Threat of new entrants. The threat of new entrants relates to the potential for new organizations, such as another association, to enter the market to provide similar or directly competing programs. The greater the barriers to entry into a market, the more difficult it becomes for new organizations to enter the market.

- Bargaining power of suppliers. The bargaining power of suppliers relates to the ability of suppliers to affect the organization's flexibility to configure or provide their services. The more powerful the supplier community in a market, the less flexibility the association has in configuring product or service options because powerful suppliers can dictate terms.

- Bargaining power of customers. The bargaining power of customers relates to the ability of customers to affect the organization's flexibility to configure or provide its services. The more powerful the customer base, the less flexibility the association has in configuring its portfolio of programs, products, and services.

- Substitute products. Substitute products relate to service options different from existing solutions but which still meet the needs of customers. For example, virtual training, using advances in technology, represents a substitute educational product that reduces the market for face-to-face, hands-on training.

Understanding the relationship of Porter's Five Forces and developing specific strategies to deal with each area is central to developing a successful strategy that reflects the realities of the competitive environment.

American Society for Gastrointestinal Endoscopy Competitive Analysis

In 2007, the American Society for Gastrointestinal Endoscopy was considering options for its hands-on training facility for endoscopy, the ASGE Interactive Training & Technology Center, located in Westmont, Illinois. Many strategic options were being considered, including expanding the existing facility, building a new facility, establishing relationships with other providers, and developing mobile training facilities.

As part of the strategy development process, the ASGE conducted a study of the competitive environment for hands-on training in endoscopy using Porter's Five Forces as a model. The study identified factors critical to selection of a training provider, new entrants into the market, and a potential substitute offering on the horizon, virtual training.

By understanding the relationship between all five areas, ASGE considered an integrated strategy combining in-place training facilities with a network of association and academic medical center partners to create a more robust training environment that maximized the utilization of the ASGE facilities while providing more accessible, affordable training to members locally.

The preceding areas of inquiry provide a general framework to guide your research efforts. By considering the membership audience, member environment, competing forces, and the association's relationship to members, the association develops a comprehensive picture to guide strategy development. This framework helps you understand and prioritize in which areas you need to collect information to make strategy decisions.

Research Methodologies for Associations

The development of the research methodology can be simple or complex, depending on your research needs. A complete discussion of research methodologies is beyond the scope of this chapter, but some guidelines and concepts can help you narrow your focus.

A specific market research methodology balances the following:

- Data type. What type of information are you trying to collect?

- Direct costs (e.g., postage, data entry). What are the direct costs of conducting the research and are these costs fixed or variable based on the methodology?

- Professional fees (if using external expertise). What type of external assistance are you engaging and what will these services provide and cost?

- Time frame (e.g., one month, several months, ongoing). What is the time frame for conducting the study, analyzing the data, and providing the report?

The optimal market research process may incorporate different methodologies designed to balance the strengths and weakness of each method while respecting the financial resources and time frame of the association.

Types of Market Research

Each specific tool for market research has advantages and disadvantages.

Primary and Secondary Data. Research collects data. Generally speaking, there are two types of data: Primary data is new data collected specifically to address the problem at hand, and secondary data is data that has already been collected through another research project. Both types of data are important. The membership executive needs to evaluate the value of existing secondary data so that new, primary data collected does not duplicate this information and adds to the association's knowledge base.

Qualitative versus Quantitative Research. There are two general methods of research.[2] Qualitative research is not subject to quantification or quantitative analysis. Quantitative research is subject to mathematical or statistical analysis.

Qualitative research is used to help the association understand the in-depth motivations and feelings of a target audience. Focus groups represent a common form of qualitative research. Qualitative research is best used in conjunction with quantitative methodologies. Qualitative research provides the analyst with a more in-depth understanding of complex issues, which is helpful during analysis. Qualitative research is also used to identify potential response options that can be tested using quantitative tools.

Qualitative research is less effective in identifying small differences in the marketing mix that may have a great impact on the success of a project or program. A second weakness is that conclusions drawn from qualitative data may not be representative of the larger membership audience.

Quantitative research is used to provide more accurate, objective information that can be extrapolated to a larger audience. Common forms of quantitative research include mail or online survey instruments. Quantitative research allows the association to specifically test precise concepts. Quantitative research uses surveys that can be mailed, posted online, or done by telephone or even with on-site intercepts, such as at a conference. The key is that the results can be quantified.

Common Tools of Market Research

In preparing for research, the membership professional should become familiar with the following common research tools.

Data Mining. Data mining is a series of tools used to study the internal database of the association which is created by the association through existing activities. For example, dues collection often provides insight into demographics. Purchase history provides insight into popular educational content or preferred delivery channels.

In 2007, the Illinois CPA Society (ICPAS) conducted a data-mining analysis of the association's data retrospectively for five years. This analysis identified key trends in participation by different age groups, which will impact how member retention strategies and retention resources should be focused. This insight was gained without surveys, or any additional information. The analysis simply compared the age of members to their event attendance, volunteer participation, and retention rate.

By creating an understanding of the situation using existing data, ICPAS also understood how to make subtle improvements in its data collection process and identified a key member market for additional, specific primary research.

The use of data mining and other strategic database analysis tools represents a growing resource for associations that have invested in the collection of data about members for many years as part of other initiatives that may not have been originally conceived as research sources.

Executive Interviews. An executive interview is a structured or semistructured format in which the researcher asks a series of questions to an individual selected as part of the study. This method is an excellent choice for collecting in-depth information from individuals who would be difficult to reach through other qualitative mechanisms or for which other mechanisms would be cost prohibitive.

In 2007, PCMA used a series of executive interviews to collect qualitative information about career aspirations from individuals active in the profession of convention management. Eight individuals were interviewed using the same five questions. The analyst identified common themes from these interviews for later testing with a quantitative instrument.

Focus Groups. A focus group is a group of 8 to 12 participants who are led by a moderator in an in-depth discussion on one particular topic or concept. Today, focus groups can be organized as face-to-face activities or as online events. The primary advantage of focus groups is the opportunity to probe for in-depth insight or understanding of the membership audience. The primary disadvantages of focus groups are the costs and the inability to quantify the analysis or extrapolate findings to the larger membership audience.

The American Bar Association's Section on Business Law conducted professionally facilitated focus groups to identify key themes important to their brand identity. Six focus groups were held in three cities, Los Angeles, Chicago, and Philadelphia, to ensure that no geographic bias was incurred. Volunteer leaders observed some of the focus groups. The focus groups identified practical resources as a key component of the relationship between the ABA-SBL and its large and diverse membership. Today, this finding is featured in the brand tagline, "Practical Resources for the Business Lawyer."

Focus groups can also be organized more informally, for example, at the association's annual conference. The key to focus groups is to establish a group that represents a diverse range of opinions relative to the research goals.

Paper (mailed) Surveys. Paper surveys are survey instruments that are mailed to a target audience of potential respondents. This method is one of the most common research tools for associations. Paper surveys are a robust method, allowing for the collection of a great deal of information. The greatest disadvantages of paper surveys are the direct costs for paper, postage, and data entry and the increase in data collection time necessary to account for the return of mailed surveys.

Paper surveys are best for collecting information from people that are difficult to reach through online mechanisms or in circumstances where the person's ability to participate online may in fact bias the data collected. The introduction of online surveys has reduced the use of paper surveys. Online surveys are often less expensive and offer the researcher greater question flexibility for less cost.

Online Surveys. Online surveys are similar to paper surveys but are administered via the Internet. The capabilities of the online format allow for a more robust data collection instrument and faster turnaround time without additional expenses for paper and postage. The primary disadvantage of online surveys exists when online access to members is restricted because of members' Internet security protocols or other technological limitations.

In 2007, the National Association of the Remodeling Industry conducted an online needs assessment of its membership. The cost savings from the online survey format allowed the association to survey all its members instead of a sample. Online surveying provides virtually every member with the opportunity to respond and yields a greater volume of data for analysis.

Also in 2007, the American Society for Gastrointestinal Endoscopy conducted a competitive environment scan for hands-on training in endoscopy. Because of the extremely short time frame (three weeks), ASGE conducted an online survey and, thus, more than 10 percent of their members provided information in just two weeks.

Telephone Surveys. Telephone surveys can be used for both qualitative and quantitative research. Commonly, members of a particular audience are contacted and led through a structured or semi-structured interview process. The primary advantage of telephone interviews is the ability to collect data very quickly. The primary disadvantage is the limitation on the number and type of questions that can be asked before respondent fatigue begins to influence the results.

In 2005, International Association of Conference Centers was in the midst of an extensive strategy development process. The association had already decided to conduct an online survey to collect information. During the research design process, IAAC determined that the information about its credential collected through this method would be insufficient. But staff decided a separate online survey about its credentialing would be confusing, since it would mean two online surveys in the field at the same time.

As a result, IAAC implemented a telephone survey of its primary member representatives to ask distinct questions about the IAAC credential. A sample of 100 members was contacted by telephone and asked a series of questions regarding the credential. This information was later appended to the online survey data to create a more comprehensive view of member opinions during the analysis.

Mixed Mode Surveys. A mixed mode survey strategy combines different types of surveys into a single process. For example, an online survey will be combined with a mailed survey. Mixed mode survey strategies are the most comprehensive form of data collection and provide a greater volume and quality of data for analysis. The primary disadvantage is the additional costs involved and the longer time frame for instrument development and data collection.

The North Carolina Academy of Family Physicians was conducting its first membership needs assessment in about a decade. The association decided it was important that each member have an opportunity to respond to the survey. However, approximately one third of the membership had not provided an up-to-date email address to the association. The result was a research methodology that combined an online survey with a paper, mailed survey. The paper survey was mailed to non-respondents to the online survey and to members who had not provided an up-to-date email.

Later analysis concluded that there were no differences in the opinions of paper survey respondents versus online survey respondents but that the association's investment in the paper survey was important for giving every member the opportunity to provide input.

Survey Deployment and Analysis

The development and implementation of the survey instrument varies by method but there are some common steps:

1. Develop a list of initial questions tied to the research goals.
2. Determine question and response format.
3. Establish questionnaire flow and layout.
4. Evaluate the questionnaire and layout.

5. Deploy the survey instrument.

6. Collect, edit, and analyze research data.

When developing the research plan, these steps should act as a guide for the creation of the specific research implementation strategy.

How to Analyze the Results

Analyzing research results is an ongoing process that creates a dialogue among the users of data. Users should look for patterns in the data and reconfigure the data as needed to address specific research goals.

Analyzing research data is a complex undertaking. Misinterpretation of research data—the researcher coming to the wrong conclusions—can harm the association's strategy development because it may encourage the association to pursue a strategy at odds with the realities of the marketplace. To minimize this risk, the association executive must take a common-sense, methodical approach to reviewing the information, developing conclusions, and communicating recommendations.

The development of your research process should be designed to produce quality information without bias. Three major types of survey bias or error in survey research should be considered.[3]

1. **Sampling bias.** These are errors that result from chance variation. Chance variation is the inevitable difference between the sample value and the true value of the sample mean. This error cannot be avoided, only reduced by increasing the sample size.

2. **Systematic bias.** Systematic bias is error that results from poor research design or execution. The development and implementation of a quality research project takes specific expertise and experience. If the project is poorly designed or executed, flaws in the data may result.

3. **Measurement bias.** Measurement bias is error that results from a discrepancy between the information being sought and what is actually obtained by the measurement process.

The following steps are important to the analysis:

- Determine the quality of your research data. As discussed earlier, sampling bias is addressed by managing the size of the sample. Systemic bias is addressed through the creation and implementation of a quality research process.

- Review the results given your expectations of the response to determine the extent of any measurement error. While some error is inevitable, understand the differences between your expected and collected information, take this into account, and adjust your analysis accordingly.

- Review the data objectively, without a predetermined set of conclusions or biases. This is perhaps the most difficult step in the analysis. If the researcher approaches the analysis with a pre-existing bias, the final analysis and recommendations will reflect this bias and affect association performance.

- Review the data skeptically. The researcher must understand not only what the data says but also what is does not say. Don't look for answers that are not supported by the data collected.

- Focus not just on individual pieces of information but also on patterns of information that represent a more complete depiction of respondents' attitudes and opinions.

In summary, the analysis consists of two components; what the research knows, based on the data and what the research suspects based on an interpretation of the data. The final analysis must be clear between these two points of view.

Presenting Research Results to Decision Makers

One of the most challenging aspects of research is to make the resulting information and recommendations actionable. Too often a quality research study simply acts as an impressive doorstop because decision makers don't understand the information or don't understand how to apply the information to their problems. Membership research can fulfill three functional roles: descriptive, diagnostic and predictive.

- The descriptive role includes gathering and presenting statements of fact. For example, 20 percent of respondents are between the ages of 25 and 30 years old.

- In the diagnostic role, data or actions of a particular target market are explained. A common diagnostic question is satisfaction. A question is used to collect member satisfaction on each of the top 10 programs or services. Programs that are rated lower in satisfaction are given priority for review.

- The predictive role involves collecting data to help anticipate future behavior. For example, a study might ask, "How critical will each of the following industry issues be to your company over the next three years?"

A good market research study helps the association balance these three areas to provide the highest quality and most useful information for decision making. To provide a quality research report, consider the responsibilities of the researcher:

- First, you must determine the quality of the data. Poor data or inappropriate data should not be included in your study. If you discover that respondents had difficulty answering a question, simply remove this data from the analysis.

- Second, you must analyze the data correctly. There are a wide variety of analytical techniques to review data, but first and foremost, the researcher should use common sense. Review the data with an open, objective mind.

- Third, look for insights that lie behind the data. Consider the following metaphor. If you want to know which way the wind is blowing you don't look for the wind. Instead you look at which way the branches or leaves of a tree are blowing. A great deal of research can be categorized as showing the leaves blowing in the trees. A good researcher asks what lies behind the research. What is driving the response?

- Fourth, present the information in context to the decision being considered. A list of tables and charts is not helpful if the information contained is not directly applied to the decision. Don't force decision makers to configure the data to meet their needs; this is the job of the researcher.

- Finally, tell the story. You are responsible not only for providing information but also for telling decision makers what you think it means. Provide insight, not just data.

Engaging a Research Consultant

Many associations conduct high quality research without engaging external assistance, while others rely on external partners for virtually all aspects of their data collection, analysis, and reporting. The key is to understand the scope of your research activities and the association's internal capacity and capability to conduct research.

The market research industry is highly specialized and fragmented. A company that is outstanding at producing an online survey may have no expertise in qualitative research. An organization with substantive knowledge of one industry may have no experience in helping organizations in other industries. Within the supply chain of research there is a great deal of fragmentation. Consider the following simple example for producing of an online survey.

- First, a research company representative needs to get the research business. This is often a company principal or related executive manager.

- Second, an analyst or researcher must design the research methodology and create the questions that will be asked.

- Third, an individual will be responsible for programming the HTML language, managing the email deployment and generally overseeing the physical creation and deployment of the survey.

- Fourth, an individual may be responsible for statistical quality control and analysis.

- Finally, an individual may be responsible for recommendations and reporting.

While a separate person may not be responsible for each step, this simple example reveals the diverse steps within a research process. The process requires a human,

---

Benefits of External Research Assistance

- An exchange of money for access to research capacity. Few association staff members are sitting around with nothing to do but conduct research. By contracting with an external resource, the association trades financial resources for the capacity to conduct the study.

- Specialized expertise. Many research companies have special industry or strategy expertise. By contracting with these companies, the association gains their expertise and experience with these issues.

- Objectivity. An external resource looks at your information with a fresh eye. This provides new insight or ideas in areas where the association might be struggling.

- Independence. An external resource will be an independent voice unbiased by politics or other legacy issues that may stand in the way of effective analysis.

technological, and physical infrastructure to be successful. The more research you conduct, the more an investment in this infrastructure makes sense for the association. The more likely scenario is that the association will purchase the infrastructure and insights from an external research provider. (See Sidebar: Benefits of External Research Assistance.)

As the volume of research conducted by the association increases, the value of developing an internal capability for research increases. In addition, the more objectivity, independence, and specialized expertise are critical to the analysis and recommendations, the more an external resource adds value. For most associations, a combination of internal capability and external support are the best option.

To create an optimal research infrastructure consider the following simple process.

1. Assess the past and current research activity of the association. What research have you been doing and why? What has been the result of this research?

2. Identify desired research needs of both staff and volunteer leaders. What information is required or desired to make decisions.

3. Identify gaps between current and desired research needs. Based on the gap, develop a structure to help you meet your research needs within the resources you have available.

To determine your external support needs, it can be helpful to conduct an internal research audit. See Appendix 1: Research Audit Questions.

Membership research is a tool to help membership executives develop and implement successful membership strategy. Competent membership professionals will be familiar with the use of membership research to guide decisions and develop strategy.

References

1. Michael E. Porter. *On Competition.* (Harvard Business School Publishing, 1998).

2. Carl McDaniel and Roger Gates. *Marketing Research Essentials, 6th Edition.* (Wiley, 2007).

3. *Ibid.*

Dean A. West is president of Association Laboratory, a nationally recognized business strategy firm headquartered in Chicago. A fellow of ASAE & The Center and a former board member of the Association Forum of Chicagoland, he is a former executive director and has more than 20 years' experience in association management, business strategy, and marketing research. Email: dwest@associationlaboratory.com

Research Audit Questions

The following questions provide a simple process to assess the internal capacity and capability of the association to conduct research. By answering these questions, the association gains an understanding of what human, technical and external resources might be necessary to implement an effective, ongoing research process to guide decisions.

1. What research has been conducted within the last three years?

2. What was the purpose, reason, or rationale for this research?

3. How or by whom was this research initiated?

4. What were the goals of the research?

5. What type of research was conducted?
   a. Qualitative
   b. Quantitative
   c. Integrated or combined methodologies
   d. Other

6. What tools were used to collect the information?

7. Who conducted the research?

8. Was the research a single project or is it ongoing?

9. Who were the primary users of the information?

10. How was the research used to improve decision making?

11. What is the key decision maker or project leader's evaluation of the research?

12. What was the actual or estimated cost of the research?

13. What future research projects are currently anticipated or included within the planning cycle?

14. What challenges or opportunities are currently driving a desire for increased research, analysis, or other membership or market understanding?

15. What are gaps in the understanding of key decision makers regarding the association's products, services, or markets?

16. What is your internal capacity and capability to conduct research?

17. What external support is necessary to conduct research you believe is essential to quality decision making?

Organizing the Membership Function to Deliver Value

By Sheri Jacobs, CAE, and Sara Miller, CAE

4

IN THIS CHAPTER:

- Essential duties of the membership professional and membership department
- Staff roles and responsibilities
- Professional development and training
- Membership as a sales unit
- Providing member service

THE SCOPE AND RESPONSIBILITIES of an association's membership department can vary based on its size, type, budget, and location, yet the needs of members vary little. Members join associations because they are looking for education, credentialing, research, information, career assistance, business development, a specific product or service, peer relationships, and leadership/personal growth opportunities. They are looking for answers and they often have many resources to find them. Successful associations not only provide services but do so better than the competition. Delivering this kind of value to members is the central purpose around which every association membership department should be organized.

Essential Duties of the Membership Professional

The role of the membership professional varies in every association. Smaller associations may have only one or two staff to perform the membership functions of the association; whereas, larger associations may have a membership director or vice president and several managers as well as administrative or telephone staff to support the functions of the department. Membership might be responsible for the planning and marketing of all organizational offerings or it may serve as a call center and service department. Despite some shared goals (increased membership, increased conference attendance, increased industry certifications), organizations have different strategies for producing membership results. Below are some of the most common duties assigned to the membership function of an organization.

Member Recruitment and Engagement. Ensuring your members are engaged is essential to any retention program. This process begins with recruitment with a promise of what will come when a member joins the organization, and continues with the fulfillment of that promise. The greatest challenge most membership departments face is engaging busy members in the activities of the organization. (See Chapter 18: Engagement.) To enhance your member engagement program consider using these tools:

- A bridge program for first-year members that includes increased communication and invitations to participate and/or volunteer in association activities.

- Including more than just new members in your orientation programs, renaming them "Make the Most of Your Membership" rather than new-member orientation. Design such programs for any member regardless of tenure; include a guided tour of association benefits; and present 10 ways to participate more.

- Use your print and electronic communications to publicly recognize members for their involvement and contributions. It is often said that the most read section of an association publication is the one about people and promotions. Use this section to engage members. Actively solicit information from your membership. Don't just let announcements find you.

- Ask veteran members to participate in a welcome program to actively engage new members. The welcome program may include email, letters, or phone calls to new members from active members, new member receptions at events, or just a contact person to help guide them through the association's programs.

- For your next event, send a special invitation to members who are new or not actively engaged. Let them feel special; include them in your VIP events.

- Create a new member newsletter in print or via email. Distribute to anyone who has been a member fewer than three years.

Member Service/Customer Service. Delivering memorable customer service begins with understanding what members want and delivering it in a friendly and timely manner. The more customer service is personalized and responsive, the greater the likelihood that your members will become evangelists and actively promote your organization. The benefits of delivering excellent customer service from the standpoint of the organization include:

- More repeat business (higher likelihood that members will register for a second conference or purchase more books)

- More referrals

- Better reputation for you association

- Higher morale, happier employees (Employees enjoy delivering good service and dealing with satisfied members.)

- Fewer complaints

Renewal Fulfillment. Most membership departments are responsible for the renewal process including:

- Forecasting and reporting renewal rates and success
- Updating the database for the dues renewal
- Printing and mailing (or emailing) dues notices
- Conducting renewal phone-a-thons
- Sending acknowledgements and thank-you messages
- Conducting exit surveys
- Changing the membership status of nonrenewals

Record management. Record management includes maintaining accurate and consistent data on all members, customers, and prospects. Because all staff members may be in contact with members and receive updates or changes, it is essential that a systemized approach to updating members' records be implemented. Incorrect information in records could mean that members won't receive all their benefits and, therefore, will be at higher risk for not renewing. Once or twice a year, ask your members to check and update their contact information online.

Data Entry/Processing. The membership department, in most organizations, is responsible for processing new member applications and renewals. This role is critical to maintaining a good relationship with members, yet it is often an undervalued component of the work performed by the department. If mistakes are made in data entry, the result is a lack of communication to those members. Clean data is essential to any retention program.

Recruitment Marketing. In most organizations, regardless of size, the membership department is directly involved in the planning and execution of the marketing strategy to recruit new members. (See Chapter 15: Recruitment Strategies.) Membership recruitment tactics may include direct mail, advertising, referral programs, word-of-mouth activities, web site, trade shows, public relations, and telemarketing. The membership department should also be involved in market research, identifying prospects, conducting surveys, and hosting focus groups.

Communications. The membership department often communicates with members more than any other department because it is responsible for changes in records, customer service, order fulfillment, new member orientation, and the distribution of welcome packets. The friendliness and responsiveness of staff will reflect on the entire organization. Conduct a communications audit to identify all the information various members receive and how often it is delivered. Make sure that members are given correct information, including how to contact the association and whom to call. Finally, ask your members how they prefer to be contacted by the association.

Surveys and Research. Surveys and research conducted by the membership department will assist the organization in its strategic and tactical planning and benchmarking. (See Chapter 3: An Overview of Membership Research.)

Affinity Programs. Because of their close and frequent interaction with members, membership departments should be involved in the selection and monitoring of affinity programs. Many associations use affinity programs to leverage the buying power of their members to secure better pricing on products and services and often the revenue streams created by affinity programs can assist an organization in the delivery of its mission. However, such programs should receive continuing oversight for their value as member benefits.

Mailing Lists. The management and distribution of mailing list rentals is often the responsibility of the membership professional. Many associations have the potential to earn considerable income by renting their mailing list to vendors interested in communicating with their membership. Income from mailing list rental is not considered a royalty by the U.S. government and is, therefore, subject to Unrelated Business Income Tax. (See Appendix 1 for a sample list rental form.)

Sales. Regardless of size, many organizations rely on the membership department for sales, customer service, and product fulfillment. The data from all transactions should be recorded in the member's file.

Web site. Membership functions must participate in creating the association's online activities. Associations can increase the value of membership by being responsive to its members' needs and by engaging members in a two-way dialogue. One way to accomplish this is through blogs and wikis. By creating such social networks for members, associations can harness power as the central organizer. Whether your membership is spread across the state or the world, a blog or wiki will help your members share ideas and knowledge quickly and easily.

An association's web site should also function as an easy way to answer general questions about the organization. The Member Service area of your web site should contain the following:

- "Who to contact" with a list of departmental responsibilities
- Frequently asked questions
- Feedback form
- Mission statement
- Membership categories and dues
- Leadership
- About the organization
- Tell-a-friend
- Renewal information
- Membership application
- Ability to update personal information
- Directory of members

Staff Roles and Responsibilities

In setting your department's hierarchy, you must first understand the desired outcomes of your department. What is the association expecting you to accomplish? You must also look at how Membership supports the work of other departments. If the Meetings department is expecting your staff to work at the trade show and/or staff a booth, how will that affect your other priorities? The flow chart should reflect the roles and responsibilities of the Membership department in your specific organization.

Stakeholders. Key stakeholders are invested in what your department is doing. Consider the roles of the stakeholders in relation to membership:

- **Board of Directors.** The board may be setting the growth goals for membership and/or creating and adjusting the member benefits list. Your level of involvement in the decision making is as unique as your organization.

- **Chief Executive Officer.** The CEO may have a major role in determining the growth of your organization's constituency and may also determine the distribution of the budget.

- **Other departments.** What are the expectations of your program departments? Is the Meetings group changing how they market the annual event? Is the Public Relations staff increasing media coverage of the organization? How does the work of other departments affect Membership?

- **Membership director and staff.** You have an investment in the products and outcomes of your department. From working with members every day, you have expectations of what should be offered and how resources should be allocated.

While these groups are not present in every organization, you may have other stakeholders to consider. For example, a membership committee of the board is a major stakeholder that may replace or supplement the full board's involvement. Almost everyone affects Membership. You need to meet with all the stakeholders so you can fully understand their expectations. Your infrastructure must account for these outside influences.

Department Hierarchy. Typically membership managers are supported by staff reporting to them. The larger your organization, the more resources assigned to your department, but the basic staffing pyramid is the same. The unique components are the actual job titles and associated responsibilities. If you look through ASAE & The Center's listservers and career headquarters, you'll find many different job descriptions. Depending on the defined responsibilities of your department, the titles and associated job descriptions will reflect that work. The Membership hierarchy typically has three levels with a number of possible titles at each level.

Figure 1. Membership Department Hierarchy

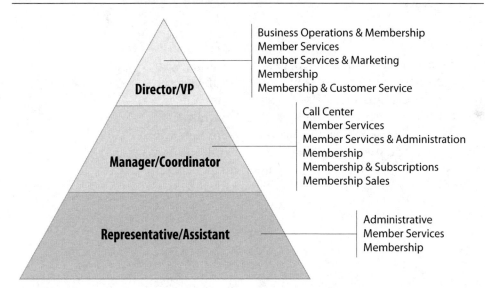

Director/VP
- Business Operations & Membership
- Member Services
- Member Services & Marketing
- Membership
- Membership & Customer Service

Manager/Coordinator
- Call Center
- Member Services
- Member Services & Administration
- Membership
- Membership & Subscriptions
- Membership Sales

Representative/Assistant
- Administrative
- Member Services
- Membership

In addition to these standard positions, some organizations have titles more specific to membership staff roles. For example, you may see positions like membership specialist, program manager, or online organizer. These positions represent a unique need within the organization. In a five-person staff, each person is likely juggling several roles. In larger organizations, the roles tend to be more narrowly defined.

In setting the best structure for your department, a major decision involves determining what the department should be three or five years in the future. The hierarchy should be well thought out so you are not constantly moving people around and changing responsibilities (aside from promotions). Staff members are often organized by functional area. Even if you don't currently have the staff to fill in all the boxes, having the vision of where you want to go will help streamline the entire process and help you identify future positions in your hierarchy. (See Figure 2.)

Figure 2. Sample Membership Department Organizational Chart

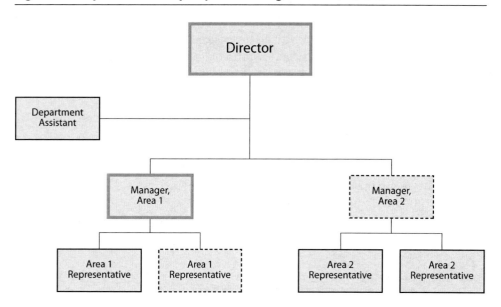

Once you understand the expectations for your department and have formalized your own departmental growth plan, you can write job descriptions. Clearly, each person needs a defined role with core responsibilities. You should also allow room for special projects and the ever-present "other duties as assigned." Your Human Relations department should have job description templates. (See Appendix 2. Sample Job Descriptions.) Additionally, you may supplement the description with a position description questionnaire that provides behind-the-scenes information. (See Appendix 3. Position Description Questionnaire.) It is important to highlight the major functions of each position as well as the skill set necessary for success.

Professional Development and Training

As managers, we do our best to hire team members who are already knowledgeable in most areas of their new jobs (the standard 80/20 rule). It can, however, be difficult to balance the things you can teach new hires with what they already bring to the table. It's also important to develop teamwork and camaraderie among staff and to empower them to work with other departments to avoid the silo mentality.

Individual Professional Development. In the groundbreaking book *First, Break All the Rules,* Buckingham and Coffman[1] write about skills, knowledge, and talents. Skills are basic abilities that can be learned; knowledge is factual information one is aware of or experiences one has learned from; and talents are the unique ways an individual's mind performs. Membership professionals must determine the areas where growth is possible and create a unique development plan for each staff member, addressing all three areas.

- Skills. Skill training relates to the daily operations of the organization or the person's particular job. If someone is responsible for corresponding with donors, you may enroll her in a computer software, customer service, public speaking, or business writing class. This will have tangible benefits on day-to-day operations and presumably increase productivity. The purpose is closely tied to improving one's efficiency.

- Knowledge. This area is at a higher level than skills. The goal is to increase one's understanding of the organization, your mission, and/or your subject matter so the individual will be a better representative of your organization. If your organization offers continuing education, you should consider the benefits of having your staff participate to gain industry-specific knowledge or even a certification. If you are trying to market a new online course, what better way to sell it than have your phone representatives speak from personal experience?

- Talents. There may not be formal classes that address an individual's innate talents like precision or creativity. Instead, you can look at new internal projects outside of job descriptions that will allow your staff to cultivate their talents. A key component in this area is the individual's exploration into who they are and what they do well. For example, someone from membership could be assigned to a committee that is exploring a new association management system.

Team Training. While it is critical that you train staff members according to their jobs and individual needs, you should also consider training that will improve the department as a whole. Customer Service may be one of the major functions of your department. Excellence in this area requires continual training and discussion.

- Online/Conference Calls. Since you are likely unable to shut down the entire Membership department for a day, outside training may not be an option. There are other ways to build your team's skills and knowledge. Online courses and conference calls are both viable options. It can be very beneficial to have your team trained at one time with the exact same material so everyone hears the same tactics and you have the opportunity for discussion following the event. With just two hours away from your desk, you could have a department potluck, attend training, and discuss the new ideas/concepts. A number of service providers offer classes that relate to your department's work.

- Group Presentations from Outside Classes. Another option is to have one or several people in the department attend a class and then present the information to the rest of the department. This may work, depending on the subject matter and the willingness of the class attendees and their office peers.

- Internal Training and Reviews. You may also conduct more formal in-house training about customer service issues. While many service guidelines are industry best practices, you still need to apply them to your own situation. You can create internal work sessions to review your organization's customer service philosophy and expectations. The exercise of writing a mission statement for your department will get everyone on the same page and serve as the foundation for future in-house projects.

Informal Training. Finally, the simple act of sharing information can serve as a component of your training program. In *The Likeability Factor*, Tim Sanders describes knowledge, network, and compassion as the keys to building successful relationships with your peers.[2] The knowledge component is particularly applicable to professional development. Membership staff can share books or periodicals that are relevant to their duties or techniques for handling certain inquiries or processes. The key is relevancy to your operations.

Informal Training Tips

Tip 1. If you are the only one in your department who is a member of ASAE & The Center or another professional organization, then you should share periodicals with your staff. You can highlight a few interesting articles. Reading the magazine isn't mandatory, but staff can take a look as time allows.

Tip 2. You may also want to have a community library where staff can do research on their own time. If you read a good book, share what you learn with your team and make the book available to anyone who is interested. *The Five Dysfunctions of a Team* is an interesting read about the pitfalls of unsuccessful teams. Share the knowledge from this book with your team, so people know what to look out for.

Training Budgets. Training is an essential line item in your departmental budget. You should determine how many classes each person will attend in a fiscal year and the associated costs. You will have to exercise some flexibility with the funds and be honest with your staff about their professional development budget. If the budget is $400 per staff member, they might choose two classes for $200 each or one $400 class. It's important for your direct reports to have ownership in their training plans. Talk with employees about their interests and how they'd like to grow and how new skills and knowledge can contribute to the department. Guide their selections in conversation, while empowering them to find options. If they suggest a class and you veto it without any discussion, your relationship and their trust in you takes several steps back.

If you don't have money or if your budget is cut, there are plenty of free ways to help develop your staff. Use the Internet to your advantage and search topics that are relevant to your work. Additionally, you can research organizations that occasionally offer free web or phone seminars.

It can be difficult to keep good staff. If you have a training program customized to each person, you continue to build their skills, thereby increasing their ability to take on higher-level responsibilities. Enable good employees to see a future with your organization that offers new opportunities and challenges. As a result, you may be able to increase the connections among employees, your organization, and yourself.

Membership as a Sales Unit

Organizations spend a lot of time trying to figure out the right marketing strategy, the right branding. During the process, if you have forgotten to include the people who actually have to communicate those messages, the process will be doomed from day one. The front-line employees (including your receptionist and member-ship staff) are the people responsible for daily interaction with the outside world. Success in this area means success for the rest of the organization.

Sales are the natural byproduct of a well-coordinated experience and increased loyalty. As a result, the membership staff are the sales people for your brand, your organization. Some membership professionals resist the idea of sales and up-selling is pure profanity to them. In truth, the membership department is naturally one of sales and you should instinctively want to increase someone's connectivity to the organization by up-selling to them. You may not like the sales terminology, but the actions are core to what membership departments do.

Up-selling Association Products. Up-selling is about getting your customers to purchase more advanced products or services than they'd originally planned to buy. For associations, traditional up-selling typically includes

- increasing the amount of a single donation
- moving up to the next membership level
- increasing the frequency of donations
- increasing the number of purchases from other areas (publications, meetings)

The focus is to change a person's purchasing behavior so you get a greater piece of the pie. This relates to "total share of customer" that Jill Griffin discusses in her book, *Customer Loyalty*.[3] Total share of customer has a direct connection to pro-ductive up-selling. If an individual has contributed the same amount for the last 10 years, what does that say about his connection to the organization? How hard would it be for a new competitor to steal that member? If the person is engaged in multiple areas, then it will be easier for him to resist the pull of the competition. As membership professionals, we all recognize that there are standard definitions for members like mail-boxer, relevant participant, cognoscente, status conscious, shaper, altruistic, doubter, and nonrelevant. If someone wants limited interaction with your organization, then you should deliver on their preferred experience, but you also should realize that such limited levels of involvement can lead to mass exodus.

Ultimately, selling is relatively simple to assess. Driven by dollars, the results are almost immediate and you can easily measure growth. If the outcomes do not match your needs, then you can make adjustments.

Up-selling Involvement. Member participation is a major resource of any asso-ciation. For many people, time is more precious than money. While up-selling to increase revenue is important, it is not the only way to up-sell. Associations look at both increasing revenue dollars and increasing participation. We conduct advocacy campaigns for which we need the help of our constituency. We rely on member participation to help accomplish organizational goals. Most associations offer a variety of opportunities so members can choose activities that fit most closely with their talents, interests and availabilities.

Your up-selling strategy should include volunteer opportunities from participating in electronic mailing lists to serving on committees to writing for publications. Your follow-up communications with members should list ways they can become involved. Some organizations need member participation in advocacy campaigns at grassroots levels by signing petitions or endorsing boycotts. It is critical for your members to know that you work on their behalf, but it is equally important that individuals have the opportunity to participate personally in the association's work.

Unlike financial up-selling, measuring the impact of your members' increased participation and connectivity to the organization may be more difficult and may take longer to be realized.

Staffing. Many membership staff and/or customer service representatives do not have formal sales training. Thus, if revenue expectations are tied to their up-selling performance, you must provide proper staff development. You will want to walk people through the different opportunities to sell and the various scripts for doing so. An important reminder for training is that not every interaction will naturally present an up-selling moment. Representatives need to be trained to read those situations and determine the best course of action. In some cases, up-selling in the initial interaction may not be the best approach.

Providing incentives to staff is a controversial issue. You must decide if sales are a core component of each person's job and, if so, if that area will be separately rewarded for outstanding performance. The idea of providing incentives for work that has some level of randomness may be difficult for your staff to understand. Additionally, if staff members have other responsibilities, they may neglect that work to increase their chance of acquiring a sales-related incentive.

Tracking. If you are going to promote up-selling and possibly connect financial incentives to a staffer's success, then you must have a comprehensive tracking system. Your membership database or other software application must allow you to identify what the person was going to buy and what you got them to buy. Alternatively, you need to be able to compare historical changes for someone before they talked with your representative with how they acted after they talked with a representative. It may take a while before you see the results, so your tracking system must account for the time lag.

Other Membership Programs. Depending on the infrastructure of your department, there may be other ways to increase sales. If Membership also handles Marketing or Subscriptions, you will naturally be able to cross-promote activities. Using knowledge from all your interactions with members, you can also generate your own correspondence and packages. You should get credit for any revenue associated with those products. Additionally, if you help another department and there are financial gains, you should receive a soft credit for your assistance. The Membership department is vital to the overall success of many activities and you need to able to quantify those contributions.

Providing Member Service

In October 2004, *Fast Company* magazine featured its first ever "Customers First Awards."[4] Recognizing companies like Progressive, Mini USA, and Trader Joe's, the magazine recorded five takeaways from the award finalists:

1. Leaders must be champions of the customer experience.
2. Employee empathy creates distinctive service.
3. In the rules of engagement, technology rules.
4. Data helps. But using it to benefit customers is crucial.
5. Cutting costs doesn't have to mean cutting service.

These lessons can easily apply to the association or non-profit world. When *The Experience Economy*[5] surfaced in the late 1990s, organizations around the world changed how they treated customers. Some businesses have a tendency to see each interaction with a member as an isolated event instead of a touch point in their overall experience. Admittedly, it is much easier to think that members don't remember what you said to them last week, but customers do remember how you treated them last week, positively or negatively. They will compare you to other businesses, which may or may not be your competition, and rate your performance against their own expectations.

In *First, Break All The Rules,*[6] four customer expectations are described:

- Accuracy—get it right
- Availability—available when needed
- Partnership—listen to the customer, be responsive, make them feel like they are on the same side of the fence as you
- Advice—customers feel the closest bond to organizations that have helped them learn

The first two points (accuracy and availability) are your base. They are the minimal expectations of your customers or members. They expect you to have the correct information and they expect you to be available. Meeting these two needs does not put you ahead of the competition but just gets you in the game. You really start to impress your customers when you satisfy the other two expectations—partnership and advice. Customers should believe you are with them in their challenges.

Although staff can not always relate, they should always empathize with the plight of your constituency. Whatever the problem, the member should know that you will work with them to find the solution. Furthermore, if members can come to you for information and education, you are filling an important void. This connection increases your relevance to members and decreases the chance that they'll forget you at renewal time.

Thinking about expectations and carefully planning the experience leads to the overarching theme of customer loyalty. While we have always heard mention of loyalty in connection with membership and customer support, we have recently seen a greater emphasis on and new metrics for determining members' connectivity to organizations. For many, experience is the mechanism for growing one's loyalty. A good experience helps connect people to the organization. The consistent interactions, the personalized service/correspondence, and continued on-time delivery of goods are all major milestones within the experience, and success in these areas helps build loyalty. Here are four major steps an organization should follow to evaluate and improve the customer experience and grow member loyalty:

Step 1: Your Mission Statement. What does it mean to provide exceptional service to your members? If your staffers do not share similar answers to that question, the first step is to draft a mission statement. Your department should have a single, concise definition of what you are supposed to do. It should be the guiding principle behind your daily work and the foundation of any new program. Without a shared mission, you can not reach your potential because everyone will be operating from different perspectives. To some, phone messages should be returned within 24 hours, while others may say 72 hours is acceptable. Without uniformity of service expectations, the members' experiences are different based on who answers the phone—and the variances can greatly affect their impression of the organization. Thus, having a departmental mission statement is a critical first step in providing member service.

The mission statement should be the foundation of every decision. Does the new or existing program help you accomplish your mission? If not, it should be put back on the drawing board. If yes, you should continue to pursue the program confident that it is in line with association and department goals. Connecting the program to your mission statement will help answer the questions, "Is this something we should do?" and "Is this worth doing?"

Step 2: The Member Experience. If possible, membership professionals should become members of their associations or at least put their names on the mailing list and seed their addresses on direct mail lists. Instead of focusing on when you send the welcome kit and the renewal notice, you focus on understanding what it is like for the member. How do the mailings read? How does the direct mail connect with the website? If a person calls, what is the availability of the membership department or program staff to answer questions? These are the elements that affect the service you provide and, ultimately, the member's experience. Few people will continue to be an advocate for the organization after a negative experience.

To get a handle on the member's experience, map what it currently is and then create a separate version of what it should be. The fictitious organization charted in Figure 3. Member Experience Compared may be vastly different from your association. The objective is to look at what it's really like for members and how you help them feel connected to your group.

Based on the variety of budgets associated with membership recruitment and retention campaigns, the above ideas may be more or less than you're able to do. There is no definitive rule here. Instead, the focus is on your unique organization, your unique members, and the unique benefits and experiences you can offer.

Once you have the real world picture and the ideal picture, the next step is to figure out how to elevate the current experience to meet your vision. Depending on the size of your membership, you will have to think creatively about how to change the experience. When funds are limited, focus on major milestones that will have the deepest reach. If you can institute a new telemarketing campaign whereby new members are called after 90 days, this may be the best way to introduce your organization to members and find out more about their specific needs. You will be surprised at the small touches that mean a lot to your members. You should always

Figure 3. Member Experience Compared

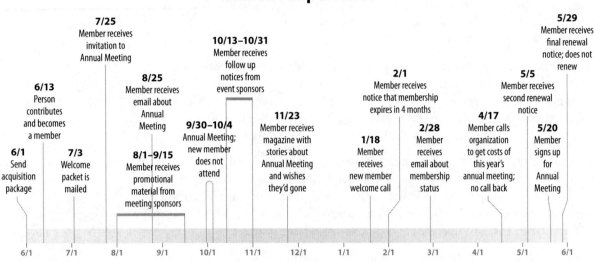

Current Experience

6/1
Send acquisition package

6/13
Person contributes and becomes a member

7/3
Welcome packet is mailed

7/25
Member receives invitation to Annual Meeting

8/1–9/15
Member receives promotional material from meeting sponsors

8/25
Member receives email about Annual Meeting

9/30–10/4
Annual Meeting; new member does not attend

10/13–10/31
Member receives follow up notices from event sponsors

11/23
Member receives magazine with stories about Annual Meeting and wishes they'd gone

1/18
Member receives new member welcome call

2/1
Member receives notice that membership expires in 4 months

2/28
Member receives email about membership status

4/17
Member calls organization to get costs of this year's annual meeting; no call back

5/5
Member receives second renewal notice

5/20
Member signs up for Annual Meeting

5/29
Member receives final renewal notice; does not renew

6/1 7/1 8/1 9/1 10/1 11/1 12/1 1/1 2/1 3/1 4/1 5/1 6/1

Improved Experience

6/1
Send acquisition package

6/13
Person contributes and becomes a member

7/25
Member receives invitation to Annual Meeting

8/1–9/15
Member receives promotional material from meeting sponsors

8/25
Member receives email about Annual Meeting

11/23
Member receives magazine with stories about Annual Meeting

2/1
Member receives notice that membership expires in 4 months

2/28
Member receives email about membership status

5/20
Member signs up for Annual Meeting

6/1 7/1 8/1 9/1 10/1 11/1 12/1 1/1 2/1 3/1 4/1 5/1 6/1

6/29
Welcome packet is mailed

8/1
Member receives personal call welcoming them to organization and explaining annual meeting

9/30–10/4
Annual Meeting; *member attends with other people from their company (your organization followed up with member to let them know of discounted rates for colleagues)*

10/11–10/29
Member receives follow up notices from event sponsors; *follows up with some of the sponsors regarding future partnerships*

1/18
Member receives 6 month follow up call

4/17
Member calls organization to get costs of this year's annual meeting; *call returned same day*

5/5
Member receives second renewal notice; *sends in renewal*

review what your competition is doing (i.e., join your competition and compare their experience to yours) but also look at for-profits for inspiration.

The experience will help you understand what it's currently like to be a member and it will help you visualize what you want that experience to be. It's important to focus on outbound communications, response time, and consistency of message. You are examining, at least, the full 12-month membership cycle. Depending on budget, you will incorporate new ideas and begin shaping the current experience to better fit your own expectations. With a smaller budget, you may have to pick the two to four major milestones that will have the greatest impact. With a more robust budget, you can address the entire experience, including considering outsourcing, revamping publications, and generating new community initiatives (listservers, networking opportunities, and more).

Step 3: Customer Loyalty. After you've created a memorable member service experience, you have to focus on the end result—loyalty. If your experience has met or exceeded all expectations, you have created a constituency that will be more loyal to your organization. You meet their basic needs, but you also offer tangible benefits beyond just being there when they call. You have entered the loyalty zone.

There are different ways to define loyalty. Who are your most loyal members? How do they act? What do they tell others about your association? As a first step, Jill Griffin[7] offers a two-part definition for customer loyalty: "Customer retention describes the length of relationship with a customer…. A firm's share of customer denotes the percentage of a customer's budget spent with the firm."

Retention. This is a common metric for membership professionals. The basic purpose is to identify how many members stick with you year after year. (See Chapter 16: Retention for more information.) The underlying principle is that if members continually renew their membership, then they must like the benefits you offer and value their membership. On an individual level, the bottom line in retention is a pretty simple yes or no question: Did they renew? For many organizations, I believe retention is too simple to be a standalone metric. Simply having a person give you the same amount of money year after year does not mean that the person is engaged in your mission.

Total Share of Customer. For this metric, you need to look at the bigger picture. Instead of a simple yes or no, you have to consider the needs of the person and how they use your organization. For associations, total share of customer is not just about whether members renew. It takes into account the other benefits and offerings you have for your constituency and the member's level of participation.

 • Does the person attend your conference or another organization's?
 • Does the person participate in grassroots activities?
 • Does the person contribute to listservers and/or special committees?

Your research would be incomplete if you didn't factor these activities into the member's experience. If you increase the person's engagement, you have, presumably, increased the value of the organization to the person and, subsequently, increased their loyalty.

Griffin[8] goes on to note that "a loyal customer is one who

1. makes regular repeat purchases,
2. purchases across product and service lines,
3. refers others, and
4. demonstrates immunity to the pull of the competition."

It is important to note that not every person requires participation in these ancillary activities in order to feel connected to the organization. The point is that if members want to participate, they are doing it through your association. You want the total share of the member's participation in your industry. If they renewed their $100 membership with you, but increased participation with another association, the retention speaks little of their loyalty. How long will it be before the other association has your $100?

In addition to mapping the experience, your organization should also understand the participation opportunities you are offering to members. The goal is to define the ideal member in terms of engagement. Create a table of all the possible activities/benefits within your organization and then determine what a sample group is doing, what the average person is doing, what you'd like people to be doing, and so on. Then, transfer the information to a simple table. You will immediately see your growth opportunities. (See Figure 4. Ideal Member Participation.)

Loyalty is based on a person's actions, not attitudes. The table should look at all types of engagement opportunities. You should arrive at a cumulative loyalty score that shows an increase in loyalty associated with an increase in participation.

Figure 4. Ideal Member Participation

	Sample member	Average member	Ideal Member	Action
Attendance at annual meeting				
Industry certification				
Committee member				
Participation in grassroots activities				
Donating at highest membership level				
Purchase of publications				
Professional development				

Step 4: Putting It All Together. By now, you should have a mission statement, an experience map of both the current situation and the ideal, and a picture of the loyal user/member who sticks with you and gives you everything he's got. You have created a foundation for all future decision making as well as an evaluation system for reviewing your current offerings.

You have undoubtedly worked with other departments to create these components, and you must share your end product with the rest of the association. You could schedule a conference call or town hall meeting to discuss the new vision and to get the buy-in of other departments. (You can't be the only one focusing on loyalty because the pieces are spread throughout the organization.) With the support of your Executive Director, work through the ideas with the rest of the staff and generate their support of your plan. Implementing, evaluating, and revising your plans is more enjoyable than looking at how your organization currently works and identify the areas where you're falling short.

While no two membership departments are exactly the same, there are commonalities that reach across all organizations. The strength of the department is in its people. The staff must have a clear understanding of your expectations and the department's goals. Furthermore, they should receive the proper training to ensure success. The department should also know the member experience and understand the connectivity between positive interactions and retention. Finally, the department's commitment to increasing member loyalty should never be compromised. A fully functioning membership department is easy to identify—staff are committed, members are engaged, and revenue has increased.

Sheri Jacobs, CAE, is managing director of McKinley Marketing, Inc., with offices in Washington, DC, and Chicago. In 2006-2007 she chaired ASAE & The Center's Membership Section Council. Email: sjacobs@mckinleymarketing.com.

Sara Miller, CAE, is the senior director of member loyalty and conferences/events with The Humane Society of the United States, Gaithersburg, Maryland. She has spent the last six years at The HSUS engaging people in the mission of Celebrating Animals, Confronting Cruelty. Email: smiller@humanesociety.org.

References

1. Buckingham, Marcus and Coffman, Curt. *First, Break All the Rules.* (Simon & Schuster, 1999).

2. Sanders, Tim. *The Likeability Factor.* (Crown Publishers, 2005).

3. Griffin, Jill. *Customer Loyalty.* (Jossey-Bass, 2002).

4. Customers First Awards. *Fast Company.* October 2004, p 81.

5. Pine, II, B. Joseph and Gilmore, James H. *The Experience Economy.* (Harvard Business School Press, 1999).

6. Buckingham, Marcus and Coffman, Curt. *First, Break All The Rules.* (Simon & Schuster, 1999).

7. Griffin, op cit, p 5.

8. Griffin, op cit, p 31-32.

List Rental Policy and Sample Order Form/Agreement

To ensure that a mailing list is used properly, it is important to create requirements and regulations. The Association Forum of Chicagoland, for example, imposes the following eligibility requirements:

- Relevant to association management
- Does not promote, market, or otherwise solicit any programs or services that Association Forum provides to its membership

Mailing List Rental Order Form

Name: _____

Address: _____

City, State, Zip: _____

Phone Number: _____

I am an Association Forum member: ☐ Yes ☐ No

Type of List Needed: ☐ CEOs only
                              ☐ CEOs & Association Professionals
                              ☐ All Members

Type of Labels Needed: ☐ Adhesive Labels
                                    OR
                              ☐ Electronic (to be used only by a bonded mailing house subject to the rental agreement)

Order of Sort Needed: ☐ Alphabetical by name
                              ☐ Zip Code Order
                              ☐ Alphabetical by association

I am enclosing the following items to complete this mailing list purchase:
        ☐ Signed contract
        ☐ Payment
        ☐ A copy of the piece to be sent

RENTAL AGREEMENT

This agreement is subject to the following conditions:

Should the mailing list renter request Association Forum's membership list on computer disk, Association Forum will deliver the computer disk to a bonded mailing house only.

The bonded mailing house is required to return the original computer disk to Association Forum within five days of completion of the mailing. By signing this agreement, the mailing list renter indicates that the mailing house they will utilize is a certified bonded mailing house.

The mailing list renter or bonded mailing house shall use the mailings lists and mailing labels provided by Association Forum only for pre-approved promotional mailings. The renter shall treat Association Forum's membership list and all mailing labels as confidential information. The renter shall not under any circumstances sell, loan, or circulate such membership lists to any third party, or use such membership lists for any other purpose.

Upon delivery of the proposed mailing piece to Association Forum's membership, the list renter shall cease using the membership list and shall immediately return the membership list and mailing labels to Association Forum.

The mailing list renter agrees that in utilizing Association Forum membership list, he/she will not disclose, transfer, duplicate, reproduce or retain any portion of the list in any form, by photocopying, electronic or any other means.

The mailing list renter agrees to reimburse Association Forum for all costs which the Forum may incur in enjoining unauthorized parties from using the membership list in all cases where such unauthorized parties gained access to the membership through the renter listed above or any of the renter's agents or employees.

The mailing list renter agrees the Association Forum will have the right to monitor the use of the membership list.

The mailing list renter agrees that the promotional piece supplied for approval with this agreement is the piece(s) that will comprise the mailing.

Only Association Forum members may address the promotional piece using "Dear Association Forum Member."

Signature below indicates complete acceptance of the above conditions and constitutes a contract between the Association Forum and the above stated mailing list renter.

APPENDIX 2

Sample Job Description Form

Job Title: _____

Department: _____

Job Code: _____ Grade: _____ Reports to: _____

ESSENTIAL DUTIES AND PRIMARY JOB PURPOSE *Other duties may be assigned.*

REPRESENTATIVE TASKS & MAJOR RESPONSIBILITIES:

QUALIFICATION REQUIREMENTS: *To perform this job successfully, an indi idual must be able to perform each essential duty and task satisfactorily. The requirements listed below are representati e of the knowledge, skill, and/or ability required. Reasonable accommodations will be made to enable indi iduals with disabilities to perform the essential functions.*

EMPLOYMENT DISCLAIMER

Position Description Questionnaire

1. Position Identification

Position Title: _____

Name: _____   Department: _____

Your Time in Current Position: _____   Today's Date: _____

2. Primary Purpose of Your Position
In one or two sentences, explain the primary purpose of your job.

3. Major Duties
Please list five to seven major job duties and the percentage of time you spend on each over the course of a year. The percent of time spent on all duties together (considering all hours worked) should not be greater than 100 percent, but may be less, since you are to list your major duties, not all duties. Indicate criticality per questionnaire instructions.

Duties	% of Time	Criticality (Hi/Med/Low)

4. Education and Specific Training
What should be the minimum schooling for a new person entering this position?

☐ High School   ☐ Some College
☐ Bachelor's Degree   ☐ Master's Degree
☐ Other

If specific training or degree is required, in what field should it be?

5. Experience
How much total prior on-the-job experience would be required for a new person with education as in question 4? This may or may not equate to your personal experience level.

☐ No experience (i.e., a capable person could quickly learn to do this job)
☐ Less than six months   ☐ Six months to one year
☐ One to three years   ☐ Four to six years
☐ Seven or more years

6. Organizational Relationship
Complete the organization chart using correct organizational titles. Include: a) the first level or management above your position; b) your position; and, c) the position(s) reporting to your position, if any.

Title(s) of positions that report to you:

7. Decision-making Authority

Give three specific examples of the types of decisions you make:

Decisions that require approval by higher or lateral authority:

8. Financial Responsibilities

9. Additional Information

Give any other information about your job not included in your previous answers that you consider important.

The Membership Department Working With Others to Accomplish Goals

By Sheri Jacobs, CAE, and Sara Miller, CAE

IN THIS CHAPTER:
- Strategic relationships among departments
- Avoiding silo mentalities
- When outsourcing works

MEMBERS ARE THE LIFEBLOOD for all associations. Their contributions are vitally important to the creation and distribution of all products, programs, and services. Likewise, good employees in the membership department will tremendously affect your recruitment and retention efforts. According to Bill Fromm[1] of the Harvard Business School, companies that distinguish themselves by the way they hire, train, and treat their employees experience growth rates from 60 to 300 percent higher than their competitors.

If a member has a great experience with your association, chances are that it is because of an interaction with a staff person or it is the result of the hard work and dedication of the association staff. As Mark Hughes[2], author of *Buzzmarketing: Get People to Talk About Your Stuff*, says, "When it comes right down to it, advertising impressions don't count. Connections count. We connect with people, not corporations."

Membership departments are successful only if they truly integrate their efforts with all other departments within the organization. Making this happen requires a clear understanding of the scope of the membership department (including staff roles and responsibilities), its relationship with other departments, professional development and training and customer/member service.

Strategic Relationships Among Departments

Many organizations use strategic alliances to maximize opportunities and make the most of limited resources. In fact, it is not uncommon for associations to rely on many partnerships to deliver their products, programs, and services to members. Strategic alliances work both internally and externally, for both large and small associations.

In any association, it is essential for the membership department to build relationships to meet recruitment and retention goals. At a small staff association, the membership director or manager should build alliances with

- Outside vendors such as contract meeting planners, human resources managers, graphic designers, printers, and other suppliers.

- Internal staff responsible for finance and/or administration

- Administrative staff

Outside vendors should be an important part of your team. They can help you stay on budget and deliver a professional message. Strategic alliances within an organization can create many benefits for each department. If your membership and marketing department consists of just one individual—you—then it is essential that you build your support staff using trusted and experienced outside vendors. Maintaining relationships with these individuals will be an important part of sustaining a consistent and professional image and message.

If you are part of a larger membership staff, the importance of building alliances with other departments is equally essential. Attracting and keeping members go hand in hand with all other association activities. Members will want to join the organization and renew their memberships if they know the value and are actively engaged. While it may appear that this responsibility falls on other departments, such as education or publications, the success of their efforts directly affect the membership department's ability to reach its goals.

Education and Meetings. Conferences and trade shows are a mainstay of association offerings, and professional growth is a common reason members join associations. Research can help assess what members need, their satisfaction with current offerings, and the gaps between the two. With this knowledge, individuals in the membership department can make better decisions when developing a marketing plan to promote these offerings.

Segmentation of membership. Marketing professionals know that one of the most effective ways to promote a meeting or event is through segmenting their audience. In most associations, the membership includes individuals or companies from various backgrounds and size. Tailoring a message to each audience will increase the likelihood of a positive response. Various elements of the meeting may appeal to one audience and not to another. The membership department can assist the education/meetings department by delivering mailing lists that are segmented.

For individual member organizations, segmentation could include

- Career stage (number of years in the profession)
- Age
- Gender

- Ethnicity
- Income
- Number of years as a member
- Level of affiliation (ad hoc, committee member, board member, no involvement)
- Customer behavior (first time or repeat buyer)
- Location
- Specialty
- Generation (e.g., Baby Boomers or Generation X)
- Position, type of practice

In addition to the segments above, a trade association may also segment its audience by:

- Size
- Employees
- Revenue
- Branches
- Business Activities

New member engagement. The first meeting attended by a new member is often the most important. The impression may last a lifetime and will affect that member's perception of the organization. It may also be a deciding factor in whether a new member attends another event. For many members, networking is one of the top reasons for attending an event. To create a successful and memorable experience, the membership department should collaborate with the meetings department to create a new member orientation or networking event during the conference. Pairing new members with longtime members will strengthen the organization's relationship with its most vulnerable group—new members.

Finance Department. A critical aspect of managing an organization is determining the monthly cash flow. During the budgeting process, the membership department should forecast when the organization will receive dues revenue from renewals and new member enrollment. By accurately projecting and updating revenue, the association is better equipped to approve expenditures and move forward with its projects. (For a more in-depth examination of the membership department's relationship to finance, see Chapter 13: Financial Management.)

Communications/Publications. Accuracy in the membership department's database is critical to the communications efforts of an association. It is a continual process involving changes and updates ranging from addresses and titles in all associations to other critical segmentation areas such as revenues and number of employees in trade associations.

Email. Email communication is one of the most common ways to communicate with members. The combination of its relatively low cost and speed of delivery makes it a highly desirable way to send messages or deliver information. However, members will not pay attention to your email if they receive too many messages or if the messages are not relevant to them. By maintaining a database with the most up-to-date member profiles, you can create more specific and targeted email communications, resulting in a higher open and click-through rate.

> ### *Email Tracking Tip*
>
> Track your association's email communications by creating a spreadsheet that includes each category of membership and lists every email that is sent from the organization. This will give you clear understanding of the content and frequency of messages members receive from your organization.

Publications. Magazine circulation numbers and advertising rates rely on accurate membership and subscription data. In many associations, this data needs to be segmented and well maintained for more effective ad sales as well as for independent audits of circulation. The membership department can assist the communications department by producing quarterly and/or annual reports for the creation of accurate circulation figures.

Administrative Staff. Administrative employees generally have the most frequent member contact. Ironically, they are sometimes the most underappreciated individuals on an association staff. They can be a source of feedback and information. Meet with the administrative staff on a monthly basis to make sure they feel like a valuable part of the team. Find out what questions members are asking.

Avoiding Silo Mentalities

Member-centric organizations understand the importance of good customer service. Good customer service begins with knowledgeable and helpful staff. While these two statements may seem obvious, not all organizations educate their staff so that they are equipped to answer or find the answer to a member's inquiry. The larger an association staff, the more difficult it may become to ensure that those responsible for different areas of member contact and services are aware of the activities of other staff.

Silo mentality is a term that refers to employees concentrating solely on their own areas and not working together in the bigger picture of the whole organization. New staff organizational formats can help build teamwork and better communications that break down silo mentalities. The membership professional can play a key role in combating the silo effect by creating and implementing a cluster system. While creating clusters will have no impact on the organizational structure, assembling leaders from departments with related responsibilities can enhance the potential for cross-marketing, set standards for communications, and establish a culture of accountability that crosses specific departmental lines.

Sharing Information. The key to all successful relationships is the exchange of information. To evaluate your association staff's knowledge of the association as a whole, consider these questions:

- If you asked staff members from any department a question about an upcoming event, service, or benefit would they know the answer or know where to find it?

- Are copies of all marketing collateral and publications distributed to every person on staff?

Sharing information among the entire staff about all events, programs, benefits, and services is essential to good customer service. While not everyone will know all details by memory, everyone should have easy access to the information and know how to find answers to commonly asked questions.

Imagine a member calls your office because he has recently moved and wants to ensure that you have his current mailing address. During the conversation he asks about the early registration deadline and fees for an upcoming meeting. What happens next?

- Is the member transferred to another individual or department?

- What if he has another question on a different issue? Is he transferred a second time?

- What happens if he reaches voice mail? Will he miss the early registration deadline because his call is not returned until a few days later?

- How many times will he be transferred before he receives the answer to a question all staff should have the answer to?

Create a distribution list of all staff members for every marketing piece created for your members. Distribute copies of all member communications to the entire association staff as soon as a mailing has been sent to members. While this can be done electronically, it is more likely to be read and referenced if a printed copy is distributed. The membership department could also create binders for all staff persons to keep on their desks so they have a place to put communication materials and will have easy access to all information. Better yet, include an FAQ for events, programs, and products and distribute it to each staff member. If your association uses an intranet or Sharepoint-type site, that is also a great way to collect important information in a location accessible to every staff member.

Items for Staff Distribution

Items that should be distributed to every staff person, regardless of position or department:

- Press Releases
- Program brochures (print and electronic)
- Magazine, journal, or newsletter
- Membership application
- Membership brochure
- Affinity program brochures

- New member kit
- List of publications and/or books
- General FAQs about the association
- Anything else that your association sends to its members to promote a product or service

---

Feedback. When associations are interested in gathering information about their members' needs, the most often neglected or overlooked source of this information is feedback. Feedback given during everyday conversations with your members provides honest and unsolicited information about your programs, products, and services. It usually happens in a simple and unplanned manner and, as a result, your staff may not have the tools to communicate this information to the appropriate department. Make sure you have a clear communication policy so that feedback is shared quickly and easily.

Cross-selling. One advantage to sharing all information about the benefits, services, education, and events of your association is the opportunity to cross-sell.

Cross-selling is a marketing term for the practice of suggesting related products or services to a customer who is considering buying something. If a member is registering for an education event, for example, you may want to suggest a publication or book on the same topic that is for sale from your organization. Cross-selling can be accomplished live or online if the association staff communicates and shares information. To create an environment where staff members routinely cross-sell other products and services, it is essential that all staff are on a distribution list of all marketing materials.

When Outsourcing Works

Have you ever looked at your budget, your strategic goals, and your staff and thought, "It can't be done?" You're not alone. Even if your association employs in-house staff to handle marketing and communications, at times you may need extra assistance. Membership departments typically outsource

• graphic design

• branding

• legal

• copywriting and editing

• web design and maintenance

• printing

• fulfillment

• public relations

- email marketing
- market research
- telemarketing services

Associations outsource for a variety of reasons:

- **Cost.** It is too expensive to employ a full-time staff person for work that is needed only periodically.

- **Expertise.** You can get the job done more efficiently and effectively by hiring someone with experience.

- **Time.** Major events and membership campaigns keep association staff extremely busy. Additional support may be needed because there simply isn't enough manpower to get everything done.

How an organization is perceived is in large measure the result of public perception, organizational image, and the totality of communications that shape the mind-set of its members, colleagues, suppliers, and the community at large. To avoid multiple messages and maintain a consistent look, associations should:

- Develop a graphics standard manual to be shared with both staff and outside vendors.
- Select only one or two vendors for the creation of marketing materials.

Knowledge sharing and collaboration between departments encourages good customer service, which in turn helps determine if members will stay and will make other purchases. While most organizations understand how important it is for departments to work together to achieve goals related to membership, not all embrace the actions needed to ensure this goal is attained.

Sheri Jacobs, CAE, is managing director of McKinley Marketing, Inc., Chicago. Her association experience includes nearly five years as the chief marketing officer and director of membership for the Association Forum of Chicagoland as well as director-level positions in membership and marketing at the American Bar Association and the American Academy of Implant Dentistry. She was 2006-2007 chair of ASAE & The Center's Membership Section Council. Email: sjacobs@mckinleymarketing.com

Sara Miller, CAE, is the senior director of member loyalty and conferences/events with The Humane Society of the United States, Gaithersburg, Maryland. She has spent the last six years at The HSUS engaging people in the mission of Celebrating Animals, Confronting Cruelty. Email: smiller@humanesociety.org.

References

1. Bill Fromm. *The Ten Commandments of Business and How to Break Them: Secrets for Improving Employee Morale, Enhancing Customer Service, Increasing Company Profit.* (Putnam, 1991)

2. Mark Hughes. *Buzzmarketing: Get People to Talk About Your Stuff.* (Portfolio Hardcover, 2005)

Membership Categories and Dues Structures

By Michael Connor and Jay Younger

6

IN THIS CHAPTER:

- A review of the types of membership categories
- Pricing structures
- Policies for billing, membership terms, and reporting

I N THE 1970S, MORE than half the revenue of associations came from membership dues. By 1999, dues as a percentage of overall revenue had decreased to 35 percent median and 38.1 percent average. And according to ASAE & The Center's *Operating Ratio Report,* 12th Edition (2003), dues comprised about one third of overall revenue (28.8 percent median and 34.3 percent average). Although associations' reliance on dues revenues has declined across time, membership dues remain the largest single source of association revenue, and membership departments are charged with important fiduciary responsibilities within their associations.

Various factors affect an association's reliance on dues. For instance, trade associations derive more revenue from dues than individual or professional membership societies (34 percent versus 25 percent). Total revenue and staff size also play into the ratio. Associations with smaller revenues and staff sizes likely will rely more on membership dues.

Most associations have additional sources of revenue, such as professional development programs, annual meetings, advertising sales, affinity programs, sponsorships, and grants, to support programmatic activities. As a membership professional, you may be responsible for some of these alternative sources of revenues, or you may be charged to work closely with other staff involved in developing such resources.

Dues are often viewed as more stable than other revenue sources, such as grants and sponsorships, which may be restricted, expire, or be withdrawn, or professional development activities, which are vulnerable to business-related travel downturns such as the one that occurred following the terrorist attacks of 2001. But dues revenues may also be influenced by outside factors. Industry consolidation can reduce the number of dues-paying members in trade associations, leading to significant losses in revenue, and economic downturns may affect corporate support of membership in individual member organizations. (If the employer does not pay an employee's dues as a part of a professional development budget, the individual member may not join or renew.)

Since a significant part of the cost of operating an association is still borne by members through the dues they pay, the leadership of the association must ensure that the dues structure is providing the amount of income needed, is seen as equitable and rational by the membership, and will sustain the association for the long term. Creating appropriate membership categories and setting dues structures and policies is critical to meeting these goals. This chapter explores the most common member categories, pricing models, and policies used in nonprofit organizations, and the next chapter will focus on initiatives to restructure categories and increase dues.

Membership Categories and Organization Types

An association's bylaws establish the legal parameters for membership in the organization by defining qualifications of who may be members. These definitions of membership are often written broadly to allow the association flexibility in determining which types of members to recruit.

For example, many associations create a category of membership that includes individuals or organizations that are "interested in" or "related to" the trade or profession that the association represents. This umbrella allows the association to pursue a wide range of prospects in its recruitment efforts. Similarly, organizations that serve a diverse population of members may opt to create different rights and privileges for various categories of membership, including

- Eligibility to vote in elections
- The right to hold office
- Participation in committees
- Different dues amounts
- Various member benefits

Chapter 1 described the types of nonprofit organizations, focusing on their scope and purpose. How membership in an organization is defined determines not only the operations of the association but also how dues are set and collected. The framework of membership provided through the bylaws usually creates an organizational dues structure following one of the models outlined below:

Individual Membership Organization (IMO). Membership is tied to an individual's name. Professional societies, unions, and donor-based organizations (for example, the American Medical Association, the International Brotherhood of Electrical Workers, and the Humane Society of the United States) are typical IMOs). In most cases, membership in an IMO is portable, in that the individual member remains a member regardless of changes in employment setting or location.

Organizational Membership (Trade Association). Membership in the association is held by an organization, which pays annual dues on behalf of its employees and constituents. The National Association of Manufacturers and the Aerospace Industries Association are examples of trade associations whose members tend to be companies involved in a particular industry or trade.

Combination of Individual and Organizational Members (Hybrid). The association's bylaws allow both individuals and organizations to join, and separate dues structures are created for each scenario. InfoComm International and The National Association of Industrial and Office Properties are good examples of hybrid associations. In some cases, unique benefits are provided to one membership type or the other. Some hybrids stipulate that employees of an organizational member must also join as individual members to participate in committees or special interest groups.

Association Membership (Federation). Associations whose members are other associations typically operate in a federated structure in which each party shares a percentage of member dues. In many cases, a federated structure includes relationships at the national, regional, state, or local level. The Federation of State Medical Boards of the United States and the Federation of Animal Science Societies are examples.

Components (Chapters, Sections). Many organizations have multiple components that members can join based on geographic location, such as Florida Chapter; content area, such as Marketing Section; or other areas of specialty. Some associations include component memberships with base dues, while others charge a la carte for additional component memberships.

A wide range of membership categories is seen within the organization types. While most of the categories below are more common in IMOs, some hybrid and trade associations also employ a variety of membership categories.

- **Active** (sometimes referred to as full or primary member). Holds all the rights and privileges of membership and typically pays the highest dues.

- **International.** Category expressly for members based outside the United States. In some cases, services are delivered electronically. (See Virtual Membership below.)

- **Student.** Offered to qualified undergraduate, graduate, and postgraduate students, usually with discounted dues and sometimes non-voting status or other limited participation

- **Associate/Affiliate.** In some cases, associate/affiliate members are vendors that serve the industry and typically join the association for opportunities to interact with the primary membership. In other cases, associate members may be employees of an organizational member or do not yet have the professional qualifications to be elected to full membership.

- **Retired.** Membership category created for non-practicing professionals. Typically includes a reduced bundle of goods and services.

• **Virtual Membership.** At a reduced fee, members receive all communications from the association through email and the web. May include restrictions on voting, participating in member discounts on products and services, or receiving publications by mail.

• **Honorary.** Membership bestowed to honored individuals, such as founders, industry luminaries, or past presidents

• **Fellow.** Members who are elected to fellowship often have met educational criteria or have distinguished themselves in the field they serve.

• **Life.** Used to denote either members who have paid in advance for benefits for the rest of their lives or for members who have eclipsed a certain formula of membership tenure and/or age (for example, at least 30 years of membership and at least 65 years old). Membership dues are often discounted or waived upon induction into life membership.

• **Component Membership.** Members are often asked (or required) to join one or more chapters or sections for an additional fee.

Pricing Structures

Whether your association dues revenue constitutes the major source of operating income or is only one of several substantial sources, pricing policies are important to calculating budgets and to building perception of value among members and prospects. As a membership professional, you should understand the variety of dues models used in associations and their implications on the operations of the membership department.

Flat Fee. In flat fee structures, membership dues are fixed for all members, regardless of their individual characteristics. Organizations that perceive their markets as relatively homogenous may use a flat fee approach to keep the dues structure simple and relatively affordable. Similarly, many organizations that use flat fees have well-developed programs and services that are available for purchase or member participation. One well known example of a flat fee dues structure can be seen at AARP, formerly known as the American Association of Retired Persons, an IMO that has membership dues of $12.50 per year, regardless of the type of membership purchased. AARP's robust portfolio of revenue-producing programs means that dues can be kept low, as they account for only 24 percent of the organization's total revenue.

Tiered Dues Structures for Individual and Organizational Memberships

Individual Membership	Organizational Membership
Job Title/Role: More senior level positions typically pay higher dues than less senior counterparts. For example, principals in accounting firms often pay higher dues than staff accountants to join professional accounting societies. **Geography:** For organizations with an international membership component, the country of residence can influence the dues amount. Many societies follow World Bank classifications to offer lower dues to members who reside in less developed economies. **Salary:** Some academic societies create levels of membership dues based on the members' annual salaries. Members typically self report to ensure that their current dues amount is accurate each year at renewal. **Job Setting:** Multidisciplinary societies often create different dues price points for members in industry, academia, and government.	**Annual Revenue:** According to ASAE & The Center *Policies and Procedures* (2006), the most common metric used by trade associations (47 percent), revenue-based dues structures assess progressively higher dues based on higher sales volumes. This regressive tax model enables an association to charge higher dues to companies that can afford to pay more. **Number of Employees:** Dues escalate based on the number of employees in the firm (or division). **Production:** Some trade associations use output from plants or facilities to calculate dues. Several association examples can be found in the lumber industry. **Organization Type:** Nonprofit organizations and government agencies are often offered reduced dues to join trade associations.
Tiered by Level of Benefit Both IMOs and trade associations can offer membership dues based on distinct levels of benefits. In this model, individuals/organization can choose the specific bundle of goods and services that best suits their needs.	

Tiered. Tiered membership dues structures vary based on some defined criteria. In trade associations, tiered dues may be determined by company revenue or number of employees. In IMOs, such as dental associations or academic societies, job titles may determine which tier of dues a member pays. Tiers can be loosely organized based on the concepts of categories or calculations.

Categories. Tiered structures that establish fixed prices based on defined criteria. For example, a trade association may structure dues based on the number of employees a member company has, as shown below:

Number of Employees	Annual Dues
Under 1,000	$1,000
1,000-5,000	$1,500
5,001-15,000	$2,000
15,001 +	$3,000

In trade associations or IMOs, a tiered dues structure may be based on the number of people from the member group who join. For instance, there may be 200 employees but only 10 qualify as members of the association. Perhaps the first three members joining are assessed one rate and any successive people in the same company who become members are charged at discounted rates.

Number of Members	Annual Dues per Person
1-3	$200
4-10	$175
11-20	$150

Calculations. Tiered structures that involve a formula or equation to calculate dues. Using the employee-based structure, a dues model based on calculation may resemble the following:

Number of employees in firm	120
Annual dues per employee	× $100
Total dues	= $12,000

Similarly, a trade association basing dues on revenues might set a structure based on 0.03 percent, with the following type of calculation:

Annual company revenues	$25,000,000
Times fixed percentage	× 0.0003
Total dues	= $7,500

Organizations using calculations must decide whether to impose a cap on dues at a certain level, a common practice, particularly for trade associations that calculate dues based on annual revenue. Establishing a cap provides the highest dues-paying members with an element of predictability, namely that dues will not exceed a given amount even if revenue increases dramatically. This provides member organizations with added foresight for budgeting purposes and is often seen as a way to level the proverbial playing field for the largest member companies.

Dues Monitoring. Similarly, the association must consider whether the member's eligibility for an appropriate category can be verified or if each member will be asked to self report. Consider trade associations that base membership dues on annual revenue or budget. In some cases, these figures become part of the public domain (Forms 10-K, 990) and can be verified. However, for most small businesses and individuals, it is likely that the members will be on the honor system to report their revenues and their corresponding dues fee truthfully. Underreporting can erode dues revenue. There are ways to police dues reporting if an association wishes to take a hard line on the issue. For example, one association lists member companies in its membership directory according to the annual revenue they

Are Dues a Fixed Price or Do They Vary?

	All Respondents	Trade	IMO
Fixed price	46%	21%	68%
Varies	54%	79%	32%

N = 572

Source: ASAE & The Center *Polices and Procedures* (2006).

report for dues purposes. In this case, it is more important to most members to accurately represent their size than to attempt to cheat on membership dues.

Policies for Billing, Membership Terms, and Reporting

Association bylaws usually dictate the parameters of who qualifies to be a member by specifying categories and terms of membership. Membership policies and procedures should spell out details, including the dues structure, billings and collections, grace periods between expiration of membership and termination of member benefits, and reinstatement processes. In some associations, bylaws address these specifics; in others, these policies are voted on by the members or set by staff, and some organizations are changing how these policies are set. For example, in one association, about 25 years old, the bylaws spelled out in detail exactly how dues were to be assessed and at what point a member in arrears should be terminated. Over time, these provisions had become outdated and constricted the association's ability to do business. In a recent revision of its bylaws, all these policies were replaced by a single clause: "The dues of the association will be determined by a vote of the membership." This left control of the dues in the hands of the membership, while allowing the staff, with board guidance as appropriate, to set policy on billing and collection procedures.

Billing and Remittance of Dues. Billing and remittance policies should consider whether memberships are based on anniversaries or on calendar years, how staff will handle processing, and how incentives may be used for both existing and prospective members. Procedures should include ways to facilitate payment, such as accepting credit cards and using e-commerce functions on the association's web site, and methods of training staff charged with interacting with members in the enlistment or renewal process.

Most associations begin the renewal process two to three months before membership is scheduled to expire. Generally, a series of hard-copy and electronic invoices are sent in advance of the expiration date. Members who have not renewed their membership are typically sent two or three reminder notices. Most associations also offer a grace period of one to three months, or up to six months, before terminating member benefits. Policies vary, and in some instances a specific member benefit may be withheld to spur payment from a member who has not renewed.

For example, in one association, a $400-$500 member discount on registration for the annual meeting is seen as a particularly valuable benefit and is a primary reason many organizations join. Because the association's annual meeting is held early in the membership year, individuals with expired memberships are not allowed the member discount for registration until they pay their dues. Other associations may offer some incentive, such as a discount off the regular price of dues, or a premium, such as a printed T-shirt, mug, or pen, to members who pay their dues early in the cycle.

Sample Renewal Timeline

November 1	December 1	January 1	February 1	March 1	April 1	May 1
60 days prior	*30 days prior*	*At expiration*	*30 days after expiration*	*60 days after expiration*	*90 days after expiration*	*120 days after expiration*
Email	**Invoice (first notice)**	**Invoice (second notice)**	**Invoice email**	**Email**	**Inactive notice (final notice)**	**Exit survey**

Membership Terms. The basic term of membership in most associations is one year, but that year is measured and dues are assessed in many different ways.

Calendar Year. Some associations renew all memberships at the same time, most often coinciding with the calendar year. However, a calendar term may also apply to the U.S. government fiscal year (October through September) or some other significant period, such as the academic year in the case of associations whose members are educational institutions or teaching professionals. The amount of dues for a new member's initial membership is often prorated for members who join at a time other than the beginning of the membership year. Some associations require full payment of a member who joins in the first three or six months of a membership year and prorate for the remaining nine or six months; others simply prorate at one twelfth of annual dues multiplied by the number of months remaining in the membership year.

For example, if an association's membership year runs October 1 through September 30, and dues cost $200 per year, here are two ways an association could deal with a member who joins in December:

• Option 1: Payment in full for full 12 months = $200

• Option 2: Prorate October and November. 10/12 = $166.67

Calendar year benefits include:

• The organization knows relatively early in the membership year how much revenue to expect from membership, particularly if accurate records are kept from year to year on the pace of incoming dues revenue.

• Some associations offer "15 for the price of 12" new member promotions three months before the start of the membership year. A new member pays a full year's dues and the association has the benefit, at a relatively low cost, of establishing itself as part of the member's life before having to bill them for renewal.

What Is the Basis for Dues Billing?

	All Respondents	Trade	IMO
Anniversary	33%	25%	39%
Calendar year	51%	57%	46%
Other	16%	17%	15%

N = 569

Source: ASAE & The Center *Polices and Procedures* (2006).

Calendar year drawbacks include:

- Concentrated, heavy workload of processing annual dues invoices and incoming payments may require additional temporary staff or outsourcing.

- If dues are prorated, new members who paid a relatively small prorated dues amount in the last few months of the membership year and are then faced with a larger bill for renewing their membership may not renew for the full term.

Anniversary. In some associations, memberships expire on the anniversary of the date the member joined the organization, which may or may not be rounded to the nearest month. In this scenario, there is typically no need to prorate, as new members receive a 12-month membership year from the date they join. Anniversary billing benefits include:

- Steady year-round cash flow from dues revenue

- Provides convenience for the member, while spreading out the workload of processing invoices and payments

Anniversary billing drawbacks include:

- The association must dedicate staff to dues processing year-round; even so, dues processing workload may be heavier in some months than in others, particularly if the association has converted from an annual dues billing to anniversary billing or if there is a surge of membership before or after trade shows or conferences.

- Complicates calculation of retention rate

- May lead to "slippage" in membership. Say a member joined in January and receives a renewal notice the following December. Life intervenes, and the member doesn't pay dues for the next year until early February. If the association then sets the membership to expire the following February, instead of January, the association loses a month's worth of dues. This can result in a significant loss of revenue over time.

- Renewal campaign is year-round.

- Perks such as annual meeting discounts are more difficult to implement.

In either case, converting from one method to another can create a series of database, accounting, and communication issues.

Reporting. Membership professionals are not usually accountants; in fact, they may be more attuned to marketing. Nevertheless, as a membership professional, you must ensure that dues revenues are being reported and handled efficiently and you may be working closely with a CFO or accountant to record and track dues. (See Chapter 13: Financial Management and Budgeting.) Depending on its needs, there are a number of ways an association may report dues revenue for benchmarking purposes. Some associations report revenues based on the membership year to which income is applied. Others report dues in the fiscal year in which is the revenue is received, regardless of the membership year to which it is applied. For instance, if an association's fiscal year and membership year coincide with the calendar year, the association usually sends dues invoices in November for the membership year that will begin January 1. Some members renew their memberships as soon as they receive the invoice, and the association receives the payments prior to the end of the fiscal year. Some associations apply that payment to the fiscal year in which it is received, and others apply it to the membership year that begins on January 1. Both are correct, as long as the same practice is applied consistently from year to year.

Also for the sake of consistency from year to year and in the interest of accurate forecasting, many associations mail dues invoices on the same date from year to year, in order to ensure that an accurate comparison can be made of the rate at which dues revenues accumulate, or the rate at which members renew.

Whatever your association's reliance on dues, as the membership professional, your attention to dues pricing and policies is critical. As your industry or association changes, you will need to monitor revenues, consider possibilities for new categories, and report accurately the affects of dues models and pricing on the fiscal health and potential growth of the association. For more information, see Chapter 7: Dues Structures, Increases, and Restructuring.

Michael Connor is director of membership at Independent Sector in Washington, DC, the leading coalition of charities, foundation, and corporate philanthropy programs. His experience includes seven years in membership at the National Association of College and University Business Officers and many years in the hospitality industry. Michael is a member of ASAE & The Center's Membership Section Council and has written and presented widely on issues related to progressive membership protocol, processes, and practice. Email: michaelc@independentsector.org.

Jay Younger is managing partner and chief consultant at McKinley Marketing, Inc., with offices in Washington, DC, and Chicago. An ASAE & The Center Fellow, he also chaired the organization's Membership Section Council in 2004–2005. Email: jyounger@ mckinleymarketing.com.

Dues Structures, Increases, and Restructuring

By Michael Connor and Jay Younger

7

IN THIS CHAPTER:
- Establishing a dues structure
- Implementing a dues increase
- Restructuring dues
- Financial modeling for dues restructures
- Other membership-based revenues

I N CONSIDERING DUES, EVERY association's leadership must first decide two major points:

- Should a member's dues fully cover the cost of providing basic member services to that member?
- Should member services be bundled or provided on an a la carte basis?

Establishing a dues structure is a multivariable equation and must be informed by a variety of considerations. A dues structure that has been in place for many years bears close examination and may be in need of revision. Over the course of time, the industry on which a trade association or professional society is based may have changed, grown, or realigned itself, and the association and the entities that comprise it may simply have outgrown the dues structure.

Establishing a Dues Structure

Whether you are setting up a dues structure for the first time or considering dues restructuring, you should consider all the implications and repercussions of the process as well as the outcomes. Ultimately, an effective dues structure should be:

- Affordable: Will prospective members have adequate funding to afford dues (regardless of the value delivered)?

- Competitive: Gather data relative to other associations with similar programs, products, and services. How are they bundled or unbundled?

- Equitable: Is the dues structure equitable for the various dues-paying members? Are there inherent inequities in the dues structure?

- Simple: Is the dues structure easy to comprehend and can it be clearly communicated to members and prospects? Will prospective members be confused by too many options?

- Well Aligned: Does the dues structure support the strategic goals of the organization and has it been developed in close relationship to other efforts?

- Scalable: Will the dues structure provide room for growth in key markets and will new categories become sustainable over time?

Bundled Structures. Nearly all associations offer some bundle of goods and services in return for membership dues. Typically, dues may include services such as

- Information (magazines, legislative updates, e-bulletins, web site)

- Membership department operations (data entry, invoicing, membership cards, membership directory)

- Programs (publication catalogs, program schedules, research, planning)

- Advocacy (lobbying, grassroots, congressional, regulatory)

- General administration (building rent, office equipment, computers and servers, phone system, administrative staff)

Most associations provide these services for members before any nondues revenue is collected. Therefore, some associations attempt to create a membership structure in which dues cover the costs of providing these basic services. However, others treat membership as a loss leader; it serves as an easy point of entry after which members can be sold additional products and services and/or the association can leverage large membership numbers in the political arena.

Of course, calculating the cost to serve a member is perhaps one of the thorniest questions association professionals face in considering their dues structure. (See Chapter 14: Financial Metrics for the Membership Professional.) Typical expenses associated with basic member service include:

- Production, printing, and mailing a magazine or journal

- Creation and maintenance of the association's web site

- Salaries and training for membership staff and cost of membership administration (renewal notices, mailing, membership cards, incentives)

- Costs associated with producing e-newsletters or other communications

- Research and/or lobbying efforts

- Discounts extended to members for association events

To calculate the cost to serve a member, should the association:

a. Add up these costs and divide by the number of members?

b. Divide its total operating budget (exclusive of fundraising) by the number of members?

c. Use another method which incorporates other costs?

Where exactly should the association draw the line at what costs to include? In some associations, including most costs would result in dues sufficiently high enough to eliminate a substantial sector of the membership. Many associations do come up with a figure, but it is generally arbitrary and may be used to support a predetermined outcome. However your association chooses to calculate the cost to serve a member, you should document exactly what costs are included so that future efforts are informed by a well-defined process. This longitudinal data (i.e., how has the cost to serve a member changed over time) is far more useful than a snapshot at any particular moment in time.

A La Carte or Cafeteria Plan. Memberships of this sort are still relatively uncommon in the association community, as most organizations find that the cost/benefit of unbundling dues untenable. Ordinarily, associations with a la carte structures offer aggressively discounted pricing on programs, products, and services. For example, organizations with a la carte structures that want to prioritize membership recruitment may create a far higher nonmember price for various programs to encourage membership in the organization. Conversely, some associations prefer to establish a "big tent" in which all members of the community at large can participate in the programs of the association. These organizations typically offer less of a discount for members to attend events or purchase products and services.

Implementing a Dues Increase

To maintain its operating budget from year to year (adjusted for inflation) or to increase organizational capacity, an association will need to increase its dues from time to time. In some associations, this happens naturally, without the need to formally institute a dues increase. Particularly in associations with organizational membership, dues may be based on the member companies' gross revenues, payroll, staff size, net profit, or some other indicator of the members' size. In such instances, as the member organization grows, the amount it pays in dues to the association will increase as well.

Types of Increases. When dues are not keeping pace with the association's operating costs or programmatic goals, an association may need to increase the rate at which it assesses dues.

Annual Increases. The most common type of dues increase is an annual increase, often tied to the consumer price index. Often these "CPI" adjustments are intended to compensate for buying power lost to inflation in such areas as staff salaries, printing and postage costs, and keeping pace with technological advances. Many associations with historically strong retention rates typically do not see much resistance to nominal increases in membership fees and may institute increases every year without major discussion.

Ad Hoc Increases. Rather than an annual increase, some associations opt for larger, less frequent increases. In some associations, this is seen as less burdensome by the membership because they don't have to vote on an increase every year. On the

Additional Dues Increases and Restructuring Considerations

- **Should dues increases or restructuring be announced or explained in all situations?** In some associations, dues are set by the board or by the staff with the board's approval, and a vote of the membership is not required for implementation. In these cases, many associations find that making too much of an issue of dues increase can be counterproductive, and choose to remain relatively quiet about the increase. Although it may not be necessary to advise the membership in advance, the process should be transparent, and staff should be well prepared to answer any questions members might raise.

- **Should dues increases be annual, biennial, or occasional?** More frequent, incremental increases to an organization's dues are less disruptive to the membership and are likely to result in less attrition. However, an association that provides frequent opportunities for its members to communicate with staff will have a sense if dues are being adjusted too frequently.

- **Forecast best and worst case scenarios.** In preparing financial models for increasing or restructuring dues, staff not only should know how much additional revenue the changes will provide to the association but also should be aware of the possibility of attrition related to dues increases.

- **Always build a case statement for why dues increases are necessary.** An association should not take for granted that its membership will quietly accept all dues increases. Staff should be well versed in explaining the need for the increase, such as increased costs, expansion of programs, broader services to members, and so forth.

other hand, more infrequent increases tend to be more disruptive to the membership because they are larger. For example, an association that generally wants its dues to keep pace with inflation and its effects on operating expenses may opt for a six percent increase every two years, rather than an annual increase of three percent. Members may be more resistant to the larger percentage, even though it is less frequent. The association's staff must monitor the attitudes of the membership in order to gauge the level of resistance to any dues increase.

Calculating Dues Increases. A direct calculation method, multiplying the dues base by a percentage with a set floor and ceiling, may be the most common way of figuring a dues increase. The difficulty with a direct calculation method of assessing dues is that it makes incremental dues increases difficult to achieve, because the decimal multipliers get very lengthy over time. For example, if the association determines its dues by multiplying the member's dues base by one quarter of one percent (.0025), and wants to increase its dues by three percent each year, the next year the multiplier is 0.002575, and the year after that, it becomes 0.00265225; the fourth year it would be 0.0027318175. Soon no one would know how the dues multiplier got to be such an odd number, and the association would have to undergo dues restructuring.

A more practical alternative to a direct-calculation method for determining dues is a tiered structure. In this model, the member looks up his dues base on a table and pays the corresponding amount. This obviates the need for minute adjustments to a dues calculation formula because it allows the dues amounts themselves to be adjusted directly. And when a major recalibration of the dues table is required, it's a relatively simple matter to manipulate the ranges of the dues base. (See Chapter 6: Member Categories and Dues Structures for more on dues calculations.)

Communicating. In many associations dues increases are implemented by a vote of the membership, either electronically or at its annual meeting, and in others it is recommended by staff leadership and approved by the board of directors. Further, if a dues increase is put to a vote of the membership and passes by a vote of 75 percent, that leaves 25 percent who voted against it—and even some who vote for it may elect not to renew their memberships when the actual invoice reflecting the increase arrives. This is why it is so important for an association to continually reiterate the value proposition it provides. In the interest of retaining existing members, the association must explain clearly why it is necessary to increase their dues and how doing so will reinforce the membership value proposition. (See Chapter 2: What is Your Value Proposition?)

The process must be transparent. Regardless of whether the association's bylaws require a vote of the membership for a dues increase, the association should explain the reason for increasing dues at all stages of the process—when publicizing a recommended dues increase, facilitating whatever vote is stipulated in the bylaws, reporting on the outcome, and sending membership renewal invoices. Failure to openly discuss factors precipitating a dues increase and ways the additional funds will be used to help the organization may create resistance.

Dues increases linked to specific tangible member benefits, particularly those that are popular with members, are typically most successful. But if the increase is tied to research or a more active role in advocacy, it may be difficult for members to see a link between increased costs and direct benefits. Even so, an association may lose members who are using a strict cost-benefit analysis to make the case for membership in the association.

Restructuring Dues

An association may outgrow its dues structure because of changes or growth in the industry with which it is affiliated. For instance, a trade association may have based dues on its members' revenue, and the dues structure tops out with companies whose annual budgets are $100 million. When the dues structure was implemented, the top dues level may have applied to only five percent of its members. But 10 years later, because of increases in populations served, mergers, and expansion into international markets, that top level of dues may include 25 percent or more of the associations' members and there may be a sizable number of companies with budgets exceeding $1 billion. This type of industry fluctuation may create three scenarios:

- A merger of two large member companies, each of which was already paying top dues, results in a single company that is paying top dues, effectively creating a loss of one top-paying member for the association.

- A company whose revenue is $101 million is paying the same dues as a company 10 times larger; this is seen as unfair, and the management may become resentful of the association's pricing policies.

- There still may be many smaller companies at the lower end of the association's dues structure for which even current dues are burdensome. These members may see value in the association but are at risk if the association implements an across-the-board increase.

Restructuring dues in response to such situations requires an approach that is both more decisive and more nuanced. There is probably room at the top of the scale for substantial dues growth, but for purposes of advocacy or other considerations, it may be in the association's interest to maintain a diverse and representative constituency. So what is really needed is a redistribution of the dues scale, assessing a more equitable proportion of revenue from the largest companies while stabilizing dues for the smaller players or even offering nominal dues relief to these companies. (See Appendix 1. Case Study: Independent Sector's Dues Restructuring.)

Involving the Membership. The association's senior staff, including you as the membership professional, may have ideas about ways to remedy dues inequities or shortages. But to ensure buy-in across the broad spectrum of the association's membership, it is important to involve a representative sample of the members from the beginning of the process. This may be a subcommittee of the association's board of directors, taking its members from different sizes of member organizations; the association's membership committee, if it contains a representative sampling of different-sized members; or a special dues restructuring committee. As a membership professional, you should be involved in whatever processes are used to analyze the possibilities of dues restructuring.

The group charged to study dues restructuring should take a step-by-step approach that will

- evaluate the cost to serve members with existing programs and to implement proposed new programs

- gather member input using qualitative and quantitative research

- create several financial models and demonstrate the possibilities of each one

- involve and communicate with key stakeholders, including the board of directors, CEO, and various levels of members

- write a proposal incorporating advantages and disadvantages of different models

Meticulous preparation and transparency are critical in the process of dues restructuring, particularly when major changes are contemplated. Accuracy of the financial modeling in the first stages is indispensable for three reasons:

- It ensures the association that the changes made to the dues model will result in the needed increase to the bottom line and will not result in excessive revenue.

- It enables members who are assisting in the planning as well as those who will ultimately vote on the changes to ascertain that they will not be unduly burdened by the restructuring.

- It enhances overall confidence in the process for members and leadership alike.

In proposing a major revision of the dues structure to a board of directors or to members for a vote, you must communicate the reasons for the changes and the increased benefit to the members. For the association in the case study at the end of this chapter, the first premise was an acknowledgement that, over time, the association's dues structure had become unfair to many of its members.

When Less is More. Even if your priority in restructuring dues is to address inequities, such changes may result in increased revenue immediately or over time. While you should explain unapologetically why restructuring is necessary, your plan should avoid the appearance of excess. For this reason, some associations actually propose a dues restructuring plan that is revenue-neutral, resulting in no aggregate increase in dues revenue, and propose a modest increase as a separate measure.

One association of 2,100 colleges and universities had for many years requested a three percent increase each year, which was always approved by the membership. But over time, as some of its members outgrew the existing dues structure, the larger institutions were paying about half as much per staff member served as smaller institutions. The association recalibrated the dues structure to increase the maximum dues by 20 percent, while reducing dues at the lower levels, resulting in a dues model that provided the same amount of revenue as in the previous year. The association clearly communicated the reasons for the recalibration, and dues committee members made personal phone calls to each of the 80 members whose dues increased by more than $1,000. The annual increase of three percent was proposed as a separate measure, and the members passed both the dues recalibration and the increase. This worked because the association staff was transparent throughout the entire process.

Financial Modeling for Dues Restructures

An association that is contemplating dues restructuring needs to know exactly how many of its members or member organizations will be affected, how each will be affected, and what the total aggregate change will be in dues revenue to the association. This is relatively simple for organizations in which all members pay the same amount of dues or in associations that have different types of members and within each type all members pay the same amount. (See Chapter 13: Financial Management and Budgeting.)

However, trade associations and other similarly structured groups whose members are organizations or companies of different sizes often assess dues based on some measure of the organization's size. It may be a company's total operating budget, number of employees, payroll cost, or gross revenue. Some associations of grant makers assess dues based on the total dollar value of grants each member awards during the year. Most higher education associations assess dues based on full-time equivalent enrollment, operating budget, or a matrix that factors in both. Associations with a sizable international contingent have an added layer of complexity in adjusting for exchange rates for international currencies. All of these scenarios add complexity to the dues restructuring process.

This discussion uses the term *dues base* to refer to whatever a given association uses as the measure of its constituent organizations' size for purposes of determining each member's dues. To determine the amount of dues that a member would pay under any proposed restructuring plan, an association must have some idea of what each member's dues base is. When such data can be obtained independently, it is commonly uploaded to the database prior to each year's dues billing. For associations that rely on the member's self-reporting of its dues base, that information should be entered in each member's record in the association's membership database each year when the member pays dues. In these cases, the data may not be reliable enough for the following year's billing, but it should suffice for financial modeling.

Associations whose members are nonprofits can purchase financial information about their members from such organizations as the National Center for Charitable Statistics (http://nccs.urban.org) or Guidestar (www.guidestar.org). Higher education associations can download the information from the Department of Education (www.ed.gov). For-profit corporations that are publicly traded typically file 10-K reports that are generally available. But trade associations whose members are private businesses may not have access to reliable information about their members' dues base. They may have to extrapolate the amount of a company's dues base from the amount of dues it has paid in previous years. (See Appendix 2 at the end of this chapter for a sample spreadsheet.)

Other Membership-based Revenues

Besides annual membership dues, some associations use additional fees to supplement member-based income. As a membership professional, your responsibility may entail administering these and communicating about them to your membership.

Initiation/Application Fees. Some associations use a one-time initiation fee that is charged at the time the member joins; it may be called a new-member processing fee. Initiation/application fees are typically a small percentage of dues and set as a fixed dollar amount. For members who tend to opt in and out of membership from year to year, the requirement of paying another application fee may cause them to renew.

Assessments. Occasionally, an association's board of directors may vote to levy an assessment, which requires each member to pay a fee (sometimes calculated as a percentage of dues and other times a flat amount) in addition to dues. Generally, assessments are designated to a particular purpose, such as paying off a mortgage on a building or funding a specific project. Assessments may be payable once by a certain date or may be spread over a multi-year period, but usually no longer than three years.

Merger and Acquisition Fees. These fees are typically assessed when two members of a trade association merge, causing the association to lose one dues-paying member. In most cases, the merger fee is calculated as a percentage of the smaller company's dues. These fees often apply for only one or two years after the merger.

Virtual Memberships. Reduced dues amounts are charged for people who are granted limited access to the association through its web site and e-communications. Such members may not have voting rights or be eligible for discounts on educational services or publications, so their files must be flagged and monitored appropriately.

The membership professional should be prepared to examine all the elements critical to determining how and when to increase or restructure the association's dues. You must follow established procedures and communicate well with association leadership and members. A well planned approach to such projects will help avoid hostile responses and ensure success of the new systems.

Michael Connor is director of membership at Independent Sector in Washington, DC, the leading coalition of charities, foundation, and corporate philanthropy programs. His experience includes seven years in membership at the National Association of College and University Business Officers and many years in the hospitality industry. Michael is a member of ASAE & The Center's Membership Section Council and has written and presented widely on issues related to progressive membership protocol, processes, and practice. Email: michaelc@independentsector.org.

Jay Younger is managing partner and chief consultant at McKinley Marketing, Inc., with offices in Washington, DC, and Chicago. An ASAE & The Center Fellow, he also chaired the organization's Membership Section Council in 2004–2005. Email: jyounger@ mckinleymarketing.com.

Case Study:
Independent Sector's Dues Restructuring

Independent Sector, a coalition of charities and foundations, had a dues structure that had been in place since its founding in 1980. It was based on direct calculation, with a ceiling and a floor. However, by 2005, many member organizations had grown much larger in the intervening years, resulting in organizations that just topped out at the ceiling paying the same dues amount as organizations many times their size. In addition, with the direct calculation method, it was impossible to implement a dues increase that would not perpetuate this inequity.

The staff began by preparing documentation for the membership committee demonstrating why the association's dues structure was outmoded and how demographic shifts in the membership had resulted in inequities in the dues model. The committee identified three major concepts that would govern their work on a new dues structure:

- The new dues structure must be fair to all members.

- It must be rational. Members should be able to determine their dues easily, and the basis on which they were determined must make sense.

- Any new dues structure would need to sustain the long-term growth of the association, both in attracting new members and in ensuring an adequate source of revenue for the future.

With these principles in mind, staff identified the following issues which would determine the outcome of the process:

- Should the dues be increased for the smallest member organizations?

- Should the dues be increased for the largest member organizations?

- Should a member's dues fully cover the cost of providing basic member services to that member?

- Staff proposed changing from the existing direct calculation method of determining dues to a category structure, where members look up their dues base on a table and pay a corresponding amount.

- The association had two different types of regular members with fundamentally different financial structures. Although the calculations were different, both had the same floor and ceiling. Staff posed the question of whether any increases imposed should apply equally to both types of organizations.

- In the past, the organization's dues had increased only every five to seven years; staff proposed a model in which dues increases could occur annually or biannually, resulting in less disruption to the membership.

To demonstrate the impact of the changes proposed above, staff presented financial modeling to show how the proposed changes would increase or decrease the dues of specific groups of members. In the chart below, the number of organizations affected at the specified level of dues increases or decreases is identified by a whole number. In parentheses, the percentage of the total membership affected is shown. In this table, variances between current dues amounts and those dictated by the proposed dues structure are expressed as a percentage of the current dues amount rather than as an absolute dollar figure.

		Scenario I	Scenario II	Scenario III
Increases	More than 500%			9 (3%)
	76% - 500%			32 (9%)
	51% - 75%		39 (9%)	12 (3%)
	26% - 50%	1 (0%)	24 (6%)	11 (3%)
	11% - 25%	70 (16%)	47 (11%)	60 (17%)
	1% - 10%	17 (4)%	2 (0%)	12 (3%)
	Less than 1%	120 (28%)	84 (20%)	60 (17%)
Decreases	1% - 10%	31 (7%)	17 (4%)	6 (2%)
	11% - 25%	91 (21%)	102 (24%)	36 (10%)
	26% - 50%	96 (23%)	111 (26%)	77 (21%)
	51% - 75%			26 (7%)
	76% - 100%			19 (5%)

Scenario III shows much broader variances being felt by a larger number of member organizations, which would make it risky to implement in terms of retention. Scenario I, on the other hand, shows fewer and less disruptive increases. The overall revenue increases (the bottom line) in each of the three scenarios is roughly the same. Scenario I achieves a revenue increase of 6 percent through increases primarily to larger members, and decreases to small and medium-size members.

Once the issues to be studied were identified, committee members and staff of Independent Sector did a series of in-depth interviews with 40 member organizations of all sizes, to gauge members' feelings on each of the issues. At its next meeting, the board concurred with the findings from the member interviews and directed the staff to recommend a proposed dues structure to the membership committee. That recommendation was accepted, with modifications, by the committee.

At this point, the committee's recommendation was shared via email with the CEOs of all the association's members, asking for feedback and noting that the proposed structure had been vetted through interviews with members, the active participation of the board, and the membership committee. All members were encouraged to participate in one of two conference calls and those who were unable to participate were encouraged to share their feedback directly with the membership director. In conference calls and direct feedback, most members praised both the process and the result. In all, approximately 20 percent of the association's members had direct input in the dues restructuring process before it was submitted to a vote of the membership. The dues restructuring proposal was accepted by the membership at Independent Sector's annual business meeting without dissent.

Sample Spreadsheet for Dues Restructure Financial Modeling

A simple financial modeling system can be set up in any spreadsheet application. This example uses an Excel spreadsheet. The spreadsheet should contain the following data elements for each member organization:

- Member ID number
- Member name
- Previous year's dues amount
- Organization's dues base
- A column showing the difference between previous and proposed dues amounts

Of course, it may contain other data elements such as demographics or location information, but these are the columns required for dues modeling.

In the column next to the organization's dues base, create a lookup formula that refers to a lookup table a few columns to the right of the data already in the sheet. The lookup table will contain a lookup vector and a result vector. The lookup vector contains levels of dues base, and the result vector contains levels of dues amounts. The lookup formula instructs the application to look up the amount of the dues base in the lookup vector and assign a corresponding value from the result vector. Once the formula has been propagated to all the rows corresponding to member records, it will assign the appropriate dues value to each member organization. Changing the values in the result vector automatically changes the dues amounts for every organization, which allows the user to manipulate the resulting dues amounts to achieve the desired result to the bottom line.

In the column to the right of the lookup formula, set up a formula that subtracts the previous dues amount from the proposed dues amount to determine the difference. In the next column, to the right, set up a formula that divides the dollar variance by the previous dues amount (expressed as a percentage) to determine the percent of increase or decrease for each member. Finally, set an auto-sum formula at the bottom of the previous dues amount, proposed dues amount, and variance columns, and you will be able to see the total increase or decrease in revenue as you manipulate the values in the result vector of the lookup table.

Further explanation in the use of lookup tables can be obtained in any relatively complete book on using Excel or other spreadsheet program.

This spreadsheet shows financial modeling for a trade association whose organizational dues are based on the number of widgets each member company manufactures annually. A "Lookup formula" in the "Proposed Dues Amount" column assigns a dues value from the lookup table based on the number of widgets specified in the "Number of Widgets" column. The "Dues Variance" column shows change between old dues amount and proposed dues amount.

Dues Per Member Organization Spreadsheet

Organization	Number of Widgets	Prior Dues Amount	Proposed Dues Amt	Dues Variance
Company A	14,217	$125	$150	$25
Company B	300,254	$3,500	$3,844	$344
Company C	152,987	$2,500	$2,563	$63
Company D	35,698	$300	$338	$38
Company E	839,876	$5,500	$5,767	$267
Company F	76,298	$1,600	$1,709	$109
Company G	26,543	$200	$225	$25
Company H	7,685	$75	$100	$25
Company I	23,457	$200	$225	$25
Company J	51,000	$725	$759	$34
Company K	47,986	$500	$506	$6
Company L	56,126	$725	$759	$34
Company M	65,223	$1,100	$1,139	$39
Company O	87,332	$1,700	$1,709	$9
Company P	14,335	$115	$150	$35
Company Q	28,977	$215	$225	$10
Total Dues		$19,080	$20,168	$1,088

Lookup Table

Lookup Vector	Result Vector
Widget Range	Dues
0	$100
10,000	$150
20,000	$225
30,000	$338
40,000	$506
50,000	$759
60,000	$1,139
70,000	$1,709
100,000	$2,563
250,000	$3,844
500,000	$5,767

Association Database Management Systems

By Wes Trochlil, Sherry Budziak, and Don Dea

8

IN THIS CHAPTER:
- Elements of an effective membership database
- Database selection and data conversion
- Database and web integration

I F DATA ARE THE currency of the digital age, the foundation for creating and sustaining value is your association's database management system. An effective system is particularly important to staff charged with the membership function. As technology continues to advance, the operative goals of managing your database management system revolve around the opportunity to shuffle the contents of the metaphorical shoeboxes of member records so that all of the possible combinations of a member record can be analyzed, indexed, pre-set, and even outfitted with intelligent reminders and notifications that anticipate and customize what members might want. The 1980s and 1990s gave traction to the term *association management systems*. The 21st century version adds the notion of customer, or member, relationship management. Hence, the term AMS/CRM.

AMS/CRM systems constitute a significant investment. This centralized system is the tool to manage the organization's day-to-day operations, including membership application and dues renewal, meeting logistics and registration, product sales, certification tracking, subscriptions, publications, fundraising, advertising sales, exhibit management, membership self-service, e-commerce, content management and activity tracking, reporting, and more. Such a system is able to track and access real-time information across functional areas. It allows the association to develop an in-house "standard" of consolidated, thorough demographic and activity-related data on all member and nonmember services. A centralized, multifunctional system streamlines operations, reduces duplication of effort, consolidates isolated data, and ultimately enhances staff productivity. In addition, most market offerings have integrated web modules that allow members to post updates, order products, register for meetings, and more—all with a direct interface to the database. This chapter provides an overview of key components of contemporary membership database systems and integration, including system and selection criteria. By understanding all of these elements, you will not only be in a better position to make the best use of your database's functionality but also be better able to inform both the evaluation of an existing system and the selection of a new one when the time comes.

Key Elements of a Contemporary AMS/CRM System

While there are many solutions from which to choose in the marketplace, most of the enterprise-wide association management systems include standard modules to support most organizations. These modules include but may not be limited to constituent management, committee management, events management, product sales, events registration, call center capabilities, and dues management. In addition to such baseline functionality, a well-designed AMS/CRM will also have the following list of attributes:

- **Centralized data processing.** Ideally, all data managed by the organization should be processed through one centralized system rather than multiple databases. A centralized system allows you to minimize data redundancy as well as provide a holistic view of your members' and customers' activities with your organization.

- **Generation and tracking of all invoices.** A well-designed AMS/CRM serves as your organization's accounts receivable package. This means that all money flowing into the organization is recorded in your AMS/CRM. This provides a good tool for keeping track of your open accounts receivable (A/R) and also provides insight into how your members and customers are spending money on your organization's products and services.

- **Linkage to your financial package.** Once all of your A/R is in your database, you need a relatively easy way to move it from your database to your financial management system (e.g., QuickBooks, Great Plains, Solomon). Your AMS/CRM should allow you to create a summary export that can then be imported into your financial package so that no rekeying of data is necessary.

- **Linkage to the web (member self-service abilities).** Today's consumers (members and users) expect to be able to interact with your organization when it is convenient for them. This means that your web site becomes a primary point of interaction with your members and customers. They expect to be able to manage their customer/member profile as well as buy your products and services. Your AMS/CRM package should provide for a strong connection between your back-office management system and your public-facing web site.

- **Flexible reporting.** The data in your database are useful only if you can get information out of it. Therefore, it is important to have a well-designed AMS/CRM that will provide several options for pulling data from the database, including query tools and "canned" and custom reports.

- **Tracking of all transactions with members, nonmembers, and customers, including information collected by outside vendors.** Transactions with your members and customers often go beyond solely financial transactions. Your members will also participate as volunteers, serving on committees; write for publications; speak at your meetings; and involve themselves in other interactions that are not based on financial transactions. A well-designed AMS/CRM will enable you to track these "transactions" as well as your constituent "activities" so that you can continue to build a holistic view of your members and customers.

- **Contact management.** The ability to track communication between your organization and your members and customers allows you to capture conversations that occur between individuals, whether those conversations were by phone, fax, or email.

- **Role-based security support.** While all staff should have access to your database, not all of them will need access to the same information or tools. A system should support setting up different roles based on the needs of each staff's role in the organization. Therefore, it is important that an AMS/CRM system support role-based security. Staff should be able log in and use the system as they need to use it, with full access to certain areas of the database and restricted access to others.

- **Tracking of changes (audit log).** Because your AMS/CRM will allow multiple users access to the system (including providing access to your members and customers), you'll need a way to track who is making what changes and when. This is what a good audit log will do. The audit log automatically captures what changes were made to the database, including the field that was changed, when it was changed, and who made the change.

If your organization's system is lacking three or more of the functional requirements in the preceding bulleted list, then it may be time to consider a new system or system upgrade.

Selecting a New System

When will you and your colleagues know that it's time to look for new association management software? Perhaps you manage multiple databases (e.g. Access, Excel, Filemaker) throughout your organization or maybe you've been using the same database system for several years and think that it's time to move to newer technology. Have your business processes changed, have you added staff and programs that need to be supported, or are you struggling with your current system's capabilities? Organizations look for new software solutions and suppliers for many reasons. However, the evaluation process and needs assessment are critical pieces in making the case for a new infrastructure.

There are easily more than 100 products on the market that claim to be association or membership management software systems. Selecting the right one for your organization can be daunting, but it will be much less so if you and your colleagues take a disciplined approach that begins with a candid assessment of your current capabilities and needs.

Typically, a well-constructed and well-disciplined methodology for selecting a new AMS/CRM follows these steps:

1. **Assess needs.** Determining the needs of the organization is no small undertaking, yet is a critical first step in the process. Whether a consultant is used or an internal project manager is assigned to this task, information needs to be gathered through interviews with each functional area. It is at this point that you and other staff will be analyzing what your organization needs in a new AMS/CRM. You will need to review your internal business processes and system support needs and then identify what functionality your AMS/CRM system requires. These functionalities should support your needs not only now but also in the near future (five to seven years). It is important that this process involve every part of your organization to develop an understanding of the complete requirements. During this phase of the process, many organizations will also give close scrutiny to how they currently do things (business processes) and consider how they might change their internal processes to get more leverage from a new database. More importantly, this is the right time to ask the fundamental questions of how we might serve our members better in the future. For example: What are core value propositions that we must support as a sustaining point of difference in attracting and retaining members? What are the supporting business processes that support these value propositions—including the key steps (inputs and outputs) for each business process? What are the implications of these value propositions to our database systems that must be addressed? Do we have international members who will need access to us 24 hours per day? Do our members expect to be able to manage their entire experience via our web site (e.g., join, renew, register for meetings, purchase products, review certification history)? Do we need to do a better job of targeting our messaging so that we are communicating with members and customers in the way they want to hear from us and about the things they want to hear?

2. **Develop a request for proposals (RFP).** Formalize the requirements identified during your needs assessment for presentation to vendors. The RFP is a list of functional requirements that communicates to prospective suppliers what you're expecting their software to do for your organization. The RFP gives vendors a detailed look at your needs and will allow them to provide you with a more accurate price for your system and identify areas where their system may need to be modified to more appropriately address your needs. Within the RFP, identify which of the functions are "must-haves" versus "nice-to-haves." Other details should include questions about the suppliers and their processes such as their implementation, project management support and training, level of system security, and ongoing support and maintenance.

3. **Identify prospective suppliers and send the RFP.** Numerous resources for identifying prospective suppliers exist. ASAE & The Center for Association Leadership's knowledge center, events, directories, and listservers; state, regional, and local societies of association executives; and consultants are all ready resources for initial research. The more you know before commencing the selection process, the better equipped your association will be to choose the most appropriate solution.

4. **Review responses to the RFP.** Once vendors have received and responded to your RFP, you'll have to review the responses to determine which of the respondents should provide demonstrations of their products to your organization. Scoring RFPs is both art and science. You can compare the responses to each question and score the RFP based on how many of each type of response was received. That is the science. The art is looking at the comments and guidance the vendors provided in their responses. Did they provide details in their answers or stick only to checking yes/no boxes? Did they provide alternatives to the functionality requested? In other words, did they really work at understanding and responding to your RFP? This is the art.

5. **Convene demonstrations.** Through the review of the RFP responses, focus on identifying one or more potential suppliers to consider. Schedule an appointment to allow them to further demonstrate the software to you. The demonstration is your opportunity to see the software firsthand, get a sense of how it works, and get a sense of how the supplier behind the product operates. Demonstrations typically fall into two categories: general overview and scenario-based (or "scripted"). General demonstrations are your opportunity to get a better sense of what the software looks like and the company behind the software. During a scripted demonstration, your organization provides in advance a script of scenarios that you would like the vendor to walk through. These scenarios reflect how your organization manages members and processes data. Scripted demos provide a much better sense of how their product can or cannot support your current data management needs.

6. **Check references and select a supplier.** The supplier will provide you with references. Try to identify other associations that are using the company's product and contact them for reference checks as well. When possible, conduct an on-site visit of references to see the product in action. Selection will be based on a variety of factors including how well the product meets your current and future needs, how well the vendor's culture matches your association's, reference checks, and of course, the price. As with scoring the RFP, selecting a supplier is as much art as science.

7. **Negotiate a contract.** Once a potential vendor has been selected, it's time to negotiate the contract. Most suppliers will provide a boilerplate contract sometime during the selection process for you to review. Prior to signing the contract, review it and get a good understanding for the terms of the contract. Does the contract lock you in to service for a set number of years? What about upgrades and maintenance? Is the maintenance fee set for a certain number of years, or can the vendor raise it without notice? Who owns the software? Who owns the customizations? There isn't a uniform answer to these questions, as differing needs and different product offerings have different contract details. For example, if you're purchasing Software-as-a-service (SaaS), you will be renting the software from the supplier for a set monthly fee. Typically, the vendor will ask for a minimum commitment of three or four years. These time commitments can be negotiated, if necessary. Some contracts will also include rates for hourly work; it is helpful to include a provision that guarantees the hourly rate for services for the period of the contract so that the vendor cannot arbitrarily increase rates without your permission.

Needless to say, legal counsel should always be engaged in supporting a contractual agreement process, given the magnitude of resources and commitments involved with your association management system. One of the key business issues that you will want to focus on is control and access to your membership data. Provisions in business terms for backups and access to data are key, assuming that you are on a hosted (application support model) where an AMS supplier is maintaining the application and the database. In instances where you control the server and your data, you want to be sure that you have access to the source code or provisions that allow you to take control of application and data should the vendor no longer be in a position to support you.

Converting Data

As described in the previous ASAE & The Center publication *Membership Operations* (2001), once an AMS/CRM is selected, a contract is negotiated, and a timetable has been set for implementation, you need to focus on data conversion. Data can be converted, archived, deleted, and cleansed. This aspect is often left to later in implementation, but experience has proven that data conversion is often a critical path item that is addressed too late in the process which leads to failed promises and schedule delays. It is never too early to address data conversion.

Converting data involves transferring information from the old database(s) into the new database. This will likely include general contact information, recent financial and transactional information such as events, purchases, and volunteer activities.

Cleansing data (which can be termed a lifetime project) is also an event-driven process. At the time of data conversion, a thorough review of data for currency, accuracy, and quality is an important practice to follow.

Archiving is moving data from the old database to a storage area that is separate from the operational database. That is, the data are not moved to the new database

---

Tips for the Selection Process

When choosing an AMS/CRM, you may want to consider a team approach, whereby an overall project leader is appointed but the evaluation and selection is a collaborative effort. Team members should represent different functional areas of the organization. Although it is not critical for all team members to participate in every aspect of the process (for example, proposal review), there are critical functions that warrant each member's involvement. These include participating in the needs assessment, software demonstrations, debriefings, and team meetings. The team approach offers representation of the association's different needs, varied perspectives when analyzing solutions, and group acceptance of the project as a whole as well as the selected solution. In addition, consider these tips:

- Align the selection of your software with your overall organizational strategy. The data about your members and customers is the lifeblood of your organization. Be sure that your new data management system can support your organization's mission and strategy.

- Consider what you need the system to do on a daily basis. What is the system most heavily used for? Do you have hundreds of thousands of members who are actively engaged, or do you have just a few hundred members that you rarely talk to? Do you process lots of meeting registrations, or very few? Do you manage certifications? Identify the most important data management aspects of your organization and make sure any system you consider can do this, and do it well.

- Should you go with a web-based or non-web-based system? This will largely depend on your organization's needs. While web-based systems are getting faster, they are still slower than traditional client/server systems for intensive, heads-down data processing. On the other hand, web-based systems are typically available wherever you have access to a high-speed Internet connection and a browser. Be sure to discuss these issues with the vendors so you have a good sense of the pros and cons of each system type.

- Should you choose a large or small software company? Again, this will depend on your needs. Typically, smaller software companies are able to provide better and more personalized customer service than larger software companies. On the other hand, smaller companies tend to have less cutting-edge technology and fewer broad improvements/upgrades because there is less research and development and not as much feedback from customers.

- What kind of support plan does the supplier offer? Be sure to ask the vendor how their annual support agreement is calculated and what kind of service it covers. Does it include upgrades, or is there an additional fee for those? Do upgrades include installation?

- Check references. Vendors will provide references for you to check. Be sure to call them and talk to them about their experiences. In addition, ask the references what other associations they know that are using the software, and call those organizations, too. Don't just stick to the reference list provided by the vendor. Ask the references what they like and dislike about the software and the vendor. Ask them how the vendor resolved problems that they've had. Ask how responsive the vendor has been.

- Don't go it alone. Many resources are available to you as you move through this process. For example, ASAE & The Center's *Associations Now* magazine typically publishes a guide to technology solutions and directory that not only lists AMS software vendors but also consultants who can help you through the selection process. In addition, ASAE & The Center's listservers are good resources for researching association professionals' experiences. Finally, remember to simply ask your colleagues. Those who have been there before will be happy to answer your questions.

but kept elsewhere in the platform file system. Examples of data that may be archived include financial records, event attendance records, and other contact information more than three years old.

Deleting data is permanently removing data from the old database, neither archiving it nor converting it. Data that can be deleted may include old contact information (e.g., individuals added to the database but with no activity associated with them, old mailing lists), temporary mailing lists, ad hoc committees, and other data that is no longer relevant.

Another consideration, also described in *Membership Operations*, is how the converted data appear in the new database. Because of differences between the structure of the old and new database, the association may have to make adjustments and/or compromises when converting data. Because of these adjustments, you will need to test the data on a prototype system before final acceptance tests and implementation. Testing your new database is a fundamental activity that will allow users to see the difference and determine whether the new system will support their core needs in the future.

The association should consider the time required to convert the old data to the new system. Data will need to be inspected and "massaged" to convert cleanly into the new system. You will want to run parallel systems for a period of time to ensure that data and systems are operating as expected.

Integrating Your Database

Databases give organizations the ability to store, retrieve, and manage information. In today's digital world, your association's database represents a core asset that sits at the foundation of your organization's management capacity.

Members expect up-to-date information and the ability to track their transactions, update their records, and manage their membership in a self-service capacity. All of this is possible with an integrated database. More importantly, integrating your web site and database will alleviate double entry. The cost efficiency and improved productivity provide administrative benefits as well.

Member expectations will continue to rise with the ever-improving levels of service and communication that they receive over the web from the private sector. To prosper, associations will need to provide similar services. Take advantage of state-of-the-art software applications that have been built with XML web services. XML web services can provide your organization with an ease of integration among your systems.

An emerging technology trend in our industry is a progression to all-web, browser-based solutions. web-based systems promise to be easy to deploy, provide an appealing interface for the user, offer centralized control, and achieve a low total cost of ownership.

Much of the complexity and difficulty of integrating different software applications across an organization has stemmed from the fact that there has been, until now, no standardization of data exchange methodology. XML web services technology provides a set of standards that allow applications to exchange information in a universally accepted format. This vastly simplifies the integration process, delivering a benefit as significant as any of the inherent technological advantages of this architecture. Associations know the cost of this historical lack of standards only too well. During the past decade, many have spent thousands of dollars integrating their web site to their back-office AMS/CRM application. If complex business rules need to be preserved across the two disparate systems, the cost and complexity only increases. Furthermore, since the two systems need to understand each others' internals, if there are separate companies involved, trade secrets and confidentiality may prevent integration from being realized at all. Products built for the association market (as XML web services) enjoy a significant advantage over those not constructed to a standard. They do not need to know internal table structures or data relationships. In fact, one web service can actually ask the other web service how it would like to have a series of data sent. Once a request or submission is sent from one web service to another, it is up to the receiving web service to know what to do with the information and where to put it. The calling web service doesn't need to care how it gets the job done or where, for that matter; the receiving web service exists in the Internet universe. The advantages to building integrations via web services should be clear: lower cost, time savings, and increased reliability.

New AMS/CRM systems have been developed to directly address the challenges posed by the trends outlined previously. This technology will assist your organization in working on integrating your disparate systems. Some of the benefits are

- **Customer self-service.** Since every action taken by your members online is captured directly by the underlying database, your organization learns from and can adapt to changing activity. From testing e-registration campaigns to automatically offering related items to orders in process, e-commerce provides the information, interaction, and mass customization that will benefit your organization and earn the loyalty of your members. The key from an operational perspective is making this technology investment meaningful. Exceptional e-commerce systems allow organizations to scale effortlessly. As an example, directly connected web sites generate real financial transactions that do not require manual intervention or, worse yet, uploaded or rekeyed data.

- **Improved information delivery.** XML allows us to effortlessly repurpose information so that magazine content can be reused in newsletter, e-newsletter, web site, fax, and/or e-alert format. For example, members could purchase a magazine online for instant download and be emailed each time that new issues were available for purchase. The association achieves a cost saving, multipurpose use of the same content, while serving members in precisely the manner they wish to be served.

Further, taking advantage of the technology is getting easier. Web technologies have enabled software vendors to provide new web-based solutions at a much reduced cost and as a hosted service. Web-based solutions have become very secure environments, and this has enabled companies to provide hosted solutions at significantly reduced costs. This is now known as "software as a service" (or a newer way to have an application service provider (ASP) model platform).

Now that Internet technologies are more robust and secure, several technology companies in the association market have developed easy-to-use and easy-to-deploy web-based systems. These solutions allow associations to manage their members, accounting, events, donations, web site, and other typical association functions.

These new, inexpensive web-based technologies provide relief to executives struggling with managing their constituents and enable them to purchase inexpensive web-based solutions that provide member self-service features, including the ability for members to update their profiles, register online for meetings, and renew their member dues, and purchase products.

There is also no longer a need to devote time and money to integrate these transactions with the back-office or the need to rekey information. Since the solutions are web-based, the forms that provide these transactions are pushed out to the web site and are automatically updated to the database when users submit their requests. Not only do these products provide members with the ability to do business with the organization in real time, 24 hours a day, they also enable the organization to streamline its processes by allowing members to help the organization administratively.

Wes Trochlil is the president of Effective Database Management, LLC, in Hamilton, Virginia. He has served as chair of ASAE & The Center's Membership Section Council and as a member of the ASAE & The Center Technology Section Council. Email: wtrochlil@ effectivedatabase.com.

Sherry Budziak is the president and founder of .orgSource, an Internet consultancy based in Vernon Hills, Illinois. Budziak previously oversaw association web and information technology divisions, with a focus on electronic communication strategies. Email: sherry@ orgsrc.com.

Don Dea is co-founder of Fusion Productions, Webster, New York. An ASAE & The Center Fellow, Dea is a recognized authority on the Internet, association strategy, online education, and technology deployment. He has served on numerous boards of directors, including that of ASAE & The Center. Email: dddea@fusionproductions.com.

Collecting, Managing, and Using Membership Data

By Don Dea and Carolyn Hook

9

IN THIS CHAPTER:

- Data management strategy
- What data to collect
- Collecting and maintaining data
- Using data for marketing, recruitment, and retention

D ID YOU EVER NOTICE how the coupons that your food store provides with your receipt are for products you actually use? Or how your dental hygienist remembers to ask you about something you mentioned during your last visit six months ago? What about those movie titles Netflix recommends? Each example is the result of data about you that the entity has collected and stored.

The ability to access, share, and use timely information allows us to make sound business decisions, enhance our marketplace position, and provide better customer service. It enables us to be collaborative, connected, and productive. The foundation for collecting and using member data is a comprehensive, organization-wide approach to management of all of the organization's knowledge, records, and/or data in such a way that it can be used to inform decisions. (See sidebar, "Key Elements of a Data Management Strategy.") Part and parcel of the broader organizational knowledge or data management strategy, of course, is collecting, maintaining, and using data most closely associated with the membership function.

Why Collect Data?

A database is an organized collection of data. An association management/customer relationship management system (AMS/CRM) will assist you in storing data about individual and corporate members and other constituents of the organization. The data contained in your database may include:

- Demographics and research data (race, age, income, gender, address, marketing results, employment)

- Segmentation data (other data necessary to segment your membership such as professional interest area, business type, professional license number, education, revenue, industry code, etc.)

- Contact data (all elements necessary to reach members such as name, address, phone, email, etc.)

- Preference data (how and what to communicate to members)

- Psychographics (personality, perceptions, values, attitudes, interests, or life-styles)

- Monetary transactional data (membership renewals, event registrations, product purchases, purchase dates)

- Nonmonetary transactional data (calls, committee participation, etc.)

- Online activity (documents downloaded, communities frequented, pages visited, click-through activities, etc.)

Why collect and store this data? To know your members as completely as possible, and thereby to enable your organization to provide benefits and services—ranging from professional development to research and statistics to networking opportunities—in the best possible way. By knowing its members, prospects, and consumers, an association can analyze data to

- Identify relevant trends

- Provide consistent operational (short-term) and strategic (long-term) forecasts

- Develop necessary programs, products, and services

- Discontinue unused and unwanted programs, products, and services

- Differentiate your members in terms of both their needs and their value to the association

- Implement customer-focused strategies (i.e., treat the customer differently based on what you know about them)

- Track, measure, and adjust communication and promotional efforts

- Turn members/customers into loyal members/customers

Respect your data as a tool to accomplish your organization's mission and purpose. Vipin Mayar, executive vice president and general manager for data analytics at MRM Worldwide, offers this warning in the June 2006 issue of *Direct Magazine,* "The smartest companies are those that start with marketing objectives and allow the data to serve as a guide to achieving them. However, if you start from the other way, saying 'Let me look at all the data [and see what it tells me],' you will be lost in an ocean of data."

Key Elements of a Data Management Strategy

Records are not merely documents that an organization produces. A record is information created and maintained as evidence and information by an organization pursuant of legal obligations or in the transaction of business. Document management may involve creating, editing, saving, reviewing, copying, deleting, and tracking documents; records management must ensure record authenticity, reliability, integrity, and usability. Records cannot be altered, and their availability, retention, and deletion must be carefully tracked and controlled.

In today's world nearly everything produces a record and serves as "institutional memory"— whether it is a document, email, or transaction. Therefore, it is important to make sure that the control, storage, and use of records occurs in the normal course of business. Comprehensive data management has taken on increased importance as organizations recognize its benefits. The benefits include

- Enabling users to track, retrieve, maintain, retain, and dispose of records according to retention schedules.
- Streamlining and standardizing records management across organization departments and locations.
- Reducing the cost of operations by streamlining rapid records retrieval—whereby information can be produced quickly and on demand when required, reducing administrative costs.

The organization's comprehensive data management strategy should reflect a clear rationale for an organized approach and process to gathering, storing, maintaining, and using information. In fact, a strategic vision that at minimum addresses these questions is a fundamental place to begin:

- How could better information help this organization perform at a higher level?
- How can we better carry out the organization's operations with greater speed, effectiveness, and efficiency?
- What obstacles do we need to overcome?

Here is a brief example of a strategic vision:

XYZ Association shall apply integrated data-driven methodologies in development of its strategies. Key elements are the following:

- Continuously track member needs and issues.

- Apply comprehensive 360-degree view of member and association's interaction.
- Provide capability for staff to access data when and how needed.
- Provide for data quality and data standards that include data that are timely, accurate, and consistent.

A data management strategy distinguishes itself as a key part of the organization's overall strategy, sets expectations for staff members' participation in the normal course of business, and identifies the responsible authority. The fundamental pieces of any data management plan are as follows:

- **Data inventory.** The process of records inventory will require the organization to identify and quantify all of your organizational records—paper and electronic.
- **Vital records protection.** Identify and protect records that are necessary to continue operations under emergency conditions.
- **Filing plan.** Your plan should include information about how documents should be filed electronically and in filing cabinets. This should include the indexing and classification schemes for arranging, storing, and retrieving records.
- **Retention schedules.** Establish a timetable for final disposition, destruction, or archival. These schedules will need to be established with each business unit.
- **Back-up and disaster-recovery plan.** Continuity planning and disaster recovery need to be a part of your overall records management strategy.
- **Security and privacy policies.** Policies, procedures, and processes must be developed to ensure protection of all confidential information when stored, accessed, and transferred. Organizations must investigate their record systems and communication to ensure proper treatment of sensitive documents. Consider having a written and communicated policy concerning email and instant messages. Employees should not commingle company and personal information.
- **Evaluation of needs for preservation.** Paper can disintegrate, ink can fade, bits and file formats can be lost, and microfilm can undergo chemical

Continued on next page

Continued from pre ious page

decomposition. For digital storage, media life and format must be carefully considered. Therefore, it is important to create a plan for preservation of important documents.

- **Destruction or archival processes.** A policy should be in place for the destruction or archival of records that no longer must be maintained because their retention period has lapsed, either immediately or at regularly scheduled intervals. Also destroy copies of documents so that the organization is accessing only one version.

- **Education, education, education.** Establish a training program that covers all aspects of the program and the role that information and records play in serving the organization. The program should be documented and included in training materials.

- **Established monitoring activities.** Organizations must preserve records concerning annual internal monitoring and external auditing activities of the records management program. Whether required or as part of a risk management initiative, you will want to monitor and recommend opportunities for improvement.

- **Data audits.** Just as outside accounting auditors are required for financial controls and policies, outside records management auditors play an important role in helping an organization improve their compliance. Governmental agencies as well as nonprofit organizations and associations can generally use a five-to-seven-year audit cycle while other highly regulated industries such as financial services may audit every three years.

Records management is a process, not an event. It is a core organizational principle, which must be adopted and incorporated into the daily working environment.

Evaluating What Data You Have and How You're Using It

Before filling your database with more data, evaluate what you have. What do you already know about your members, customers, or prospects? You may be "data rich and information poor" if you're not analyzing your existing data in relation to your organization's objectives. It may seem overwhelming, but you can start with your database field lists, screens, or modules. Categorize each field (or groups of fields) using the data type listed above. Identify which type of record or records these data are valuable for (member, student, customer, prospect, etc.). Also list how the field is currently being used and other potential uses (see Table 1). Consider analyzing frequency and monetary value of recent purchases or transactions.

Be sure to complete this exercise with representatives from other functional areas in your organization and keep in mind that some data are required as part of a transaction and may not appear useful by itself. For example, entering a check number may be required by your AMS/CRM and not seem important but knowing how many members pay by check versus credit card may be valuable. Potential uses should be discussed, developed, and implemented in compliance with your organization's priorities and strategic initiatives. In addition to finding new and creative ways to use your data, you may find you have data that is no longer valid or valuable. Consider making a recommendation to your database administrator that outdated and worthless data be removed, following any appropriate database policies that are in place. Remember to evaluate and analyze your existing data at least annually.

This is just a starting place. You may need to consider bringing in data mining experts and specialty software to meet your needs.

Table 1. Sample Data Record Types and Uses

Field or Group of Fields	Type	Record Type	Current Uses	Potential Uses
Name (first, middle, last)	Demographics	All	Communication	Create family membership
Citizenship	Demographics	Prospects		
Event Registration	Monetary transaction	All	Registration confirmation Event development Identify best customers	Non-member registrants, solicit membership All registrants—offer frequent purchaser discounts Tell members they saved $X this year
Reason for joining	Psychographics	Members	Identify and market involvement opportunities	
Contacts/ phone calls	Non-monetary transaction	All		Create membership renewal FAQ Lead generation

What to Collect

Armed with the knowledge of what is already in your database, you can identify what's missing. Ask yourself, "What would you like to know about your members that you don't already know?" Again, be sure to include other key staff in this discussion. Start by discussing your organization's challenges, marketing objectives, and any changes in the marketplace. How can having the right data in a centralized database (versus outside survey data or ancillary databases) help? What is the data's potential worth—its return on investment? Your data collection efforts should be driven by a plan to address specific knowledge gaps.

Here's a starter list of information that you may discover you want to know about members, prospects, and customers:

- How do you get information?
- When do you look at association communications?
- Were you referred to us by another member?
- What are your reasons for joining?
- Why did you leave the association? What were your reasons for not renewing?
- What is the association's role in your success? How can we help you do your job better?
- What are your expectations of the association?
- Where else are you going to get what we do?
- What do you enjoy and do outside the office?
- What do you do for a living?
- How do you like to purchase products (online, over the phone, mail)?

- What do you fear about your business or profession?
- What are your interests within the organization (outside-of-work interests)?
- Why did you get involved with this industry/profession/activity/charity?
- What do you like about it?
- What would you change?
- What kind of decisions must you make today? Tomorrow?
- What is the biggest challenge you are facing?
- What would make your membership in any organization so invaluable that you would be a member for life?
- What do you think the association thinks of you?
- If you could get the association to do one thing for you that it isn't doing now, what would that be?
- What satisfies you online, at events, when reading publications, during a registration process?

Collecting data can occur in the usual ways—through profile updates, evaluations, surveys, in-bound and out-bound phone calls, membership renewals, and registrations. Look for your organization's touch points, or contact points, between

---

Six Things to Remember When Collecting Membership Data

1. **Plan to use your data.** Don't forget that whatever you decide to collect should be added to your data usage chart. In other words, don't collect it if you don't have a plan and the resources to use it.

2. **Know the law.** In "Overview of Data Privacy Law" (www.marketingpower.com/content20159.php), Dan Goldstein, president and founder of Privacy Research and Consulting, said, "You must, at a minimum, be in compliance with state and federal laws regulating the manner in which you handle consumers' nonpublic personal information." Many privacy laws may apply to you, depending on your organization's audience and activities. A few are

   - The CAN-SPAM Act establishes requirements for those who send commercial emails and consequences for violations.

   - *The Children's Online Privacy Protection Act (COPPA)* imposes requirements on organizations operating web sites and online services directed to children under 13.

   - *The Fair Credit Report Act (FCRA) & Gramm-Leach-Billy Act (GLBA)* regulates the collection, dissemination, and use of consumer credit information.

   Detailed information about these privacy acts can be found on the Federal Trade Commission web site at www.ftc.gov/privacy or visit the Better Business Bureau website at www.bbbonline.org/understandingprivacy.

3. **Keep it secure.** In addition to keeping data private, certain data, like credit card or social security numbers, may need to be encrypted in your AMS/CRM and accessible to only key users.

4. **Tell members it's private.** Establish what data is confidential. Let members know that information that is considered personal and intimate will not be made available for rental, sale, or exchange. Include your privacy policy (or policy location) on your organization's web site, in your online and print membership directory, wherever members update their profile and on any forms that request member data. Awareness and transparency are vitally important.

5. **Avoid data overload.** Make a clear distinction between what's nice to know and what is of key strategic importance. The more data you have, the more you have to maintain.

6. **Put members first.** Members are still asking, "What's in it for me?" Make sure members will be willing to give you the information you're looking for by telling them what it's used for.

the organization and its customers. Overlooked touch points may include when a member visits your web site, changes jobs or addresses, has a birthday, upgrades membership, sends an email, visits your office, attends a meeting or event, joins a committee or chapter, makes a purchase, opens and reads mail, or refers a member.

Maintaining Data

Along with your plans to use your data (whether existing or new), you'll need procedures and policies for maintaining your data. Working with your IT personnel or database consultant, you'll want to establish strategies for making sure your data are consistent and valid.

At the New Jersey Society of Certified Public Accountants, a database work group meets at least two times a year. The work group consists of staff from various functional areas who are decision makers in regard to "their" data. When a new functionality is needed or before fields are added or removed from the database, the group discusses the potential organization-wide implications of the change. Whether you have a team or a consultant or it's all up to you, maintaining data integrity means developing and implementing strategies for

- **Validating data.** Do phone numbers have the right number of digits? Do all of your email addresses have an @ and a period? Do all your male records have a Mr. and your female records have Ms. or Mrs.? Are there events that are missing locations or food options? Are all subcommittees linked to a parent committee? Do you have duplicate records?

- **Removing/replacing outdated data.** Can records without valid addresses be deleted after a certain number of years? How long are you keeping prospect records? Will you purchase new lists to replace outdated data? Do you have data that need to be in a new format?

- **Updating the organization's various databases.** If you have multiple databases, how will a change in one database affect another? Are all your data compatible?

- **Developing data entry standards.** Are you following United States Postal addressing standards? Does your mailing house run your data through a CASS (Coding Accuracy Support System) correction program? How will you enter college degrees: BA or B.A.? Will you use abbreviations in company names? If members are updating their own data, will they be required to follow these standards?

- **Staffing and training.** How will staff be notified of new procedures? How is new staff trained? Do you have a manual or documentation outlining procedures? How will staff be assigned responsibility and ownership for specific transactions and procedures? Who can make changes and who can't?

- **Preparing for future AMS/CRM needs and selection.** What data is your system unable to store today that you'll want to store in your next AMS/CRM or AMS/CRM version?

- **Evaluating data and how it is used on a regular basis.** Do you know what you have and how it's used?

Ensuring Data Quality

Without a high level of data integrity, results produced from the system may be misleading or difficult to interpret. Poor data entry includes misspellings, typos and transpositions, variations in spelling or naming, data missing from database fields, and using multiple databases scattered throughout different departments or organizations.

The goal of establishing quality data is to bring consistency to various data sets that may have been created with different, incompatible business rules. The Healthcare Financial Management Association, for example, protects its database against inadvertent insertions, deletions, and updates through commitment control, constraints, and triggers (e.g., SQL procedures, etc.). For example, commitment control allows you to define and process a group of changes to resources, such as database files or tables, as a transaction, which helps to ensure data integrity. This minimizes the possibility that a single set of data might not be detected, whereas a complete transaction or file that affects multiple areas will flag inconsistencies.

Specifically, established constraints govern how, which, and by whom data values can change or be changed. Triggers are automatic actions based on the criteria of a transaction updating specific tables.

Ensuring data quality requires a shared sense of responsibility within the organization and never-ceasing vigilance. Every time data are entered to the system, the person doing the entry should feel responsibility for and pride in the quality of the data and success of the mission. Managers responsible for a business unit must be aware of their responsibilities for the data around which their work is structured. Quality data are, simply put, data that meet business needs for accuracy, completeness, consistency, and timeliness. Quality data are measured and monitored and meet a set of quality expectations. For example, data quality standards look at validity of the data, accuracy of descriptions, accuracy of counts, and timeliness. A standard around consistency would require that all females should have a salutation that reflects Ms., Miss, or Mrs. Another example would be that all fields that use a second address line should have completed address line 1.

Quality standards may be communicated in several ways. For example:

- Publish rules.
- Ensure that the system warns the user of potential missing data sources, especially for users who are entering information through your web site.
- Clearly establish update schedules.
- Publish accuracy results.

Human Resources for Effective Database Management

There are no absolute guidelines for how many employees are needed to effectively manage an association database. What is important is that the association does assign ownership of the database system to the staff member who is responsible for it. In most associations, management of the database falls naturally to the membership department, but in many cases it is a shared function.

Having one employee who is responsible for overseeing all aspects of managing the database goes a long way toward ensuring the integrity of the data it holds. These functions include managing data input, thoroughly training both permanent and temporary employees, assigning security levels to individual employees, and serving as a primary resource for managing and collecting new types of data. That person may or may not have the technical expertise to tinker with the back end of the database but should have a thorough understanding of its workings, its importance to the association, the effective use of policy to manage data collection and entry, and the ability to communicate these concepts effectively to other staff.

A technical person should also be working with the database. This individual, or individuals, must be thoroughly conversant with SQL (Structured Query Language, pronounced *sequel*), Oracle, UNIX, or whatever programming language regulates the underlying structure of the database. This person may be the same as the database manager, or in a larger association it may be an employee from the information services or information technology department.

Finally, staff members should be assigned to do the actual data entry. You have to have enough staff to ensure that data changes are entered in the system in a timely manner. They may be part of the membership department or spread across several different departments, but they must all be thoroughly trained by the database manager, and their work should be regularly monitored.

Managing security levels among staff and volunteers who have access to the association's database is one of the more difficult issues a database manager faces. In some associations, many or all staff members have read access to the system, which allows them to look up individual records or query for groups of records. Before gaining write access to the database, an employee must be thoroughly trained in all aspects of data entry and, thereafter, should be continuously reminded of the association's data entry standards. Even so, not all employees would have either read or write access to members' financial records stored on the system. This information should be limited to those with a need to know. The ability to void or change invoices might be limited to only those individuals in the association's accounting department. The availability of security levels that would grant access to only those parts of the database that an employee needs to do his or her job is an important factor in choosing a database system. Assuming that security levels are available, they should be scrupulously monitored by the database manager who assigns them.

Many associations grant volunteers read access to parts of the database; some grant write access to volunteers. There are several factors to consider in allowing access to members who do not work directly for the association. First, all employees and volunteers should be asked to sign a confidentiality agreement stating that they will not rent, sell, or otherwise divulge information in the database to outside parties. If an association also grants volunteers write access to the system, it should be aware that volunteers may not be entirely rigorous in adhering to data entry standards, and the association does not have the same leverage in these cases as with employees. The only recourse an association has with volunteers who fail to meet standards is to monitor and correct all of their data entry or revoke access and risk losing an otherwise valuable asset. Most associations steer around this thorny issue by instituting a policy of read-only access for volunteers.

Reporting Data

What you report on will depend on your organization's initiatives and priorities—and is discussed further in chapters 10 and 14. By applying the following guidelines about how and why to report, your organization can rely on a valuable history of knowledge to assist in meeting its objectives:

- **Run reports for a reason.** Go back to your marketing or operational strategies and see what reports are needed. Identify who will review and act on the report. Resist the urge to start running a report just because a board member likes statistics. Create reports that support program metrics, objectives, and goals. For example, if you were charged with increasing attendance, profits, and member satisfaction levels of your annual convention, prepare a report for the conference planning committee or education foundation that demonstrates growth or drop-off from year to year.

- **Consistently report at regular intervals that make sense.** Look at the timing of your reporting seasons. Will the report be more or less valuable at any specific time? For example, does reporting retention make sense before your annual membership drop-offs are processed?

- **Look for trend development and behavior changes.** Look at your regular report results side by side for steady and abrupt increases or decreases and lack of movement. Use your reporting tool or other software and formulas for trending, data forecasting, and analysis.

- **Don't report in a vacuum.** Sometimes outside influences may affect your member activities. Make sure you know what else may have been going on during your reporting period. Was there a shift in the economy? Were your members affected by high oil prices, natural disasters, political decisions, or terrorist activities?

• **Present it in a readable format.** Raw data can be cumbersome and overwhelming. Use your reporting tool to import data into software, like Excel, that can create pie charts and bar graphs.

Using the Database for Marketing, Recruitment, and Retention

You should collect, manage, and maintain data for one reason: to use it to better your organization's offerings. Your database and data are particularly essential to your organization's marketing, recruitment, and retention efforts.

Marketing

Perhaps the greatest value of the association's database is the marketing data collected. One way to use the data is to apply recency/frequency/monetary value (RFM) analysis to identify information about its best members or customers. Simply put, RFM suggests that the best customers/members in the database are those who have recently purchased a product or service, purchased several products and/or services, and spent greater sums of money on these products and services. With a well-maintained database, the association can analyze the buying habits of its members and customers and develop a target list of those members and customers most likely to purchase another product or service from the association. Generally, it is relatively easy to look at RFM for your most recent time periods, such as a past year. Looking at your member data across a three-to-five-year period is challenging because data comparisons become more difficult.

Here is an example of applying RFM to develop a membership segmentation strategy.

Recency, Frequency, Monetary Value—Member Segmentation

What does RFM do? It analyzes three parameters for each member:

1. Date of last purchase (recency)
2. Number of purchases (books, articles, meeting registrations, webinars, etc.) per month/quarter (frequency)
3. Average amount of money spent per purchase (monetary value)

You can perform a cluster analysis of the numbers (or in the simple version, a membership person decides based on gut feeling) and define boundaries for each parameter, in order to split them up into categories.

Example:

• Recency: R1 is everyone who purchased in the last 12 months, R2 is everyone who bought in the past two years, and R3 is the rest.

• Frequency: F1 is every member who purchased on average three or more times per year, F2 purchased at least one time per year, and F3 is the rest.

• Monetary Value: M1 are those who purchased more than $100 per visit (including meeting registration) and M2 are the rest.

In this scenario, you have split up your heterogeneous member group into 18 ($3 \times 3 \times 2$) more or less homogeneous subgroups that you can address in different ways. Your super-members (R1-F1-M1) don't need the same approach as the R3-F2-M1 (the big spenders that haven't been around to your shop in the last year). And you hope you can predict the behavior of members by analyzing their past behavior.

See the following for futher explanation on RFM:
http://en.wikipedia.org/wiki/RFM

An association's data, along with other primary and secondary data, can also be used to help identify growth areas, new products, and maturing or dying products. This information is gleaned from sales data but gaining insight from it requires creative thinking and analysis on the part of association staff. To identify growth areas and new products, staff must analyze the trends in the types of products and services being purchased. Do the products and services with greater sales have a common theme among them? For example, if a printed piece on a particular subject is selling well, is there an opportunity to develop a seminar or educational sessions around the topic? Could complementary software be created? Is there a particular format that sells better than others? Do the members and customers prefer electronic formats to printed material? Do they prefer videoconferencing to on-site meetings? Are there common themes from our own data that we can see across other industries or professions? All this information can be gleaned through analysis of existing data as well as through other external research, survey information, and historical data.

Finally, sales data can provide insight into products and services whose appeal is waning. Analyzing the sales trends of a particular product may show that sales are decreasing. Before concluding that the product has matured, association staff must weigh other factors, including quantity and quality of marketing for the product, timeliness of the issue addressed by the product, and other issues, such as pricing. At the same time, consideration should also be given to the product's relationship to the membership value proposition (public awareness, advocacy, etc.). Keeping in mind all these considerations, association staffers can use sales trends to help decide if further efforts should be made on maturing or dying products.

Recruitment

Associations can use their data to develop a profile of ideal members. By collecting a variety of demographic data, the association can determine what the best prospective member looks like and then target nonmembers who look like the ideal member.

Depending on the type of association, demographics for trade associations could include company size (sales and staffing), industry served, and geographic location. For professional societies, demographics might include profession, experience, level of education, age, gender, geographic location, household income, specialty area, and more. The types of demographic criteria to consider are limited only by your imagination. By examining demographic data with elements of designation such as CPAs or MDs, further segmentation can help to refine and help to target segments with more customized offerings.

In addition to the ideal member, associations can also use data to identify non-members who purchase a lot of products and services and approach them about membership.

Retention

In addition to telling staff how many current members there are, the association database can track how often members are touched by the association throughout the year. Association staff should record each contact made with members, whether through direct mail promotion of a product or service, notices about upcoming business meetings, or email announcements about legislative issues. Each time the association speaks to its members, the database can track what was said and when it was said. These data can be used to ensure that members are being communicated with in a timely and appropriate manner.

The database can also provide clues about when a member is most likely to drop membership. If the association has been tracking join data and drop dates for an extended period, these data can tell the association at what point in a member's membership life he or she is most likely to drop membership and can provide the association an opportunity to address the issue before the member drops. Consider a hypothetical example. By analyzing the join and drop dates of its members during the past five years, the XYZ Association finds that the average member drops in the seventh year of membership. Armed with these data, XYZ Association creates a special program whereby all members entering the seventh year of membership are personally contacted by a member of the association's board of directors to ensure that members' needs are being addressed.

Tracking

Directly related to marketing, recruitment, and retention efforts is tracking. Like all other promotions, membership promotion is a sales cycle. Thus, the cycle and promotion efforts can be tracked through the use of source codes, which should be recorded in the association's database for effectiveness. For example, a professional society might do a direct mail promotion to 10,000 potential members. A source code is printed on the reply form, so when a new member joins from that form, the source code is recorded in the database, showing from which promotion the new member was acquired. In addition to the response form, the letter that is part of that direct mail solicitation lists a special department number with a phone number so that the source code is tracked in the database when a new member calls to join. By vigilantly tracking the source of all new members, the XYZ Association is able to identify which membership promotions are effective and which are not.

It's All Worthwhile

Without question, identifying and collecting the right data, ensuring its quality, and managing and maintaining it is a considerable, ongoing undertaking. And it's all worthwhile—if you put the information to use. When you have all the data you need, don't treat it like your telephone book that sits unopened on a shelf or under your child at the Thanksgiving table. Use your data and use it wisely. As the technology experts at Gartner, Inc., remind us, "After the analysis has been done, there is no business benefit until the results change the organization's or member/ customer/prospect's behavior." For example, by identifying underserved segments with more targeted and customized offerings, you can address new prospects who in the past have not connected with mass messages or services that did not resonate with their specific needs.

Don Dea is co-founder of Fusion Productions, Webster, New York. An ASAE & The Center Fellow, Dea is a recognized authority on the Internet, association strategy, online education, and technology deployment. He has served on numerous boards of directors, including that of ASAE & The Center. Email: dddea@fusionproductions.com.

Carolyn Hook is the director of membership and operations at the New Jersey Society of Certified Public Accountants, based in Roseland. Part of NJSCPA since 1989, in her current role, she manages efforts to recruit and retain members, maintains the membership database, supports NJSCPA governance and strategic planning initiatives, directs Young CPA efforts, oversees volunteer activities, and trains staff on customer service and database skills. Email: chook@njscpa.org.

Recommended Resources

American Marketing Association	www.marketingpower.com
CIO Magazine	www.cio.com
Direct Marketing Association	www.the-dma.org
Federal Trade Commission	www.ftc.gov
Gartner	www.gartner.com
The Privacy Rights Clearinghouse	www.privacyrights.org
TechSoup	www.techsoup.org

A CEO's Perspective on Membership Data and Its Use

By Tom Hood, CPA

10

IN THIS CHAPTER:

- Association data: your association's most important asset
- Reporting capacities needed to effectively use data
- Applying data to recruitment, retention, and marketing

MANY ASSOCIATIONS BREATHED A collective sigh of relief when the dot.com era ended with the dot.com bust and the association community was still standing. Many of the Internet start-ups were entering the information and services business and threatened the existence of some associations. Yet despite the loss of many direct competitors, a fundamental shift in the way businesses are operating continues to widen the gap between the business and nonprofit sectors.

According to the U.S. Census Bureau, the average annual growth rate for associations was 3.8 percent—barely above the 3.2 percent real growth in the U.S. Gross Domestic Product (GDP) for the 10-year period between 1992 and 2002. The U.S. Chamber of Commerce's Survey on the Future of the Competitive Association found that 62 percent of associations actually performed below the average GDP rate, with a total growth rate below 20 percent for the same 10-year period. Yet the for-profit commercial sector grew by more than 52 percent during the same time frame. While a few fast-growing nonprofit organizations are exceptions to this rule, most are struggling to maintain flat or slightly declining memberships. Relevancy is being questioned and many associations have started to look for other sources of revenue to shore up flat or declining budgets. Yet most for-profit organizations would love to have a captive membership base that freely shares preferences and other demographic information. What is the key to unlocking the hidden value in your membership database? The answer is the right data about your members and the right tools and training to use that data.

Data: Your Most Important Asset

Associations are in an ever more competitive and difficult environment, as members and customers demand more and more targeted services and information and more personalized experiences. This trend is being driven by the members' experiences in the real world, where personalization, customization, and 24/7 service have become the norm. All these features are driven by customer or member data and matching member profiles with the products and services that are offered. Ultimately, the idea is to capture the most important data about your members and the products and services you provide and to be able to use that information to create membership growth in your organization or increases in products and services consumed by your membership.

So what do you need to know about your members? The answer starts with your organization's purpose and strategy. Start with the organization's highest priorities and determine how they are relevant to your members. Also, consider new initiatives and strategies. What future products and services are you planning to provide? Is yours an individual membership organization, a membership made up of organizations and corporations, or both? What specific, targeted members are you planning to recruit? What are your major products and services to your membership—whether individuals, corporations, or both—and the public? It is important to consider all of these elements in your planning.

Start With Your Best Customers

A great starting point is to identify your best members and customers. Can you list the members who use the most products and services in your organization? Make sure to include committee and chapter volunteers, speakers, authors, and others as important groups of members you need to support and interact with. Next, include future-targeted groups or categories of members. Identify the critical data that identify these members and that are critical to communicating with them.

Our experience at the Maryland Association of Certified Public Accountants (MACPA) shows that even if your association is based on individuals, you should consider how to capture and relate individual members and transactions with the member's organization. Often the true customer is the person or organization paying the bill. For example, the MACPA noticed contributions to its PAC were declining. A deeper look at the data showed that the CPA firms, rather than the individuals who are our members, were paying the dues and, therefore, eliminating the PAC check-off. The reason: PAC contributions cannot be made on behalf of individuals through a CPA firm check. Only individuals may contribute to a PAC. This insight led the association to implement a new focus on serving the CPA firms and beginning to form relationships with the decision-makers at those firms, since they were influential in decisions ranging from membership to product and service purchases.

Match Your Priority Products and Services to Your Members

Another way to look at your data and data needs is to map your primary products to your members. Here are the basic steps:

- Identify the different types of members and audiences you have.
- List all of the priority products and services you have.
- Map them to your member types and audiences.
- Identify relationships by how they are searched for by your members.
- Capture the categories and classify the data into hierarchies.
- Use that classification system in your data structures where possible.

Some questions to explore might include the following:

- Do these products and services relate to all of our members, or are specific segments targeted?
- Can you identify the key traits in the segments that can lead to categorization?
- Who is the real decision maker when buying or signing up for our services and products? The member? The member's boss? Or even the member's company?
- Can you effectively reach those members and decision makers?
- What data are important in targeting those relationships?
- How do your members search for the products and service you offer?
- What terms do they use when looking for items?
- What new programs, products, or services is your organization developing, and what type of member segments need these services?

The key is to work from the point where the member is transacting with you and to work backward inside your organization. Look at the structure and types of data you currently capture about members and the transactions they have with you. Don't forget to consider all the channels through which members are doing business with you: for instance, the member call center, fax or phone orders, in-person at conferences and events, and, of course, the web. All these member entry points are valuable places in which to explore potential data that will help you match your products and services to your members. Another important aspect to consider when mapping out your products and services is your content: the numerous articles and other information that you provide to your members. Even if it is free, it may be a benefit that members value highly and can help you determine what their needs are.

Creating a 360-Degree View of Your Members

The goal is to create a comprehensive view of your members and all the ways they interact with your organization. An example of how this would look is to sort your database by all the ways members interact with you. Start with the easy, measurable transactions like event purchases, product purchases, and membership purchases, and then add volunteer activities, leadership positions, PAC contributions, and so forth. Then aggregate that data by organization to capture concentrations of members, if you are an individual membership organization. Sort this data from highest (most revenue) to lowest (nonfinancial transactions) and you will have a listing of members who are the most engaged with your organization. The for-profit world would identify these as preferred customers and usually would have special programs and customer relationship management techniques and benefits to maintain and grow the relationship with these loyal, high-use customers.

Just as described earlier, check this list against your organization's strategy and priorities. Are these members the right target? Are there groups of members who are missing from this list that the association needs to research further to target its products and services to them? The insights from this type of analysis are the natural starting point for developing a targeted marketing strategy.

All the data about your members and all the ways they interact with your organization and each other creates a 360-degree view of the member. This is the critical database of information that will allow you to personalize web and self-service applications, organize your content, and target market the right products and services to the right members. Many of the newest association management system/customer relationship management products have included this functionality under the banner of customer relationship management, or CRM. CRM systems automate the tasks for capturing and organizing all the data around this concept of a 360-degree view of your members.

Several stand-alone systems for customer relationship management are available for nonprofits to use to supplement their association management systems (AMS). These systems are particularly helpful in capturing relationship information about organizations with multiple points of contact. These systems should be considered if your organization is based on individual members or donors and you are considering new products and services for your members' organizations in addition to individuals. Salesforce.com has been a market leader for some time. This group also has an extensive nonprofit program that offers free enterprise licenses for qualified nonprofits. Microsoft also has a CRM system for the .Net platform. These systems can supplement your existing AMS systems and offer added features like sales force automation (SFA) that can be critical in offering new products and services to specific targeted segments.

However, if you do not have this type of system, even basic systems like Microsoft Outlook or ACT! can help you capture extra data about your members that, when combined with your transaction details and volunteer activities, will give you all you need to analyze your membership to identify patterns that will help you become more targeted in your approach to recruitment, retention, and growth in products and services. The next critical step is to study and comprehend the potential market available for growth.

Understand the Market

Understanding the market surrounding your membership is an important step in understanding the potential to grow your membership and products and services. Start with your membership base. What are the total potential members available to your organization? Depending on the size and scope of your organization, this data may be easy to obtain or may require professional market research. You need to determine the entire universe of your membership types. For instance, most professional associations start with the number of licensees in their market (national or state-based). These data are often available from regulatory authorities that issue licenses or permits. Other sources of market data are trade publications, census, and economic data. Trade associations may want to identify all the companies in their industry. If you divide the number of members you have by the total available members in the marketplace, you get your percentage of market share or penetration rate. This number offers you insight into whether you have growth potential. If your penetration is at 90 percent or higher, you should probably explore other avenues of growth.

Calculating Market Share: An Example

A national organization of certified public accountants determines its market share as follows: Number of existing members = 350,000 divided by the number of CPAs licensed in the U.S. = 560,000 (a 62.5 percent penetration or share of the market). Thus, the organization has the potential to recruit a maximum of 210,000 members, or 37.5 percent.

There are only four basic ways to grow your association:

- Increase the use of existing products and services by existing members, often referred to as growing the share of the member's wallet.

- Increase the number of dues-paying members or donors, also known as recruitment.

- Increase the number of members that renew their membership (retention).

- Add new products and services that members need.

Understanding your existing membership and the potential market with this perspective is the foundation for developing your future growth strategy and the data you will need to execute that strategy.

Using the Data: Capacities for Effective Reporting

Your systems should have the capacity to easily produce reports and distribution lists without the need for requesting report development from your information technology, or IT, department. Standard reports should reflect the key metrics that membership, meetings, publications, marketing, and other departments require for managing the day-to-day operations of the association. It should provide the basis for performance reporting of membership operations and campaign management as well. Standard reports should be those reports that can be generated routinely from the membership system or be easily developed by staff. Some of these reports would be

- Accounts receivable/cash
- Ad sales management
- Back orders
- Billing
- Campaign tracking and management

- Certifications
- Chapter leadership roster
- Collections and refunds
- Committees
- Customers
- Donations
- Event calendar
- Exhibitor sales
- Exhibits
- Expirations
- Fundraising
- General ledger journal summary
- Inventory
- Legislative tracking
- Members
- Member demographics
- Nonmember prospects
- Opportunities
- Orders/sales
- Partners
- Referrals
- Registrations
- Rosters
- Sales commissions
- Sponsorships

Information is one of the most important assets of your association. An organization generates a significant amount of data on a daily basis across orders, customers, members, meetings, books, publications, subscriptions, marketing, and more. All of this information is somewhere in your organization. Ideally it is in your AMS/CRM. How do you make sense of this information and data? How do you organize it to help you understand the following?

- Who joins and why?
- Who renews and why?
- Who declines to renew and why?
- Who is buying and why?
- What is the annual value of membership benefits to a member?
- What is the lifetime value of membership to a member?
- Who is most likely to attend the annual meeting?
- What is the deadline and what requirements still need to be fulfilled to complete your member's professional development or certification requirements?

Reporting, whether strategic, ad hoc, or in an executive dashboard, can provide some of the answers. However, reporting reflects a point in time. It can tell you what your member or customer data look like as of today or at a snapshot in the past but further work is required to understand patterns and trends. Organizing data that may not come from one database but that is pieced together from several different databases becomes the work of data mining and data warehouse tools. Looking at the effectiveness of a campaign to a selective segment of your database is the work of campaign analytics tools. More advanced versions of this work are sometimes referred to as business intelligence. The goal is to provide your association with strategic insight to patterns about your membership and customers.

Using the Data for Recruitment, Retention, and Marketing

Assuming that the association is keeping track of its members in the database, and assuming that data are up to date and accurate, association executives have immediate access to two key measurements: total members and total membership revenue. Depending on the type of association, this benchmark may occur as infrequently as annually or as frequently as monthly or weekly. Whether the association is a trade, professional, or philanthropic organization, it can track its progress with periodic benchmarking of these two numbers. The association's growth can be measured in terms of current membership compared with one week, one month, one year, or five years ago (or whatever is appropriate) as well as total membership dues revenue measured against the same time period.

Other statistics are also easily accessible from the database, provided records have been kept accurately for some period of time. These include

- Membership retention
- Market penetration
- Lifetime value (LTV)

Membership retention is a relatively easy formula that requires only three numbers: the number of members from some date in the past, the number of new members added since that time, and the total number of members now. One simply subtracts the number of new members form the current members and divides that number by the number of members in the past. For example:

> On 1/1/99, XYZ Association had 575 members. On 1/1/00, XYZ had 612 members, 77 of them being new members. Thus (612-77)/575=0.930 or 93 percent retention.

Retention is an important number because it tells the association whether it is keeping members that it is acquiring or whether it is losing an unusually large number of members. Retention is also key because research has shown that acquiring new members and customers can cost anywhere from 8 to 16 times the cost of retaining an existing member or customer. (For more about member retention, see Chapter 16: Retention.)

Market penetration is another relatively easy formula, assuming the association has two key numbers: current number of members and the universe of potential members. For many associations, determining the universe of members can be difficult, especially if the association has a broad range of membership categories. But assuming a universe can be identified, the formula is simple: number of current members divided by the number of the universe. For example:

> On 1/1/2000, XYZ Association, representing accredited higher education institutions in the United States, has 2,512 members. The universe of accredited higher education institutions in the United States is 3,215. Thus, 2,512/3,215 = 0.781 or 78 percent. XYZ Association has a market penetration of 78 percent.

Market penetration can be important for several reasons. If the association lobbies on behalf of the industry, with higher market penetration, it can claim to be "the voice of the industry." High market penetration also increases the value of advertising space in the association's publications. Market penetration also demonstrates growth potential for the association in terms of membership numbers and revenue. High market penetration (greater than 90 percent) may not allow for much future growth in terms of member numbers and dues revenue; thus, the association may need to look beyond membership dues for additional revenue. On the other hand, low market penetration may be an opportunity for increased dues revenue or may indicate the association is not providing enough value to the market it is serving.

A third statistic that can be mined from the database is *lifetime value,* or *LTV.* Simply defined, LTV is the total dollar value of a member for the life of his or her membership. That is, if the association adds all revenue received from a member (dues, products, and services) over the entire period of time that the member is involved with the association, this is the LTV of the member. (See Chapter 14: Financial Metrics for Membership for more about lifetime value of members.) Association executives should calculate LTV for their membership to measure whether their recruitment and retention efforts are effective. The key statistics to calculating LTV are average number of years a member stays with the association and the average amount of money (including dues) spent by the member each year.

Multiplying these two numbers together provides the LTV. For example:

> At the XYZ Association, the average member stays in the association for 11 years. The average member spends $2,150 per year with the association, including dues, meeting attendance, and publication purchases. Thus, the LTV of the average member is $11 \times \$2,150$ or $23,650. This is important because while dues for the new member may be only $1,500, the association may choose to spend several multiples of $1,500 to acquire a new member, because the LTV is much higher than one year's dues.

"Growth is the oxygen of associations and nonprofits," to paraphrase a quote from best-selling author and business guru Michael Treacy. Growth means member satisfaction—members are selecting your association over other choices. Growth in an association means increased strength and power, a stronger voice, and the ability to exert more influence over the industry, profession, or even the world that your members operate in. It also means growth for the dedicated association professionals who have chosen your association for their careers. Your membership data, the systems that capture and record that data, and the staff competencies to use and interpret that data are fundamental to unlocking the hidden growth inside your association.

Tom Hood is a Certified Public Accountant and the executive director and CEO of the Maryland Association of CPAs, in Towson, Maryland. Email: tom@macpa.org.

Web Sites and Membership Directories: Their Key Roles in Membership

By Don Dea

11

FROM A MEMBERSHIP OPERATIONS standpoint, your association's web site is the primary channel for awareness, knowledge, and engagement. Your web site is both a strategic and operational endeavor. While the principles and strategies for the web extend beyond the scope of membership operations, outlined in this chapter are some of the key considerations that should be addressed by the membership function in an association or other membership organization. Also included is a basic primer on effective web strategies that support member value delivery. Because membership directories, whether delivered in print or online, are key tools for supporting member value, their role and deployment is explored as well.

Web Sites: Organizing for Engagement

From a membership operations perspective, what do you want to accomplish via your association web site? As in most things, the first step in organizing your use of the association web site for membership is to define a clear set of goals. For example, organizations will identify that the primary purpose of the web site is to be the primary information portal for their specific industry or profession. Supporting goals would include expectations around the specific scope of the domain area that will be covered. This helps staff, volunteers, and users understand what to expect and sets benchmarks that staff can support. Another goal for the web site might be to create value for members' interaction in ways that permit them to take advantage of the association's data, knowledge assets, and services with full integrity, accessibility, currency, and automatic online delivery. The natural extension of the purpose or goals for use of the web site in a membership context are a set of objectives, audience segmentation, and a description of the expectations you'll address via the web for each of the audience segments. Without a clear statement of purpose, objectives, and outline of your audience and the expectations that will be set for them, the project will begin to wander off course and bog down or may go on past the point of diminishing returns. Careful planning and a clear sense of purpose are the keys to success for sustaining your association web site.

Setting Objectives. A clear, short statement of objectives should form the foundation of your membership operation plans. This is where you expand on the goals in your statement of purpose, and it will be the tool you will use to analyze the success of your association web site. For example: "We expect the association's web site to accomplish these goals during the next 12 to 18 months."

Remember, the web is nonlinear and to truly be an effective tool for your members and audience, you need to provide information in a logical and clear manner in which your members and other audiences would engage with you, not the way that your association is organized or by function. While this may require more coordination, ultimately your ability to integrate your information and tools in a manner that is self-evident to your members and users will determine their degree of success or dissatisfaction with your web site.

Defining Audiences and Expectations. The key to effective membership operations via the web is to identify and segment the potential members and users of your site so that the web site design meets their needs and expectations. The knowledge, background, interests, and needs of members and users will vary from new members—tentative novices who need a carefully structured introduction—to expert power users who may chafe at anything that seems to patronize them or delay their access to information. A well-designed web site should be able to accommodate a range of user skills and interests. Develop your own model of the various ways that members and users will want to use the association web site. Make sure that you understand and can articulate what your member/user expectations are for online and offline engagement. On your web site as part of a site tutorial for first-time visitors, or when introducing a new redesign, state how best to use the site and what the association promises the value of the site to be. For example, "To best use our site, check back weekly; you will find a digest of news articles, press releases, and publications that affect YYY. Each month you will find both our newsletter and BBB journal along with a round up of other professional peer review summaries. Check back daily to see what information your colleagues are interested in by reviewing most frequently used search terms."

When you have identified and segmented your target audiences, take these steps:

• Create a statement of purpose for each constituent group. For example, "The XXX community of practice proactively advocates the importance of XXX in the PPP product delivery process with the objectives of providing a forum for members to discuss issues of common interest through education and training; listserver e-discussions; regulatory cooperation; information dissemination; establishment of links to internal and external groups with common interests."

- Know your main objectives and key outcomes that your constituents desire and that you can fulfill.

- Define a concise outline of the information your site will provide and maintain.

- Characterize the types of users/members in each segment, who are they, what are their online access settings, and what are the conditions that they most likely will engage your web site.

Establish metrics and know your web statistics about your site and usage. Web site metrics and analytics help you to understand how your users/members and public are using your web site. For example, tracking visitors, unique visitors, members, where they go on your site, what search terms they use to get to your site, what pages are most frequently viewed, what pages members view, and so forth will help you recalibrate how you organize your site, what content should be enhanced or added, and what area should be reviewed for enhancement or replacement, etc.

Here are some of the metrics that are core elements to keep track of:

- *Visits/sessions.* A visit is an interaction, by an individual, with a web site consisting of one or more requests for a page.

- *Unique visitors.* The number of inferred individual people (filtered for spiders and robots), within a designated reporting timeframe, with activity consisting of one or more visits to a site.

- *Entry page.* The first page of a visit.

- *Exit page.* The last page on a site accessed during a visit, signifying the end of a visit/session.

- *Visit duration.* The length of time in a session.

- *Referrer.* The referrer is the page URL that originally generated the request for the current page view or object.

- *Search referrer.* The search referrer is an internal or external referrer for which the URL has been generated by a search function.

- *Page views per visit.* The number of page views in a reporting period divided by number of visits in the same reporting period.

Using metrics and measures to track user activity on your web site, in combination with membership profile information, can provide the foundation for helping to customize information for users on the web site. For example, knowing what special interest groups that a member belongs to can then be used with web site content that is tagged for that special interest group. When a member logs into the members-only area of the web site, specific information that is related to the special interest group can be highlighted. The same process can be extended by examining the web site metrics to highlight frequently viewed pages that contain the key words of the special interest group to provide a filtered view of information to the web site user.

Helping Members Help Themselves

The core elements of the web and membership form the foundation of what is now called "member self-service." Many of the elements are transactional in nature. Some involve e-commerce, others deal with secure information, and many involve the product, program, and services that are accessed, discovered, and obtained via the web. Often many of the elements are member benefits that then require a method of authentication to provide access to information that needs to be secure for member-only access. Following is a list of key member engagement functions or elements typically inherent to or delivered via the association web site:

- Access to various member benefits (both association-delivered and those delivered for the organization by third parties, such as advocacy or job banks)
- Authentication for members-only access
- Continuing education profile and history
- Donations
- Electronic product delivery
- Meeting registration
- Member join and renewal functions
- Member profile updates
- Member purchases
- Membership directories
- Member transaction history including payment history
- Publications
- Subscriptions
- Survey forms
- Volunteer activities and engagement

Your association web site will reduce the demands on the staff for routine information on association activities, deadlines, dues and fees, frequently asked questions, and information about association meetings and events. You should expect your web site to save a significant amount on postage and processing of routine member correspondence. The association web site will carry all of the content that currently goes into your association's newsletter, new member welcome kit, and a multitude of marketing collaterals, but will also carry more timely information as events warrant. Maintaining your organization's web site is an ongoing process, not a one-time project. Sustained editorial, knowledge management, database management, data mining, campaign management, and technical maintenance must be covered in your membership plans for putting the web site to work.

Your association's web site in effect becomes a 24/7 extension of your association staff. A fully integrated membership system and web site provide the essential information that members need to interact with the association and in addition can provide the added value of customized information based on the demographic needs of each member. Self-service association web sites, while still in their infancy, will be the operative capability as associations develop the appropriate security and processes to provide accurate and up-to-date information for members and users to conduct business.

Other Uses of Your Association Web Site

Your association's web site, of course, provides myriad opportunities for engagement with members and other constituents. Here are a handful:

- **Online collaboration, community, and networking (Communities of Practice).** Communities of practice are groups of people who come together to share and learn from one another face to face and virtually. They are held together by a common purpose; they contribute to the body of knowledge and are driven by a desire and need to share problems, experiences, insights, templates, tools, and best practices. Community members deepen their knowledge by interacting on an ongoing basis.[1] Whether communities of practice take place online or face to face, the core aspects of knowledge sharing and networking remain at the foundation for engagement and interaction. The online world provides access and leverage that complements or substitutes for the face-to-face element. Recent advances on the Internet have introduced online social networking tools such as blogs and wikis that have enabled users to easily publish information on the web without the need to understand HTML coding. New online capabilities such as Facebook, MySpace, Flickr, and so forth have created rapidly growing online communities that have attracted wide participation by youth, high school, college, and young professionals. Associations have begun to also introduce these tools as an approach to futher supplement their online channels.

- **E-learning and professional development.** Web-based training applications tend to be linear in design and present few opportunities to digress from the central flow of the presentation. Most online training presentations assume a contact time of less than one hour or are broken up into sessions of an hour or less. Inform your users/members about how long the session will last and warn them not to digress from the required material if they are to get credit for the training. Training applications typically require a user log-in and often present forms-based quiz questions in true/false or multiple-choice formats. User log information and scores are typically stored in a database linked to the web site. The formats vary from synchronous programs, often called webinars, that are event driven with a specific time and format to asynchronous, or on-demand, which are courses that users can access 24/7. The types of material are varied and depend on your association's unique education and professional development assets and mediums. Examples include workshops and seminars from your annual or regional conferences (synchronized PowerPoint and audio), customized courses developed on unique curricula about the specialty areas, and peer reviewed journal articles with online assessments. Depending on the administrative and management requirements, these types of applications could be addressed by your association's content management system with custom application support or with a learning management system that is fully integrated with your association management system.

- **Reference and Body of Knowledge.** The best-designed reference/body of knowledge web sites allow users to quickly pop into the site, find what they want, and then easily print or download what they find. Typically, there is no story to tell, so the usage patterns are totally non-linear. Content and menu structure must be carefully organized to support fast search and retrieval, easy downloading of files, and convenient printing options. Keep the graphics minimal to speed download times, and you may want to investigate search software instead of relying exclusively on index-like lists of links. Contact time is typically brief, and the shorter the better.

Membership Directories

Another key tool for membership operations is the membership directory. According to ASAE & The Center for Association Leadership's 2006 *Policies and Procedures in Association Management Volume 1 (Membership)*, the association membership directory is one of the top four core key benefits organizations provide. The others are newsletters, magazines, and information or reference services. Directories provide a listing of the primary constituents of the organization. Starting from the basic information about the individual or organization, a membership directory may extend to more detailed information regarding capabilities, specialty areas or capabilities, credentials, and so forth.

Membership directories serve as a means of communicating to the membership and in some cases to the public who the organization's constituency is and how to reach them. Membership directories are a valuable resource for members or those within a profession to identify resources for peer-to-peer networking or development of business opportunities. Many organizations believe that one of the primary benefits of membership is to enable networking or connecting with other professionals. In this case, membership directories take on an expanded role in providing additional information to help distinguish members based on various demographic or professional considerations.

For trade organizations, the membership directory provides a convenient system to identify members for business-to-business or business-to-consumer communications and often serves as the official listing of the contact information for the firm or organization. From a marketing and industry perspective, such an official listing in a directory signifies the participation of the organization in the marketplace or economic sector. Membership directories may be an explicit requirement in the bylaws of an organization.

As a membership professional, you need to bear in mind that the membership directory can be a significant asset for the organization. It represents the visible access to the core constituency of the organization. The policies and procedures and practices of an association ultimately determine whether the membership directory is an asset or a liability.

Directory Development, Deployment, and Use

Membership directories are typically a member benefit (free or at a discount) and available generally in print, and as the web continues to expand, most organizations have an online version. In many cases, associations are replacing the print with online; however the hard copy is still a valuable asset for many organizations. The advantages of online beyond the lower publishing costs include the timeliness of changes and the expanded search capabilities that online directories can have. For many organizations, membership directories also serve as a source of nondues revenue. In the 2002 ASAE & The Center benchmarking guide *Generating & Managing Non-dues Revenue in Associations,* half the organizations indicated that the membership directory is a source of nondues revenue through sales of the directory and advertising within the directory.

The key to a membership directory's value proposition is the accuracy, timeliness, and quality of the information that is made available. The challenge that associations face is to keep up with the dynamic changes that take place with their membership. Ensuring that members update their association profiles requires a concerted effort to remind them and an easy-to-administer process that is seamless for members. As more and more avenues for member self-service open up online, unifying the various interactive and print channels requires careful organization and technical competence.

Protecting the Information in the Directory. An association's core membership information is one of its most critical assets. It is important to protect it physically and legally. In the past, the most common and yet potentially valuable proprietary association asset has been its mailing list. While you would think that legal safeguards are in place, generally this is not the case. Unlike an association publication whose intellectual creations and intangible assets can be protected by copyrights, databases do not enjoy the same level of copyright protection. Be sure to consult legal counsel in determining the extent to which copyright protection can apply to your association mailing lists and membership directories.[2] Additionally, consider certain language that you should consider for deployment for your association membership directory.[3] (See sidebar, "References and Resources.")

Updating the Information. Maintaining your association's membership data is part of the core responsibilities that association staff provide. Detailed process and thoughtful strategies must recognize that members who are willing to share information expect it to be used appropriately, kept secure, and deployed in an explicit and transparent manner. Keeping information up to date also requires tenacity and diligence, following up to ensure the accuracy of data and information and providing appropriate self-service and mail opportunities that do not confuse members when they take the initiative to make changes.

Members' Use of the Directory. The old adage that garbage in is garbage out takes center stage when looking at membership directories. If the directories are not current or correct, the credibility of the database becomes questioned and can spiral into a credibility issue. Additionally, if information is misused—whether directly or indirectly—that misuse can tarnish the integrity of the membership directory and the association. Like any asset, it must be managed. Risk assessments must be periodically conducted to determine if any vulnerability may exist and what plans and actions can be taken to mitigate or neutralize any exposures. For example, conducting periodic audits of the directory data to check consistency of address information, most recent updates to a record, completeness or incompleteness of information, area code changes, and so forth should help to flag records that require further exploration. This periodic audit helps to ensure that the quality of the data in the directory is up to date and consistent.

Production and Deployment Options. Print publishing processes continue to evolve, with more flexible and dynamic mechanisms for information exchange as well as formatting. So, too, is the online directory process continuing to undergo major changes. As membership management systems add enhanced functionality, some membership directories can be published as a separate application launched from the membership system. Third-party application directories can provide enhanced searching and display functionality as well as experience in marketing, data capture, and self-service that can supplement an association staff and its membership system.

Simple membership directories that do not require significant search capabilities and special formatting and display considerations often can be handled internally, assuming that the membership system can provide user-friendly survey/database programming capabilities. If the membership system requires more advanced database access and programming tools, special technical skills, or a requirement to incorporate data from other parties, then you are well advised to consider using your membership management vendor resources or third-party application developers.

Don Dea is co-founder of Fusion Productions, Webster, New York. An ASAE & The Center Fellow, Dea is a recognized authority on the Internet, association strategy, online education, and technology deployment. He has served on numerous boards of directors, including that of ASAE & The Center. Email: dddea@fusionproductions.com.

References

1. APQC: Communities of Practices Association: June 2006.

2. See article: "Are Your Association's Membership Directory and Mailing Lists Protected by Copyright? Think Again."

3. See reference and resources model: "Shrink-wrap License for Association Membership Directory."

References and Resources

List Server Discussion: Asking Members' Permission before Adding Them to Your On-line Directory
Membership Developments, May 2000
ASAE & The Center, *Policies and Procedures in Association Management, A Benchmarking Guide, Volume 1 Membership,* 2006

Are Your Association's Membership Directory and Mailing List Protected by Copyright? Think Again.
By: Jeffrey S. Tenenbaum Esq. Venable LLP
jstenenbaum@venable.com
Source: Center Collection
Published: June 2002

Shrink-wrap License for Association Membership Directory (PDF)
Organization: Venable
Web site: www.venable.com
Description: Did you know that most association membership directories (printed or online) are not subject to copyright protection and, unless otherwise protected, generally may be freely copied and used by marketers and others? This model shrink-wrap license can help protect one of your organization's most valuable assets by placing contractual restrictions on the use of this information.
Contact: Jeffrey S. Tenenbaum Esq., jstenenbaum@venable.com

New Member Contact, Renewal, and Communication Processes

By Katie Jones and Don Dea

IN THIS CHAPTER:

• New member communication

• Renewal processes

• Members' access to the association

ESTABLISHING A POSITIVE RELATIONSHIP between a member and an association begins even before an individual or entity becomes a member. The bond begins to form not only on the strength of a clear expression of value to the member and a welcoming environment but with clarity around the myriad details that come with joining a new organization. And that relationship evolves—pro or con—with every touch thereafter. Consequently, professionals responsible for the membership function need to ensure that the information and processes are in place to ease new and continuing members' understanding and navigation of the organization. This chapter focuses on the vital processes related to new member communication and renewal processes as well as on easing members' access to the organization.

Informing the Prospective or New Member

It's fundamental but essential. Make sure prospective and new members clearly understand what is involved in joining. Among the information to cover:

• How much do they pay?

• Do you offer corporate memberships, individual memberships, or both? If you offer a corporate membership, does it include everyone at the company or only a specific number of individuals?

• Is there an application fee? If so, make sure members understand why. What does it cover?

- Do they need to wait for approval or do they become members as soon as the application is submitted?

- As new members, will they receive anything right away?

Once they have joined, make sure you have processes in place to ensure that they receive what you've promised. Your first contact should immediately acknowledge their payment/application. People expect instant confirmation of payments, especially if they join online. When you acknowledge, reaffirm what they should already know as the process for joining. Make a point to understand and document why they joined. If you can establish why, you will then be in a position to align your member benefits appropriately.

Your second contact should be some sort of new member packet or welcome kit. The packet can include a broad range of information about your organization. Likely contents are a welcome letter that highlights the main benefits of being a member, membership cards and/or certificates, information about state and/or local chapters (if appropriate), and any materials that spotlight programs that may be of value to new members. With access to online capabilities, a quick start guide about how to use your association's web site is a big plus for new members.

From there, you can take your new member contact program any way you'd like. Here are some suggestions for further contacts:

- Send invitations to new member welcome receptions or local events.

- Use a new member mentoring program; have new members' mentors call them and encourage them to get involved.

- Hold scheduled new member orientations.

If yours is a local organization, you may have success with simple, in-person new member events. Make sure to host as many existing members as new members, so that new members can talk to experienced members as well as staff to get acquainted. If you are a national organization, you may want to take advantage of web meeting technology to hold live webinar orientations. webinars allow members from anywhere to sit down at their own desks and watch and listen to a live presentation by association staff or maybe a member. Once the presentation is complete, attendees can ask questions of the presenter. And since it's online, new members may feel a little less awkward about submitting a question, since it's a little less visible audience. The best part of webinars is the ability to record and store them. Then new members can watch the orientation sessions at their convenience. If you allow that, make sure that members who watch the recorded sessions know who to contact if they have other questions.

A general note about member communications: The days of "Dear Member" are over. Associations are about community, and no one feels like they belong when they are referred to as "member." This is especially important in any communication in which you are asking a member to contribute time or money. Think about how you'd respond to an appeal for money that's just addressed to "Dear Member." The current versions of Microsoft Word and mail merge functionality in general make it easy to personalize, so don't skip that step. For smaller organizations, if you don't have the staff, outsource the project to a mail house. With your member list they can create personalized communications.

Renewal Process

One of the first decisions associations must make is the type of renewal cycle they'd like to follow. There are really two primary options: anniversary cycles and calendar cycles. There are positives and negatives to both.

In an anniversary cycle, if a member joins on June 1, he or she pays the full membership amount and the membership then runs from June 1 through May 31 of the next year. The membership would be divided into 12 smaller groups to be invoiced each month. While this approach allows for more personalized attention, it also means staff would continually be focusing on renewing members. Dues revenue would be spread out over the course of the year, eliminating the potential need to amortize dues.

In a typical calendar cycle, if a member joins on June 1, he or she would be invoiced a prorated dues amount and the membership would expire December 31. In December, the member would be billed, along with every other member, for the full amount for the next year. With this approach, staff can ramp up for a once-a-year renewal effort, which makes it easier to ask volunteers for help. Since all dues revenue would be received in the same few-month span, it would make sense to amortize that revenue (divide it up and recognize smaller amounts at several different points, usually on a monthly basis).

Regardless of what type cycle you follow, when renewing members, you will want to use as many communication methods as possible to grab their attention and focus it on the fact that it's time to renew. A well-written letter emphasizing the benefits of membership is a great accompaniment to a paper invoice, but don't stop there. Consider allowing your members to pay their renewal invoices online. If you do, a reminder email with a link to your web site and the payment page can catch the attention of someone who may have missed their paper invoice. And if letters and emails don't work, consider asking member volunteers to help staff make phone calls to delinquent members. By combining approaches, you're bound to reach more members than just by sending a printed invoice (or two or three or four).

Another question to ask is, "How many invoices should I send?" One way to best answer this question is to add a source code to printed invoices as they are sent out. When renewals are returned, staff can track the source code on the invoice and then you can look at the trends. Do your members respond only to the final notice? Or did 50 percent of members respond when you sent the reminder email and allowed them to pay online? Once you have an idea of member behavior, you can revise your approach for the next cycle. Maybe you don't need to send printed invoices any more. Or maybe it isn't worth it to send three advance invoices if members respond only to the final notice.

Your grace period factors into this process, too. Do you have a long grace period or a short one? Do your members know how long the grace period is and do they take advantage of that? When determining the length of your grace period, take these questions into account. In many ways, a longer grace period encourages members to pay later. After all, if they are still receiving services, why should they pay sooner? If you are on an anniversary cycle, do you recognize the membership term from when they are billed or when they pay? If you are recognizing the membership cycle from when they pay, members are actually able to get free months of service by waiting to pay until the end of the grace period. Make sure your grace period does not shortchange your association.

Once your members have renewed, you have to determine how you are going to recognize that fact. As a member, there is nothing worse than sending off your money and getting no response whatsoever, so it's important that you let members know that you appreciate their renewal. You have several options.

If you allow members to renew online, you should at the least set up an automatic "Payment Thank-you" page to display once they've paid. A nice second step would be to send an automated thank-you email. Manual thank you's include mailing a thank-you note or letter or maybe even a whole packet of information on the association.

Many associations send dated annual membership certificates as part of the renewal process. You'll need to get a feel for whether a certificate is important to your members or not. If you do send them out, they can be an added reason for members to renew. Members like to display certificates. They often think it adds credibility to their job or business. If your certificates have an end date on them, they'll want to have a valid certificate to display. Even better, instead of mailing certificates, you may want to set up a print-on-demand option so members can print their own certificates online and have them instantly.

Just like membership certificates, many associations send a membership card to each member as well. It's a great chance to put important information on a card they might carry with them at all times, such as a User ID and password to your web site or information about discounts they may receive as members of your association. You should be able to get a feeling about how important a membership card may be to your members. If they are important, they are worth doing. If not, it could be a cost saver to discontinue the practice. If you can offer a print-on-demand option so members can print their own, that's great, too.

Ensuring Member Access

One of your top priorities is to make sure it is easy for people to get the information they need, whether it's via phone or your web site. We all know that if it's not easy, people won't use it. They just won't get the help they need, and that always makes the decision to renew or not much easier.

Phone Access

The ability to access staff via phone generally boils down to one main decision: using a live receptionist, an automated system, or call center. This is actually a more difficult decision than you'd think because there really isn't a right answer. It all depends on your organization and the members you are trying to serve. There are pros and cons to each option.

With a live receptionist, callers tend feel a more personal connection. It's easier to help people who don't necessarily know what they want, and it's an additional resource for the organization. However, a rude or unhelpful person in the position can negatively affect the member experience, and there is the additional expense of another employee.

From a cost perspective, an automated system is usually a one-time cost to purchase and install, and then members can call at any time because your switchboard is never closed. However, members may complain that they never speak to a person or have trouble getting to a person.

Once your association reaches a critical mass where there is specialization, then the added dimension of looking at how your members/users can effectively engage you becomes a key consideration. When calls have to be routed to several different people to address a question, members will become frustrated. Call center strategies require careful analysis and setup. If a call center becomes a viable option, then getting outside consulting resources should be considered, as you will have process, systems, and management considerations.

If you are choosing between a receptionist and automated system, here are some considerations:

- If you are selecting a receptionist, the first priority is to make sure your organization creates a detailed job description for the position. Here are some things to consider: Do you expect the receptionist to actually handle calls or just direct them to other staff? If so, include detailed explanation of any tasks outside of answering the phone (managing packages or mail, greeting guests, etc.). Define performance standards ahead of time (number of calls allowed to go to voicemail, responsibilities regarding the general mailbox, etc.). Once you have created the job description, you can begin the hiring process. The main thing to consider here is the personality of your job candidate. Remember, this is who will be greeting everyone who calls and visits your organization. If they do not impress you at your first meeting, do not hire them.

- If you do select an automated system, you can set up that system to function at its highest level. Set up a corporate directory that someone can navigate based on the first name of the employee. Really, how often do you know the last name of the person you are trying to reach? Then make sure to include general options for membership, accounting, events, and any other area that may get lots of calls. There are lots of times when members don't have a specific employee name, but they know the general areas. You can route these calls to a specific employee mailbox or a general box. However, if you use general boxes, make sure a specific staff member is assigned to monitor each box and return the calls. Otherwise, members will be angry that they never received a response.

- Most importantly, with an automated system, your job is not over as soon as it's installed and operational. You need to test the system often to make sure your members are getting the attention they deserve. At least once a month, do a test call and see if you are able to navigate the system the way you'd need to if you were a member and had a specific question.

- Also, because you can't answer every call, use your outgoing voice mail message to the member's advantage. Make sure your outgoing message includes the name and extension of another staff person members can reach in your absence. If it's easier or faster for you to respond to email, include that information, and your email address in the outgoing message. If most information can be found on your web page, include the web address as well.

- Most importantly, give an idea of when you'll be able to answer the call. Have a policy for all staff that calls have to be answered in a certain time frame, and make sure members know what that policy is. That will set a manageable expectation in their minds, and they will be happy to receive a call within that time frame.

Online Self-Service

Member self-service, as mentioned earlier, is the 21st Century model of empowering members/users to engage directly with your association. The web has established expectations of member/user engagement on their terms. While it is still very important to provide human contact, online self-service 24/7 is part of the minimum conditions of operation.

Supporting member self-service is the need to have access to up-to-date information from your association management/customer relationship management system. This applies to your phone access support as well. Maintaining an up-to-date "frequently asked questions" area on your web site is also key. Access to this information is important for your members/users as well as staff who support your phone information capabilities.

Getting these points of engagement right is vital to the success of membership operations. Members expect to have accurate, up-to-date access to data about their relationship with the association. They also expect to get to people or information that will effectively address their needs. Service and systems are the cornerstones of effective engagement.

Katie Jones is an associate with Integrated Software Solutions, in Reston, Virginia. She worked in nonprofit organizations for nearly a decade, most recently as vice president of membership for the National Mortgage Brokers Association. Email: kjones@issimpak.com.

Don Dea is co-founder of Fusion Productions, Webster, New York. An ASAE & The Center Fellow, Dea is a recognized authority on the Internet, association strategy, online education, and technology deployment. He has served on numerous boards of directors, including that of ASAE & The Center. Email: dddea@fusionproductions.com.

Financial Management and Budgeting

By Susanne Connors Bowman and Lori Gusdorf, CAE

13

IN THIS CHAPTER:

- Accounting methods
- Invoicing and collections
- Projecting revenues for budgeting
- Sources of revenue

M ANY FUNCTIONS OF AN association's membership department and its accounting department overlap and having synergy between the two is vital to the success of both. From budgeting, to cash flow, to processing of payments and sending out renewals, responsibilities can shift back and forth between the two departments. As the person responsible for the membership department, you must have an understanding of each of these tasks and manage financial goals and timeliness in processing of membership. This chapter introduces accounting methods, collection and budgeting processes, and nondues revenue sources. The next chapter will help membership professionals judge the health of the organization by tracking a series of metrics relating to membership.

Accounting Methods

Two forms of accounting are used by associations: cash basis and accrual. The difference between the two methods is the recognition timing of the revenue and expense received. Membership professionals should be aware of how these accounting principles specifically relate to membership dues income because of the impact to examining dues structures and potential dues increases.

Cash Basis. Cash basis accounting is based on real time cash flow. Income is not recorded on financial statements until it is actually received and expenses are not recorded until bills are paid.

From a membership perspective, this means that your association does not carry the dues owed for your memberships as an accounts receivable and dues revenue is not recognized until the dues have actually been collected. When renewals are sent out, no corresponding accounts receivable entry is made in the general ledger. The balance owed resides in just the membership module of the association management system with no corresponding entry in the accounting module.

Accrual Basis. An accrual basis of accounting records income when it is earned, rather than when it is paid. The same principle applies to expenses; they are recorded when obligations arise, not when you pay them.

From a membership perspective, the accrual method of accounting allows the association to record the amount of dues owed at the time of invoicing your members as an accounts receivable and, therefore, an asset on financial statements. When your membership renewal is processed, it creates a general ledger entry against accounts receivable in this model. This method of accrual accounting for membership revenue is used most often by trade associations or other types of associations that have an extremely high retention rate.

Deferred Income. When a payment is received for membership dues, it is recorded in the general ledger as cash received and income. Some associations recognize the entire amount of payment in the month that it is received. Others use a deferral system where one twelfth of the dues income is recorded as actual income each month. If a deferral system is used, then general ledger entries are made each month, taking income out of the deferred income and placing it in current income. If a member pays dues prior to the expiration date, the income is not realized until the membership year begins. If a member pays after their expiration date, the number of months that they are late is calculated and recognized as income at the time of payment.

For example, a member has an expiration date of December 31. If he pays early, the general ledger entry would be

Cash	$120
Deferred income	$120

Then in January, when the new membership year begins, income is moved from the deferred revenue to current revenue.

Current income	$10
Deferred income	$110

If a member pays two months late, the general ledger entry would look like the following:

Cash	$120.00
Current Income	$20.00
Deferred Income	$100.00

Hybrid. An association might take a hybrid approach to accounting, using the accrual basis of accounting but recording membership revenue on a cash basis and deferring the income throughout the year. Alternatively, another association might accept partial payments for membership dues, recording as accounts receivable the balance owed for the membership dues once the initial payment is received.

Essentially, that approach uses an accrual basis for membership dues once the first partial payment is received but uses a cash basis if the entire amount is sent at once.

Uncollected Dues. Whether cash or accrual accounting is used by your association, in most association management software programs, you still need to reconcile your uncollected dues. If your association records membership renewals as accounts receivable, you will need to determine a schedule for when you will write off the amount owed from members who have not renewed. A general ledger adjusting entry will remove the receivable from your financial records.

If the association operates on a cash basis of accounting, the uncollected dues invoices are not actually recorded on your financial statements. However, most association management software systems require that some type of renewal record for members is set up before they are billed. If the member does not renew, then you need to cancel that membership at some point in time and no longer show a balance due on the member record. This is usually an automated process that needs to be performed on a regular basis in the membership module of the association management system.

If you fail to cancel a lapsed member's outstanding record, you may wind up billing that same individual for the next year. For example, if first renewal notices are sent out to members three months before to the expiration date, reconciliation should take place for the prior year's membership of those members who have not renewed within those nine months. If you do not do this step, in most software programs, you will then bill the lapsed member for both years. Say for members having a 12/31/xx expiration date the first set of renewal invoices are sent in September. All the members that were billed with a 12/31/xx expiration date the year before but did not renew must be cancelled before the next year's billing is sent so they do not receive another bill. An effective method of following up with these extremely lapsed members is to do a targeted follow-up mailing to try and get them to renew.

Internal Controls. Most associations are audited annually. Usually during the audit, a random selection of membership payments are chosen and it is the membership or accounting department's responsibility to go back through your systems and records and find the backups showing the membership entries and the payments that were received for them.

Whether the data entry of membership payments is done in the membership department or in the accounting department, it is imperative that membership payments be processed in a timely manner. One advantage to the membership department's being responsible for this function is that generally there is more control and a greater sense of urgency about handling membership records. Processing membership payments as efficiently as possible allows questions to be answered in a timely manner.

However, a segregation of duties or accounting controls is necessary to avoid any appearance of mismanagement or the possibility of theft. For example, payments are received in the accounting department and a batching process records the receipts and establishes a basis for tracking. The manager of the accounting department posts receipts to the General Ledger so that the same person who enters the payments is not posting the payments. The membership staff performs the data entry of the payments, and the membership manager records that the batch is complete on a spreadsheet that was set up by accounting so that reconciliation can take place between the departments.

Invoicing and Collections

A mix of mailed and emailed reminders is the most effective way to handle the renewal process. Although many organizations allow individual members to self-renew and update member information online (see below), some individuals and many organizations still pay membership dues by check, so it is imperative that you continue to mail membership renewals to your members to facilitate payment in this manner.

Annual and Calendar Year Differences. Membership can be on an anniversary or calendar year basis. (See Chapter 6: Membership Categories and Dues Structures.) If your association operates on a calendar year, invoicing is tied to the beginning of the fiscal year and all members are on the same annual cycle. Calendar year renewal processing makes the administrative billing cycle more compact. It also makes the payment processing more compact and can adversely affect processing time unless systems are in place to accommodate the large amount of data entry that occurs as payments are received. Depending on the percentage of revenue that your dues comprise, you may have to manage a large influx of cash at one point during the year.

If your association operates on an anniversary basis, your membership billing is disbursed throughout the 12 months of the year and your members can have 12 different expiration dates. An anniversary membership spreads out the invoicing, payment processing, and cash flow during the year.

Here is one scenario for an anniversary billing cycle: Send up to five renewal notices to members. The first one is sent three months prior to the expiration date. If they do not renew, send a notice every other month up to five months after expiration. By generating renewals every other month, you allow enough time for the renewal notice to reach them and for payment to be received, minimizing the number of payments crossing in the mail with notices. See Appendix 1 at the end of this chapter for a sample spreadsheet of this model.

Lapsed Member Mailing. An effective method for approaching long term lapsed members is to plan an annual marketing initiative. When it is a quiet time of year, send a special mailing to all lapsed members from the previous year. For example, in August you can target all members who had an expiration date of January through December of the prior year. The mailing should be different from other solicitations, letting the member know you want them back as a member. Additionally, it can include an exit survey for those who have chosen to not renew and you can find out the reasons why. This process can capture the attention of new employees who may have replaced the previous member at their place of employment.

Online Processing. Allowing members to join or renew online with a credit card payment saves staff time because the data entry component of the process is essentially eliminated. The only additional steps necessary are payment verification and data entry integrity checks. Most association management systems are configured to communicate with both accounting and membership functions to process online submissions. The use of online join and renewal systems also saves postage and processing time involved in renewal reminders.

Projecting Revenues for Budgeting

Whether your association is on an anniversary or a calendar year for membership, you still must develop a fiscal year budget. Likely you will be involved not only in developing an operational budget for your department but also in contributing your revenue projections to the association's overall budget.

Calculating Membership Revenues. Budgeting for a calendar year is simpler because all your memberships have the same expiration dates for their terms. Most associations record their dues on a deferral basis, meaning that one twelfth of the dues revenue is recognized each month. Working with an anniversary membership is more complex because you need to determine how many members expire in a given month, base your retention and acquisition numbers on those numbers and determine the variations.

Table 1. Sample Anniversary Dues Spreadsheet

Membership Start Date	Membership Expiration Date	81% Active Members	$220 $ Projection	Budget Recognition
Feb 06	Jan 07	# of members	(# of members × dues amount) × 1/12	12-Jan
Mar 06	Feb 07	# of members	(# of members × dues amount) × 2/12	12-Feb
Apr 06	Mar 07	# of members	(# of members × dues amount) × 3/12	12-Mar

You also have to figure in the various dues amounts that your association charges. Table 1 is a sample anniversary spreadsheet for several membership categories with varying dues amounts and retention statistics. In some situations, the membership term for a new member is different from a renewing member so the deferral and budget must be calculated accordingly. To calculate the entire year of membership revenue, for an anniversary system, the revenue being recognized is actually spread over 23 months. This is because you have to account for the one twelfth spread of membership 11 months prior to the start of the year and eleven months after the end of the year. However, one single membership is spread over a 12-month period.

The example in Table 2 details the 2007 budget for one membership category that costs $220 and has on average an 81 percent retention rate. The formula to calculate the amount to be budgeted is Number of members × 1/12 of $220 = budget projection amount, where the budget recognition reflects the number of months in the current year that are being recognized for revenue.

Table 2. Budget Projections

Membership Start Date	Membership Expiration Date	81% 10 Members	$220 $ Projection
Feb 06	Jan 07		
Mar 06	Feb 07		
Apr 06	Mar 07		
May 06	Apr 07		
Jun 06	May 07		
Jul 06	Jun 07		
Aug 06	Jul 07		
Sep 06	Aug 07		
Oct 06	Sep 07		
Nov 06	Oct 07		
Dec 06	Nov 07		
Jan 07	Dec 07		
Feb 07	Jan 08		
Mar 07	Feb 08		
Apr 07	Mar 08		
May 07	Apr 08		
Jun 07	May 08		
Jul 07	Jun 08		
Aug 07	Jul 08		
Sep 07	Aug 08		
Oct 07	Sep 08		
Nov 07	Oct 08		
Dec 07	Nov 08		
Totals			

Cash Flow. Appendix 2, Renewed Membership Budget Calculation, is a spreadsheet tied to Table 2 that will calculate automatically the amount projected for each month for each member category. This illustrates how you can determine a month–by-month budget projection.

When planning long-term or short-term cash requirements, it is important to factor in the cash from your membership dollars. By using the budget chart on Appendix 2, you can estimate when those dollars should be received. If your organization has calendar year membership, you can expect a large influx of cash during a short time just before and after the start of the membership year. For anniversary billing, the cash flow will fluctuate based on the number of members expiring each month.

Cash flow budgets estimate cash receipts and cash disbursements. Your accounting department may prepare a comparative statement of cash flow, and one of the comparisons is membership dues dollars from year to year. This may include both actual income and deferred income.

Cash flow can be affected by marketing initiatives that outlay a large expense in producing materials or paying for advertising prior to receiving the income from the generation of new members. During the first year of a large-scale membership campaign, costs can outweigh income and should be anticipated and budgeted appropriately. If new members are retained for several years, the initial expenses will be recouped and positive cash flow will result over time, but the impact to cash flow in the short term should be considered.

Revenue Mix

ASAE & The Center's *Operating Ratio Report,* 12th edition, indicates that revenue from dues is generally decreasing in proportion to total association revenue. Participants in the report averaged membership income as 40.9 percent of total revenue and a median of 35 percent, compared to 42.7 percent and 35.5 percent, respectively, in the 10th edition. This compares to the 95.7 percent of revenues in 1953, the first year of the *ORR*), and 52.3 percent in 1977, representing a precipitous drop.

Nondues Revenues. In addition to dues, associations derive revenues from a variety of sources, including

- Sponsorships
- Exhibit Fees
- Nonmember Customers
- Affinity Programs
- In-kind Donations
- Advertising
- Publication Sales
- Conference Registrations

In larger associations, these other sources of revenue may not be in the prevue of the membership department; nevertheless, it is important for a membership professional to understand the role of membership dues in context of other revenue sources, particularly since associations exist to serve members. A membership professional usually has a closer feel for members' wishes and needs and can advise other departmental areas that are responsible for generating nondues revenues.

Unrelated Business Income Tax. Unrelated business income for nonprofit organizations is taxed if the gross income is more than $1,000. Associations must file a Form 990-T within 5 ½ months of the end of the fiscal year. This UBIT tax does not apply to dues revenues, of course, but can apply to some of the other revenue sources listed above.

Revenue Mix. Revenue mix is the balance between the level of dues revenue and revenues coming from various nondues programs and services. It is a concept membership professionals should understand because it can alert you to potential financial concerns. Revenue mix is an important part of the budgeting and dues management process and should be reviewed annually. As a membership professional, you may be involved as part of a team that determines revenue mix or you may be under pressure to attain a certain percentage of growth in membership to maintain a balance of revenues approved by the board. Often membership departments in larger associations may deal strictly with dues revenues and have little input about nondues funding in the association.

Table 3. Sample Graph Showing Association Revenue Sources

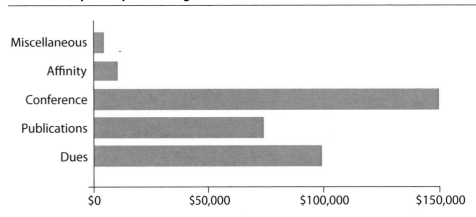

In Table 3, dues are an important source of revenue but not the single largest source. The largest source of revenue is the organization's conference. Consider what the financial ramifications of a revenue mix like this might be. What if the conference must be postponed or doesn't happen at all, as was the case for many conferences immediately following September 11 or Hurricane Katrina? The association's revenue would be markedly affected.

In many organizations dues are the single largest source of revenue. If your organization is small, serving a relatively discrete population, a decision to make dues your single largest source of revenue usually will create a high per-member contribution to the overall bottom line.

Table 4. Sample Pie Chart Showing How Membership Dollars Are Spent

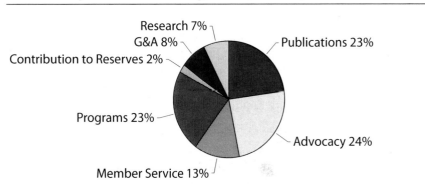

Communicating How Revenues are Spent. Often members question how the association manages its resources. An effective way to communicate that is by creating a graph that illustrates how dues dollars are used. (See Table 4.) This can be kept at a general level or may be specific, depending on the organization and how the finance area keeps information.

This sample includes the general areas of advocacy, publications, research, member service, general and administrative costs (G&A), and contribution to reserves.

In many ways, the membership professional must be a financial professional not only because membership dollars are important sources of revenue but also because other programs of the association and, indeed, the association's measure of success often hinge on the membership function.

Susanne Connors Bowman, is co-owner of The Haefer Group, Ltd., a membership value consulting firm, located in Reston, Virginia. Sue has served the association community as a consultant for more than 10 years. Her previous employment included 16 years as a senior level manager at AARP and several years as a manager at the American Pharmacists Association. She chaired the ASAE & The Center's Membership Section Council in 2005-2006. Email: sbowman@thehaefergroup.com.

Lori Gusdorf, CAE, is vice president of Membership and Chapter Services at the Association of Fundraising Professionals in Arlington, Virginia. She has worked there for 17 years and prior to that installed software systems for associations. She is a member of ASAE & The Center's Membership Section Council. Email: lgusdorf@afpnet.org.

Sample Anniversary Renewal Billing Cycle

Renewal Processing Month	1st Notice expiration date	2nd Notice expiration date	3rd Notice expiration date	4th Notice expiration date	5th Notice expiration date
Jul 07	Oct 07	Aug 07	Jun 07	Apr 07	Feb 07
Date sent	7/15/2007	7/19/2007	7/18/2007	7/17/2007	7/15/2007
How many sent	2,247	1,467	852	630	514
Aug 07	Nov 07	Sep 07	Jul 07	May 07	Mar 07
	8/10/2007	8/11/2007	8/12/2007	8/13/2007	8/14/2007
	2,606	1,714	791	519	516
Sep 07	Dec 07	Oct 07	Aug 07	Jun 07	Apr 07
	9/29/2007	9/22/2007	9/23/2007	9/24/2007	9/25/2007
	4,200	1,544	856	655	534
Oct 07	Jan 08	Nov 07	Sep 07	Jul 07	May 07
	10/17/2007	10/18/2007	10/16/2007	10/15/2005	10/19/2007
	1,963	1,793	1,103	551	458
Nov 07	Feb 08	Dec 07	Oct 07	Aug 07	Jun 07
	11/17/2007	12/1/2007	11/18/2007	11/19/2007	11/20/2007
	1,994	2,542	1,002	1,064	572
Dec 07	Mar 08	Jan 08	Nov 07	Sep 07	Jul 07
	12/14/2007	12/15/2007	12/16/2007	12/17/2007	12/18/2007
	2,182	1,338	1,219	885	479

In the scenario above, an average of 36 percent of the membership pays on the first notice. By the second notice, 58 percent of the membership has paid; by the third notice, 69 percent; and by the fourth notice, 73 percent have renewed.

Renewed Membership Budget Calculations

The table on the next page shows sample budget calculations based on membership renewal. The CD-ROM accompanying this book contains this and three additional worksheets that provide renewed membership budget calculations and the formulas used to reach those calculations.

About the table

- This example assumes that ABC Association has six membership categories, each with different annual fees. The annual fee for each category is listed below the membership category header (see key below).

- The historic retention rate for each category is listed below the membership category header (see key below).

- The "$ Projection" column (abbreviated "$ Proj.") is the membership revenue per month. It is calculated as the number of members that month × the annual fee / 12 months.

Historic retention rate for this category

Annual membership fee for this category

Membership Category 10		
HRR 77%	$220	HRR
# Members	$ Projection	Memb
1,614	29,590	
1,658	60,793	
1,725	94,9	

Projected revenue for this month =
 # of members this month
  × annual fee
  / 12

ABC Association
2008 Renewed Membership Budget Calculation (based on 08/31/07 membership)

Membership Start Date	Membership Expiration Date	Membership Category 10 HRR 77% # Members	Membership Category 10 $220 $ Projection	Membership Category 20 HRR 81% # Members	Membership Category 20 $75 $ Proj.	Membership Category 30 HRR 48% # Members	Membership Category 30 $100 $ Proj.	Membership Category 40 HRR 57% # Members	Membership Category 40 $150 $ Proj.	Membership Category 50 HRR 68% # Members	Membership Category 50 $220 $ Proj.	Membership Category 70 HRR 25% # Members	Membership Category 70 $35 $ Proj.	Total Budget Members	Total Revenue Budget
Feb-07	Jan-08	1,614	29,590	10	63	265	2,208	143	1,788	63	1,155	22	64	1,974	33,080
Mar-07	Feb-08	1,658	60,792	5	63	272	4,533	121	1,513	52	1,907	19	111	2,006	67,407
Apr-07	Mar-08	1,725	94,875	6	113	268	6,700	137	1,713	61	3,355	25	219	2,085	105,261
May-07	Apr-08	1,597	117,113	10	250	219	7,300	106	1,325	74	5,427	5	58	1,905	130,148
Jun-07	May-08	1,299	119,075	5	156	246	10,250	91	1,138	61	5,592	5	73	1,616	135,146
Jul-07	Jun-08	1,523	167,530	9	338	213	10,650	94	1,175	52	5,720	5	88	1,802	184,325
Aug-07	Jul-08	1,374	176,330	3	131	220	12,833	79	988	50	6,417	5	102	1,652	195,813
Sep-07	Aug-08	1,325	194,333	3	150	244	16,267	114	1,425	53	7,773	5	117	1,630	218,640
Oct-07	Sep-08	1,401	231,165	5	281	225	16,875	83	1,038	30	4,950	5	131	1,666	253,403
Nov-07	Oct-08	1,521	278,850	12	750	225	18,750	118	1,475	30	5,500	5	146	1,793	303,996
Dec-07	Nov-08	1,601	322,868	7	481	225	20,625	91	1,138	26	5,243	5	160	1,864	349,378
Jan-08	Dec-08	2,683	590,260	88	6,600	225	22,500	110	1,375	45	9,900	5	175	3,046	629,435
Feb-08	Jan-09	1,730	348,922	8	557	0	0	81	1,012	65	13,165	7	209	1,810	362,852
Mar-08	Feb-09	1,616	296,309	5	304	0	0	67	834	61	11,220	6	182	1,689	308,015
Apr-08	Mar-09	1,682	277,477	7	365	0	0	74	926	51	8,415	7	190	1,746	286,447
May-08	Apr-09	1,566	229,705	8	405	0	0	60	755	67	9,874	2	35	1,643	240,020
Jun-08	May-09	1,398	179,352	7	319	0	0	67	841	63	8,029	2	36	1,469	187,735
Jul-08	Jun-09	1,486	163,471	7	243	0	0	57	713	48	5,236	2	31	1,542	168,981
Aug-08	Jul-09	1,478	135,449	3	101	0	0	60	755	46	4,239	2	26	1,529	139,815
Sep-08	Aug-09	1,446	106,044	3	81	0	0	62	777	61	4,438	2	20	1,512	110,584
Oct-08	Sep-09	1,435	78,898	5	91	0	0	43	534	37	2,057	1	11	1,478	81,057
Nov-08	Oct-09	1,522	55,817	7	81	0	0	68	855	43	1,571	6	35	1,578	57,504
Dec-08	Nov-09	1,462	26,808	4	25	0	0	62	770	48	885	2	7	1,517	27,725

Financial Metrics for the Membership Professional

14

By Susanne Connors Bowman and Lori Gusdorf, CAE

IN THIS CHAPTER:

- Calculating acquisition costs
- Lifetime value formulas
- Costs to serve a member
- Membership renewal calculations

FINANCIAL METRICS ARE AN important tool to judge the current financial health of your organization, project future needs, and identify problems. Some of the most common questions on ASAE & The Center's list serve are about how to calculate various metrics. This chapter discusses a variety of financial metrics, gives examples showing how they are calculated, and explains situations where they might be most useful. Remember, use metrics with caution. They are an important tool but often don't tell "the rest of the story."

Acquisition Metrics

New members are important to the financial health of any membership organization. But it's important to understand how much acquiring new members is costing the organization. The rule of thumb says it is cheaper to keep members than get them. No acquisition is free. For instance, members who join through your web site or through direct mail have been affected by marketing, advertising, or word of mouth.

The most basic fundamental for acquisition metrics is to first understand how members are learning about your organization. Knowing how members learn about your organization is the only way that you can judge the effectiveness of each acquisition method separately. That allows you to make the case to invest in certain strategies over others. How do you accomplish that? Every member who joins your association should be tagged with a source code. Ideally, your association management system should be the place where that is tracked. If that's not happening, development of a simple Excel spreadsheet will do.

Basic Components of Direct Mail. Direct mail remains a successful medium for marketing membership. Direct mail acquisition programs are relatively easy to measure. Typical costs include:

- List cost (if list is purchased from an external vendor). This cost would not apply if you are using internal lists of former members.

- Data processing, including merge purge and personalization of a letter

- Package cost relating to production. Typically these are quoted in "cost per thousand."
  - Outside envelope
  - Letter
  - Brochure (Costs will vary based on size, paper quality, use of color.)
  - Application form
  - Return envelope

- Agency fee (if applicable)

- Creative fees for photography, illustrations, layout (if applicable)

- Lettershop costs (to assemble the elements and prepare for mailing)

- Postage (outgoing). May be first class, third class, or third class nonprofit rates.

- Postage (business reply envelope)

- Fulfillment costs (package costs for sending membership card, thank you letter, handbooks, or other materials.)

Additionally, some organizations factor in the cost of staff people who are devoted to membership acquisition and some percent of those who provide member service. Rarely do organizations factor a percentage of overhead into the costs, sometimes because doing so takes a sophisticated allocation system and sometimes because organizations prefer to expense general overhead separately.

Terminology and Theory. Acquisition costs are considered on a per-member basis. For direct mail, the first calculation involves calculating how much you will spend to produce and mail each piece. Fixed costs for a membership campaign, such as agency or creative fees, do not change based on the volume of a mail campaign. Variable costs, such as paper, printing, and postage, will change based on volume. Adding more pieces may reduce the per-piece cost for printing but would increase your mailing costs. Typically, the overall per-piece cost goes down when volume increases.

Then you must forecast your response. In calculating the success of a direct mail membership campaign, consider these outcome metrics:

- Gross acquisition costs are total acquisition costs divided by the number of members who respond to a particular campaign.

- Net acquisition costs factor in the number of people who request a refund or, in a "pay-later" situation, ultimately do not pay dues.

Calculating Direct Mail Costs. The Association of Widget Manufactures has decided to conduct a direct mail campaign. They purchase a list of prospects from a list vendor. They ask an ad agency to create a package that has a four-page invitation letter from the association's Executive Director; a six-panel, two-color brochure; a membership application; and a return envelope without postage. New members will receive a membership card, welcome letter, and new member handbook. The association plans to mail 4,000 packages and expects a three percent response rate.

The estimates for costs in this campaign come from the Direct Marketing Association's *Statistical Fact Book*, which is produced annually. It is an excellent source of information to develop direct mail budgets and forecasts.

Table 1. Calculating New Member Acquisition Costs—Direct Mail

Element	Cost Per Thousand	Total Cost
Agency fee		$2,500.00
Other creative		$200.00
Letter printing, four pages, black and white	$28.05	$112.20
Brochure printing, six-panel, two-color	$108.00	$432.00
Membership application printing 8½" × 11" – two sides	$55.00	$220.00
Outside Envelope (No. 10)	$28.69	$114.76
Business Reply Envelope (No. 9)	$15.49	$61.96
Mailing list	$100	$400.00
Lettershop production (insertion, application of postage, pull samples	$26.25	$105.00
Postage (third class, non-profit mail rate)	0.17 cents (per piece) or $170	$680.00
Variable per thousand cost	$531.48	
Fixed costs	$2,700.00	
Cost to mail (per piece): $531.48 x 4 = $2,125.92 + fixed costs $2,700.00 Sum divided by 4,000	$1.21	
Total mail cost		$4,825.92

If you factor in the additional cost of internal staff time, the calculation would look like this:

Variable costs per thousand ($531.48 x 4)	$2,125.92
Fixed costs	$2,700.00
Staff cost (one month of manager and one support staff salaries/benefits)	$7,500.00
Total costs	$12,325.92
Cost to mail per piece ($12,325.92/4,000)	$3.08

The addition of internal staff time to the acquisition campaign increases the cost to mail dramatically. In smaller organizations where no staff supports the membership function full time, these additional costs usually are not reflected. (See Appendix 1 for a sample table you can complete.)

Calculating Gross Acquisition Costs. When you have figured the costs to mail your campaign, the next step is computing your results against costs. You are mailing 4,000 packages and you are expecting to have a three percent response rate, or 120 new members. Using the first calculation, you've spent $4,825.92 to obtain 120 new members. So by dividing $4,825.92 by 120, you'll see that the cost of the campaign to acquire each new member was $40.21. But you are not finished. Next, you must factor in the cost of fulfilling that new member—the membership card, the welcome letter, the handbook, the postage, the processing. For sake of example, let's say that is an additional $2.00 per member. So your total acquisition cost per member response is $42.21 per member.

Return on Investment Metrics for Associations

For membership professionals, return on investment (ROI) is most commonly applied when looking at acquisition costs. However, ROI formulas can and should be applied to renewals and to programs and services, such as conferences, publications (in total or individually), and advocacy efforts as well.

Simply put, ROI is the ratio between expenses and expected revenue. In commercial entities, ROI is a much clearer calculation. For instance, if you spend $4,000 to develop a product, the sales price is $50, and you sell 600 units, you have generated $30,000 from your $4,000 investment. So your return is $30,000/$4,000. Your ROI in this instance is 750 percent. If you had sold only 45, making $2,250, your return would have been 56 percent. To recoup your costs, your ROI must equal 100 percent.

Examining the Net Results. Is $42.21 to acquire a new member a good number or not? That depends. How much are your dues? How long will it take to recover the acquisition costs? Compare the acquisition cost to your dues. In the case of the Association of Widget Manufactures, dues are $30 per year. That means that it will take approximately 1.4 years of membership for the acquisition expenses to break even if you consider only dues from the member. However, if the association's dues were $300, the campaign would be judged a great success. Another thing to consider is that a new member might invest hundreds more dollars in purchasing association publications or attending the association's conference in the first year of membership. Every way a new member contributes revenue to the association might be calculated into how the association views its return on investment from the acquisition campaign.

Other Types of Marketing Campaigns. Calculating acquisition costs for programs other than direct mail apply the same basic methodology but use different elements to develop the costs. (See Chapter 15: Recruitment Strategies, Table 2 Marketing Media Compared for relative costs of various media.) For example, elements to consider for telemarketing campaigns include

- Outbound phone costs
- Human resource costs (either internal or outsourced)
- Data processing expenses
- Follow up materials, including postage

A common error is for organizations to believe that email campaigns are free. They're not! If your email campaign includes having members go to a micro site—and it should—development costs for the forms should be included as well as a portion of the time for IT staff. Development time for the campaigns should be included in the costs, as well as any fulfillment materials that are provided in response.

Costs to include in Member-Get-a-Member (MGM) campaigns include materials provided to members to aid their work, incentives such as prizes, print ads, and fulfillment materials.

Print ads in publications can be an effective way to acquire members. Outside advertising may be effective, depending on your association's target member. Acquisition costs for print advertising should include:

- Cost per page (In internal publications, revenue foregone should be included.)
- Agency costs
- Costs for a reply device (if applicable)
- Fulfillment costs including postage

Remember, in evaluating any acquisition cost, you need to judge effectiveness in light of the lifetime value of your member, as well as the break even point against your dues.

Lifetime Value

The lifetime value of a member (LTV) is one of the most important membership metrics. LTV estimates a member's financial contribution to the organization over the life of membership. The LTV calculation takes into consideration both dues and nondues income, such as publication sales, conference registrations, and fees from affinity relationships.

The pieces of information you need to calculate LTV are

1. Dues level. If you have multilevel dues, you can do separate LTV calculations for each member type or you can average the dues level by multiplying the number of members by their dues (at each level), totaling those numbers, and dividing by the total number of members. Use last year's full-year calculation.

2. Average member tenure.

3. Total nondues revenue. Include conference registrations, publication sales, and any other member purchases. Use last year's full numbers.

4. Cost of serving members. There are many variations of this element. (See Chapter 7: Dues Structures, Increases, and Restructuring.) A simple version is total expenses divided by the number of members. You may want to consider excluding some expenses or just including membership-related expenses.

Lifetime Value (LTV) Formulas. Following this list of formulas, you will find a sample chart. At the end of the chapter is a blank chart you can use to calculate the numbers for your own association.

Table 2. Lifetime Value of Membership

LTV Measurements	How to Calculate
Lifetime Dues Value of a Member	Yearly dues per member times average member tenure
Annual Nondues Revenue per Member	Total nondues revenue divided by number of members
Lifetime Nondues Value of a Member	Annual nondues revenue divided by number of members times average member tenure
Gross Lifetime Value of a Member	Lifetime dues value plus lifetime nondues value
Lifetime Cost to Serve Member	Annual cost of serving members times average member tenure
Net Lifetime Value of a Member	Gross lifetime value of a member minus lifetime cost to serve member

Table 3. Example of Lifetime Value Calculation

Number of Members	12,000
Annual expenses	600,000
Average dues level	$230
Annual nondues revenue	$2,000,000
Average member tenure	7.5 years
Lifetime dues value	$1,725
Annual nondues revenue per member	$167
Lifetime nondues value	$1,250
Gross Life time value	$2,975
Annual cost to serve a member	50
Lifetime cost to serve a member	375
Net lifetime value of a member	$2,600

What Does the Lifetime Value Calculation Help You Do? It helps you determine how much you can spend to acquire new members because it allows you to see where your break-even point is. It is a fair measure of what a members' financial contribution is because it takes into consideration the nondues revenue that a member contributes to the organization.

What Should Your LTV Look Like? Typically, LTV will be 7 to 10 times your annual dues amount. It is dependent on the relationship between the dues amount and the amount members contribute via participation in events, purchase of products and services, and other ways members are involved in creating association revenue.

How often should you examine LTV? Review LTV at least annually, but more often if you are introducing new products and services or if you're seeing major changes in renewal trends.

Cost to Serve a Member

Associations do not simply divide total operating costs by number of members to set dues. Doing so would probably make participation cost-prohibitive to many potential members. It is expected that nondues revenues will offset much of the operating expenses of an organization. However, at a minimum, the following costs should be included in the costs to serve a member:

1. Printing, production, and postage costs for the renewal series
2. Costs to produce, print, and mail membership publications/communications
3. Costs of membership staff—including salaries, benefits, and training
4. Technology and data processing costs for member service, such as T-1 lines, call center equipment, and so forth
5. Web site expenses relating directly to membership
6. Research relating directly to membership, such as member needs or satisfaction surveys

Some organizations may want to include other costs such as:

1. Portion of rent, G&A, executive salaries, and technology expenses for the entire organization
2. Advocacy expenses
3. Communications and public awareness expenses
4. General research expenses
5. Revenue foregone from discounts extended to members for association events
6. General web site expenses

What does your cost to serve a member calculation help you do? The cost of serving members is one of the important calculations in considering what your dues level should be. Whether or not to cover the full costs to serve a member is a basic philosophical decision to be made by the organization's leaders. If dues do not cover the costs to serve members, then additional products/services will need to be developed and sold to members to ensure the organization's continued financial viability. (See Chapter 7: Dues Structures, Increases, and Restructuring for a detailed rationale.)

Table 4. Calculating Costs to Serve Members

Cost to Serve Member	How to Calculate
Annual cost to serve a member	Yearly expenses divided by the number of members
Lifetime cost to serve a member	Annual cost to serve a member multiplied by the average tenure of membership

What should the relationship be between your dues income and your cost to serve members? This will vary by organization and organization type—professional, trade, or philanthropic. A rule of thumb is that your cost-to-serve should be no more than 50 percent of your dues.

How often should your examine your cost to serve? Cost to serve should be examined at least annually, usually during budget preparation time.

Membership Renewal Calculations

Key metrics concerning membership renewals are the renewal rate and the lapse rate; they are the inverse of each other. Renewal rates reflect those who remain with the organization; lapse rates reflect those who do not continue their membership. The terms renewal and retention often are used interchangeably.

Some organizations simply compare membership numbers at the beginning of two consecutive periods (BOP). Other organizations are more detailed in examining the members eligible to renew, eliminating members who do not renew because of death or because they no longer meet the organization's membership criteria.

Renewal Calculation Example. For this example, we'll make two assumptions: Membership is billed on a calendar year basis, and membership eligibility is based only on whether full dues are paid. In this example, we are assuming that the new members are pro-rated and therefore, aren't paying the full years' dues. At the beginning of 2006, XZY Association had 425,000 members who were in paid status. At the end of 2006, the Association had 405,000 members who were in paid status. Renewal rate plus lapse rate always equals 100 percent.

Table 5. Calculating Membership Renewal Rates

Renewal/Lapse Rates	How to Calculate
Renewal rate 405,000/425,000 = 95.29 percent	Divide current number of paid members by number of paid members a year ago.
Lapse rate 425,000 - 405,000 = 20,000 20,000/425,000 = 4.71 percent	Subtract current members from last year's members; then divide by number of last year's members.

Segmented Renewal Example. Association CDE has an overall renewal rate of 81.64 percent, a number their board is very proud of. However, when the membership director pulled out new members from the average calculation, CDE learned that of a membership of 25,000, 3,000 members fit the new member definition. New members had membership tenure of two years or less. A re-examination of the numbers revealed:

1. The number of members who were in the first two years of membership—3,000.

2. The more tenured group numbered 22,000.

3. Of the 3,000 new members, 1,050 (35 percent) renewed.

4. Of the 22,000 tenured members, 19,360 (88 percent) renewed.

Why is it important to look at segmented renewal rates? As this example shows, focusing on an average rate can mask a reasonably serious problem with new members and underestimate the loyalty of tenured members. Look at retention by different terms and categories, not just overall rates.

Table 6. Examining Renewals by Tenure

Number of members	25,000
Number of new members	3,000
Tenured members	22,000
Total number renewing members	20,410
Average	81.64%
Number new members returning	1,050
Number tenured members returning	19,360
Longer tenure renewals	88%
Renewal rate of new members	35%

What Should your Renewal Rate Look Like? "What's the right average renewal rate?" is probably the most often asked question on ASAE & The Center list serves. The answer is: It depends. Renewal rates are affected by:

- Aging of your members
- Changes in your profession
- Dues increases
- For trade organizations, mergers/acquisitions in your industry, regulations
- Unexpected world events, such as natural disasters, terrorist attacks, and changes in the economy

Developing trend data for your organization will help you to quickly identify potential problems and negative trends and take actions to remedy them. Appendix 2 at the end of this chapter is a sample statistical report that determines the retention rate, the growth rate on a calendar as well as year-to-year basis, and past statistics.

Caution

Focusing on average renewal rates can mask problems or trends. Always examine renewal rates according to segments of your membership. Members with short tenure are often the most vulnerable. If members with shorter tenure are lapsing at significantly higher rates than members with longer tenures, it is an indication of problems with member value or with communication processes.

Examining Renewal Rates. A case can be made that your renewal rate should be looked at monthly. Here are some handy comparisons that you can make to identify trends.

Anniversary Renewals
- Compare this month to the same month last year.
- Compare this year-to-date to year-to-date last year.

Calendar or Fiscal Year Renewals
- Look at early payers. Who is paying from the first notice, before the actual calendar or fiscal year begins?
- Examine renewal rates in the first three months of calendar/fiscal year. Compare to last year.

Cost to Renew. Much the same as examining acquisition costs, an organization should examine the cost to renew members (CTR). The cost to renew a member is significantly less than the cost to acquire a member. Why? In member acquisition, you spend resources to identify names/contact information and you generally spend more on creative and printing. However, the biggest variable is the total response rate. Direct mail, at best, will generate a four percent response rate. A single renewal effort can easily generate 50 percent of your total renewal, depending on your members' response patterns. By eliminating those who respond to prior efforts, you reduce costs dramatically. In addition, current members are more receptive to email renewal notices than prospects are to email acquisition efforts. Email and web-based renewal programs are an excellent strategy to manage renewal costs. You can apply the same methodology to determine your CTR as you do your acquisition costs. Factors to be taken into consideration are:

- Agency costs for creative
- Print costs for the various communications
- Postage
- Telemarketing cost (if applicable)

It is atypical to place staff costs into the renewal expense calculation. Most nonprofit financial statements do not consider "renewal" as a program/activity expense or accounting line item. The renewal process cuts across the organization, usually involving a relatively small piece of several individuals' time.

Calculation methods related to the functions of getting and keeping members and using dues revenues for budgeting are basic skills required of membership professionals. Using them will enable you to anticipate problems and measure successes.

Susanne Connors Bowman is co-owner of The Haefer Group, Ltd., a membership value consulting firm, located in Reston, Virginia. Sue has served the association community as a consultant for more than 10 years. Her previous employment included 16 years as a senior level manager at AARP and several years as a manager at the American Pharmacists Association. She chaired ASAE & The Center's Membership Section Council in 2005-2006. Email: sbowman@thehaefergroup.com.

Lori Gusdorf, CAE, is vice president of Membership and Chapter Services at the Association of Fundraising Professionals in Arlington, Virginia. She has worked there for 17 years and prior to that installed software systems for associations. She is a member of ASAE & The Center's Membership Section Council. Email: lgusdorf@afpnet.org.

Suggested Reading

1. ASAE & The Center web site archives 2006.

2. Nat G. Bodian. *Direct Marketing Rules of Thumb.* (McGraw-Hill 1995)

3. *Direct Marketing Association's Statistical Fact Book 2004.* 26th Edition. (Direct Marketing Association, 2004)

4. Malvern J. Gross, Jr.; Richard F. Larkin; and John H. McCarthy. *Financial and Accounting Guide for Not-For-Profit Organizations,* 6th Edition, (PriceWaterhouseCoopers, 2000)

5. Jerry Kaup. Make Member Lifetime Value Work for You. *FORUM Magazine.* Association Forum of Chicagoland. January/February 2006

6. Philip Kotler and Gary Armstrong. *Principles of Marketing,* 11th Edition. (Prentice Hall, 2006)

7. *Operating Ratio Report,* 11th Edition, 12th Edition, (ASAE & The Center for Association Leadership, 2003)

8. David Shepard Associates. *The New Direct Marketing.* 3rd Edition. (McGraw-Hill, 1999)

Worksheet: Calculating New Member Acquisition Costs—Direct Mail

Element	Cost Per Thousand	Total Cost
Agency fee		
Other creative		
Letter printing, four pages, black and white		
Brochure printing		
Membership application printing		
Outside Envelope (No. 10)		
Business Reply Env. (No. 9)		
Mailing list		
Lettershop production (insertion, application of postage, pull samples		
Postage		
Variable per thousand cost		
Fixed costs		
Cost to mail per piece. (total variable costs + fixed costs) divided by number mailed		
Total mail cost		

Sample Examination of Retention Rates

	2002	2003	2004	2005	2006	2006 New Members	Year to Year Growth	Calendar Percentage Growth	Renewal Rate	Renewal Rate
Jan	24,693	25,600	25,034	26,374	26,881	654	1.9%	(0.7)	76.5%	75%
Feb	25,131	25,610	25,190	26,628	27,114	632	1.8%	0.8	76.6%	76%
March	25,396	25,298	25,391	26,956	27,491	677	2.0%	1.4	77.0%	77%
April	25,466	25,041	25,351	27,001	27,264	506	0.9%	(0.8)	75.8%	77%
May	25,563	25,291	24,988	26,963	27,205	530	0.8%	(0.2)	75.7%	
June	25,661	25,377	25,355	27,132						76%
July	25,836	25,591	25,549	27,180						76%
Aug	26,054	25,666	25,713	27,248						76%
Sept	26,189	25,623	25,896	27,275						76%
Oct	26,372	25,761	25,963	27,252						77%
Nov	26,406	25,619	26,057	27,329						77%
Dec	26,218	25,499	26,191	27,097						77%
Total (Year to Date)					27,205	2,999		0.5	76.3%	76%

Recruitment Strategies

By Tony Rossell

15

IN THIS CHAPTER:

- The target market—who you want to reach
- The membership offer—what a member will receive
- The marketing message—why a member should join
- The promotional tactics—how a member will be reached
- The testing and tracking—where to take future efforts

WITHOUT RECRUITING NEW MEMBERS, it is impossible for an association to grow. Every association leaks members. Members of professional associations retire or pass away; companies in trade associations merge or close; and members of avocational associations change their interests. These members need to be replaced and more added to result in membership growth.

Associations that have had great success in recruiting new members have systematically applied the five disciplines of target markets, membership offer, marketing message, promotional tactics, and testing and tracking.

Target Market—Who

Savvy marketers will agree that whom you target with your promotion is the single biggest factor in the success or failure of your efforts. Whether you are using viral marketing, direct mail, telemarketing, email, broadcast fax, or any other media to recruit members, the *who* you are reaching is defined by lists—and the selects within those lists—that you choose to use in your recruitment efforts. Here are three strategies to find the best member targets for your organization.

Do List Research. All list research should start with your internal database. Conduct a census of your database and identify prospective members for whom you already have a record. These will include lapsed members, nonmember conference attendees, nonmember buyers of products (e.g., books, professional development), and inquirers. Without a doubt, these are some of the best prospects to contact for membership because they are already aware of your organization.

When you begin to look for lists outside your organization, ask your members what other organizations they are members of and what professional magazines they read. The lists that best match the behavior of your current members are likely to work in attracting new members.

You will also want to take a look at where organizations like yours advertise and exhibit. Chances are the subscribers or members of these organizations also will be good prospects. Likewise, if an organization is renting your mailing list, it is likely that their customer list will also have good prospects for you.

To go even deeper in your search for lists, you can investigate some outstanding online subscription databases that are excellent tools to help identify specific files. The two most recognized online sources are the Marketing Information Network (MIN) and SRDS DirectNet. SRDS also publishes a print directory called the *Direct Marketing List Source* that includes most commercially available mailing lists.

Finally, help from list professionals can be very valuable. A good list broker will help you find the lists that have worked successfully for other associations. Brokers also have subscriptions to the major list databases to help you locate the most appropriate lists. Because the list owner pays the sales commission to the broker, working with a list broker does not add any costs to your outside lists.

Use the Best Selects. It is wise to always try the best segment or select from a test list first. If this select does not work, then you can assume that the remaining portions of the file are unlikely to generate an acceptable response. But how do you know what the best segments of a list are? Even if you know very little about a list you plan to test, you can be fairly certain that you are receiving the best portion of the list by remembering three letters, "RFM," and incorporating them into your list selections.

- The "R" stands for recency (i.e., Hotline Names). This select is usually the best bet to increase your response rate because a recent purchase indicates someone is in transition or in a buying mode.

- The "F" stands for frequency (i.e., multiple transactions in the last 6 to 12 months). Frequency of purchase can also be described as a multibuyer select.

- Finally, "M" stands for monetary amount (i.e., larger order size). This select is important if you are trying to sell a higher-priced item because it indicates purchasing authority.

Based on RFM, for example, you would want to try your most recently lapsed members or the most frequent nonmember book buyers for a membership promotion.

The Offer—What

There are two levels to consider when looking at what to offer in membership recruitment:

- The larger question affects the value equation of the products and services included in the membership package that members are offered.

- The second question is what incentives or special offers are used to attract members, to move them from shoppers to buyers.

The Membership Package. Making the membership package more attractive to members usually means either unbundling the normal membership benefits (offering an a la carte approach) or bundling additional products and services into the membership package. Both packaging options have their supporters.

However, an alternative membership packaging strategy that is gaining favor to bundled or unbundled membership is to develop a tiered membership package. In marketing vernacular, a tiered membership is called product line extension. Many industries have used this strategy over the years. For example, in 1914, when Model Ts began to roll off the assembly line at Ford Motor Company, all of them were black because black paint dried faster than other colors. As customers asked for different colors, Henry Ford reportedly proclaimed, "They can have any color they want, but just make sure it's black." Today, car manufacturers offer a breadth of options to meet customer needs and demands. If they did not provide a full product line, they would be out of business."

The same concept is behind offering a tiered membership. The ideal tiered membership allows members to choose from a set of established membership packages the one that best satisfies their particular needs, professional designation, or budget. It is an alternative to providing members a "black Ford" only because it is the easiest to manage and fulfill. And since the benefits that make up the tiers can often be drawn from existing programs and services, the cost to service the higher tiers is limited to the incremental cost of shipping the items. (See Table 1 for an example of a tiered membership product.)

Incentives or Special Offers. Many prospective members are aware of your association. They have thought from time to time of joining. However, year after year they remain on the sidelines. Special offers or incentives to join can be effective in moving people from shoppers to buyers. Everyone loves a sale. A special offer can be effective in any media used to acquire members from mail to radio to a web site.

Creativity comes into play with matching the offer to the sales objection that a prospect might have. For example, if an association has a strong product offering, but low market awareness, a free trial offer may be appropriate. Here are some examples of special offers used by membership recruiters to help acquire association members:

- A discount off of the regular first year dues payment. The amount of the discount must be appropriate to the product/situation. Generally, a discount should be 15–35 percent. Too small a discount does little to increase response; too much can cheapen the product and dampen response. In membership acquisition, a properly developed discount will produce both more new members and more revenue than a full-price offer.

Table 1. Tiered Membership Options

An example of a tiered membership program is the membership structure established by the Association for Supervision and Curriculum Development (ASCD).* ASCD membership offers four major membership categories that allow prospects to select the value package that best meets their needs and budget.

ASCD Membership Category				
Benefits	Premium ($219)	Comprehensive ($89)	Basic ($49)	Express ($29)
Educational Leadership (8 Issues)	●	●	●	Online
Education Update (12 Issues)	●	●	●	Online
Member Prices on Resources & Meetings	●	●	●	●
Access to Online Library	●	●	●	●
Member Books	9	5		
ASCD Infobrief (4 Issues)	●			
One PD Online Course	●			
$100 Professional Development Voucher	●			

* Source: ASCD web site (www.ascd.org)

- Discounting is most effective when it lowers the dues amount to what pricing strategists call a "price point." Prices points, like those that end in a 7 or a 9, typically get higher response rates than other dollar denominations. That's why store items sell for $7.99. A $39 membership dues offer typically will be more successful than a $41 offer in total dollars and in the number of responses.

- A no-risk offer or free trial allows prospective members to sample membership with an agreement to receive an invoice which may either be cancelled with no risk or paid. This offer is a favorite in magazine circulation development and will almost always out perform a hard, or up-front, payment offer. Since it gives the association the right to invoice the individual or company, it usually works best with organizations that deliver a lot of visible benefits, known as "mail box benefits," to members. A tightly managed billing system is required to administer this offer effectively.

- A sweepstakes to win a trip or some other prize will increase front-end response but may require additional sweepstakes with renewals. Sweepstakes work best for impulse memberships like a magazine-based membership or a contribution/donation membership. Sweepstakes offers must meet specific regulations and legal requirements established by the United States Postal Service and the Federal Trade Commission.

- Premiums or gifts for joining can be effective. The best premiums appeal to the self-interest of the prospective member (e.g., salary surveys, special reports, and survey data). If they are off-the-shelf items already produced by the association, then the cost to fulfill offer comes at very little added expense.

- Offering more of the product can sometimes increase response (e.g., 15 months of membership for 12). This is especially appropriate when an association operates on a calendar year membership. It avoids prorated dues confusion. Extra months of membership works best in markets where the product is already well known to the prospective member.

- Offers with deadlines outperform offers without them. But be careful not to make the deadline too short or it can prematurely truncate response. Generally, use a deadline of 90 days from your launch date.

- An installment payment options will increase response, especially on a high-ticket membership. This offer would typically require a credit card that can be debited at regular intervals (monthly, quarterly, annually) and a system to manage credit card rejections.

The Marketing Message—Why

Once you have decided whom to direct your promotion to and what membership product and incentive you are making available, you need to decide what you want to say to the prospective member.

Addressing Needs. Developing your marketing message begins with gleaning information about your prospective members from market research. A wide variety of research tools are available to gain quantitative and qualitative data related to recruiting new members. It is outside the scope of this chapter to present a full list of research opportunities; this is discussed in detail in Chapter 3: An Overview of Membership Research. However, it is important to note that useful information can be gathered inexpensively and in a relatively short time through the use of focus groups and simple phone interviews. These tools effectively provide qualitative information that can help in understanding what is going on in a prospective member's mind when it comes time to join. Excellent questions to ask in researching might be:

- "What would prevent you from becoming a member?"

- "How would you convince a colleague or friend to become a member in this association?"

- "Can you tell me the thought process or evaluation that you go through when choosing to join an association?"

Another source of insight for developing your marketing message comes from ASAE & The Center's 2007 study *The Decision to Join: How Individuals Determine Value and Why They Choose to Belong*[1] (DTJ). This survey recorded feedback from 16,944 members, former members, and prospective members of eighteen professional associations. DTJ reported that the three most important personal benefits in the decision to join were:

- Opportunities to network with other professionals in the field

- Access to the most up-to-date information available in the field

• Professional development or education program offerings

DTJ highlighted that "the decision to join an association reflects an expanded understanding of what constitutes a benefit. Members do not simply make a calculated self-interest decision but also join based on benefits the association provides to the field or profession including:

• Promoting a greater appreciation of the role and value of the field among practitioners
• Providing standards or guidelines that support quality
• Maintaining a code of ethics for practice

To recruit members, you need to take the information the market research has provided, and craft it into what marketers call the value proposition or the unique selling proposition. The membership value proposition succinctly answers the question, "Why should I join your organization?" Think in terms of the very real and practical needs that are met by your organization.

Crafting Benefits Copy. Once you have determined the major reason that someone would want to join your organization, it is critical to translate all the key selling points or features for your organization into benefits. For example, a feature approach to an association newsletter might read, "As a member, you receive 12 monthly issues of our *Alert* newsletter." A benefit copy approach might read, "Our *Alert* newsletter gives you instant access to job critical reports."

Similarly, feature-based copy about your magazine might say, "Receive the flagship magazine of the ABC association." But translating this into benefit copy may result in, "ABC's magazine tells you the real story you won't find anywhere else." Benefit-based copy includes a promise to your member.

Finally, remember these copywriting tips as you write your promotion.

• Think of your membership promotion as a conversation between a salesperson and a prospective member. Ask and answer the questions any prospective member would ask. And be sure to deal directly with typical sales objections (e.g., It seems too expensive, or I'm not sure it will be useful to me.")

• Specifics are what make copy effective. Use real examples, numbers, product data, and testimonials.

• Often the best lead is buried somewhere deep in your promotion. Pull the buried lead to the beginning to help the reader get to the point quickly.

Promotional Tactics—How

Now it is time to determine what marketing tool(s) or media should be used to reach your target audience with the offer and message that you have developed. Your selection of media is chiefly driven by the reach-ability of your market segment and the expected return on investment.

Reaching Prospects. Reach-ability means you can get your message to your prospects and they can respond. You will need to obtain email addresses to send emails, phone numbers to do telemarketing. These may or may not be available in your database or from outside lists for your particular market.

Your prospective members also must have the ability to respond to your promotion. For example, if your prospective members are classroom teachers, their names, addresses, emails, and school phone numbers are available in commercial databases, but since they are in classrooms, they are not easily reachable during the day for telemarketing.

Return on Investment. Return on investment may drive your selection of media. Some media, such as face-to-face sales, are very expensive and are used chiefly for high-dollar, low-volume membership sales. For example, a sales call to a prospective trade association member across the country may be worthwhile because the dues payment would be very high, but a personal sales visit may not be economical for a low individual dues payment.

Table 2 lists media options regularly used for membership recruitment and some of the advantages and disadvantages of each. They are listed in relative cost order from most expensive to least expensive per impression.

Testing and Tracking—Where to Go in the Future

Perhaps the most important, but most overlooked, discipline in membership recruitment is testing and then tracking the results of marketing tests. Effective testing and tracking points you to where you can best deploy your resources most effectively and economically among the vast array of marketing options available.

The renowned marketing professor Philip Kotler said, "Successful companies are learning companies. They collect feedback from the marketplace, audit and evaluate results, and take corrections designed to improve their performance. Good marketing works by constantly monitoring its position in relation to its destination."[2]

This recommendation was affirmed in the research undertaken for ASAE & The Center's book *7 Measures of Success*, "If there's one phrase that sets remarkable associations apart from their counterparts, it's 'Data, data, data.' They gather information, analyze it, and then use it to become even better."[3]

A successful membership recruitment test may change response rates by the following percentages:

- List tests can impact response by 500 percent.
- Offer tests can impact response by 200 percent.
- Creative tests can impact response by 100 percent.

Without testing, a marketing program is likely to substantially underachieve on potential returns. If testing is so important, then how should it be done?

The Art of Testing. There are two aspects of testing, the art and the science. The art of testing involves thinking outside the box and creating a new way to do

Table 2. Marketing Media Compared

Media Type	Advantages	Disadvantages
Face-to Face-Sales	Allows for true one-to-one communication. Each sales presentation is customized for the prospect.	One of the most costly marketing options available ranging from $100 to $300 per sales call. It requires higher dues and a high close rate to be an economical option.
Telephone Sales and Telemarketing	An excellent medium to reach former members and higher dues prospects.	Costs can range from $3 to $9 per prospect contact. Legal "do not call" requirements apply to some associations.
Direct Mail	The historical work horse of membership recruitment. Highly selectable direct mail lists are available to help reach specific targets.	Costs can range from $.50 to $1 per piece mailed. This will be lower for associations that can take advantage of USPS nonprofit postage rates.
Member-Get-A-Member Programs	Takes advantage of members' network and an integrated print, mail, email, and web approach to engage members in the recruitment process.	Requires time and expertise to build a supporting web infrastructure to manage the program, and only a minority of members may participate.
E-Mail Broadcast Fax	Very economical, especially if the e-mal address is held by the association. Outside email lists are increasingly available for rental with targeted selects. Recipients' behavior can be tracked. Faxing is economical—$.15 to $.25 per page—and timely. Faxes tend to break through the clutter and get noticed when sent to businesses.	Low delivery and open rates can mean your message will not be read. Legal requirements for opt-in and opt-out apply. Rented email lists may cost in excess of $.35 per name. This medium requires managing regulatory requirements, including previous business relationship and opt-outs.
Search Engine Ads	Since payment for ads is based on those who actually click through to your web site, you pay only for those who choose to view your message.	Requires ongoing staff time to monitor and optimize key words. Costs are somewhat unpredictable, driven on bids and clicks.
Web Advertising	Often web ads are available for trade or at low negotiated rates.	Usually generates only a low volume of new members.
Print Advertising	Effective tool to build awareness about the benefits of membership.	Usually does not generate enough tracked new members to cover the cost.
Word of Mouth	Creatively intense, but very low cost. Builds awareness by producing a buzz about your association.	Unpredictable. You may get people talking about your organization, but this may not translate into paid memberships.

things. Each membership recruitment project should start with a brainstorming session that asks,"What if?" or "How about?"

Bob Stone, in his landmark book, *Successful Direct Marketing Methods*,[4] suggests asking the following questions to get the creative thought process going:

- Can we combine?
- Can we add?
- Can we eliminate?
- Can we make an association?
- Can we simplify?
- Can we substitute?
- Can we reverse?

In addition to brainstorming, there are some specific high-leverage areas to consider testing, including:

- **Lists.** One of the easiest and most productive tests is trying new lists. Test the membership list of another association or a subscription list of an industry magazine. For most marketers, list testing is the place to start. If list selection is the single biggest factor in the effectiveness of a promotion, it makes sense to test the lists that you are using.

- **Frequency.** Try marketing more frequently to top prospects and customers. This is a test that almost always produces a profitable outcome.

- **Discounts.** Try different dues discounts to see whether there is price resistance in your market. Remember that psychological price points are real. As a rule of thumb, a dues rate ending in a 7 or 9 will generate more orders and dollars.

- **Packaging.** Test a one-price-gets-everything membership bundle instead of selling each membership option separately.

- **Media.** Many media are available and every one you plan to use should be tested. Split your list three ways and try a mailing compared to a broadcast fax compared to an email to see which generates more members.

The Science of Testing. Equally important is the science of testing. The science of testing starts with creating proper test structures. The key is establishing a control package and testing against it. This is done by drawing a portion of names from a control group of the marketing effort and using them for the test. Then structure the test by holding everything else constant except the variable that is to be tested. For example, if the test is for a special discount offer, then on the test segment, use the same format as the control package and send the test promotion to an equal number of the control names in the mailing.

A test obviously does not always produce better returns than the existing control. That's why tests should go to small segments of a larger promotion. However, in each test cell you need a minimum of 40 paid responses to get a statistically valid test. Therefore, the number of anticipated responses will dictate the size of each test segment. For instance, if a 0.5 percent response rate is expected, then the test cell should include a minimum of 8,000 names (40/0.005 = 8,000).

Tracking. The other challenging yet critical component of the science of testing is tracking. Despite the difficulty of tracking, the potential returns of testing are so great that an organization needs to build some kind of mechanism to track returns. Membership professionals will have to work with the organization's IT staff and order-processing staff to find the best way to track returns from a test. Coding options include personalizing the membership reply form with a promotion code for each list and test, requiring a promotion code to receive a special offer on a web form, and setting up unique URLs with links from email solicitations.

Once returns come in, compare the responses in the control group against the test cell. See which cell generated a higher return on investment and make the best-performing test your new control.

Testing and tracking are ongoing processes. Over time, they become part of the culture of an organization. A focus on testing ensures the flow of new ideas and products to keep an organization entrepreneurial and growing. And it also provides a methodology for validating each new idea and product.

"If you build it, they will come" is the famous line from the 1989 film *Field of Dreams*. It also can apply to some associations when it comes to membership recruitment. Associations can do a wonderful job in building world-class publications, creating exciting networking events, and sharing timely information on their web sites but mistakenly assume the job stops with the creation of the membership product.

In reality, having a great membership product that meets the needs of those in the marketplace is the entry point today for doing business. Associations that will thrive are those that successfully target the best prospects with membership offers and messages that are compelling. And they will rigorously test and track their promotional efforts to build a highly effective recruitment program. In short, they will use the best membership marketing practices available to them to attract new members and grow the association.

Tony Rossell serves as the senior vice president of Marketing General, Inc., in Alexandria, Virginia. A frequent writer and speaker on association marketing topics, he blogs at http://membershipmarketing.blogspot.com. Email: Tony@marketinggeneral.com.

References

1. Dalton, James and Dignam, Monica. *The Decision to Join: How Individuals Determine Value and Why They Choose to Belong.* (ASAE & The Center for Association Leadership, 2007).

2. Kotler, Philip. *Kotler on Marketing: How to Create, Win, and ominate Markets.* (The Free Press, 1999) p. 34.

3. *7 Measures of Success: What Remarkable Associations Do that Others Don't.* (ASAE & The Center for Association Leadership, 2006), p. 38.

4. Stone, Bob and Jacobs, Ron. *Successful Direct Marketing Methods.* 7th edition. (McGraw-Hill, 2001) p. 468.

Retention

By Tony Rossell

IN THIS CHAPTER:
- Benchmarking—Determining, comparing, and tracking retention rates
- Communicating Value—Marketing techniques to communicate value to members

MEMBERSHIP RENEWALS FOR AN association have a profound impact on the direction of the total membership number. If an association, for example, adds 10,000 new members a year, the steady state of the association will vary greatly depending on the renewal rate achieved by the association. With 10,000 new members a year:

- At a 65 percent renewal rate, an association has a steady state membership of 28,571 members.
- At a 75 percent renewal rate, an association has a steady state membership of 40,000 members.
- At a 90 percent renewal rate, an association has a steady state membership of 100,000 members.

But what drives these renewal rates and how can an association increase them?

Calculating Membership Steady State

A Steady State Analysis shows the destination or equilibrium for the total membership of an association. To do this analysis, start with how many total new members you have added to your association in the past year. Next, take the reciprocal of your current membership renewal rate for the association (the percentage of nonrenewing members) presented as a decimal (.30 for 30 percent). Plug each number into the following formula.

- New Member Input / Reciprocal of Renewal Rate (or Lapse Rate) shown as a decimal = Membership Steady State
- For example, 10,000 New Member Input / 0.20 Lapse Rate = 50,000 Membership Steady State.

Any discussion of renewing members must begin with the understanding that the association needs to deliver value to members in order to keep them. Membership renewal represents a member's chance to vote on how well the organization has served the member's needs over the previous year. A positive or negative response is measured through membership renewals. ASAE & The Center's *The Decision to Join* highlights this in findings that report the number one reason that members do not renew their membership is that the member "did not receive the expected value to justify the cost of dues."[1]

Once an association has built a valuable membership product, the next steps required for retaining members are to benchmark and track renewals and effectively communicate the value of the membership product to members. Done effectively, an association can increase its membership renewal rate.

Note that definitions for the words *renewal* and *retention* vary widely in the association field. The terms are used synonymously in this chapter to mean members who continue with the organization for an additional year. Based on this definition, the number of members eligible to renew is not how many renewal notices will be sent out. Instead it is the total number of paid members in the association including multi-year members (who may not receive a renewal notice this year) and life members, since these members have remained with the association. Not including these members in the renewal numbers would artificially suppress membership statistics like the steady state analysis.

Benchmarking

Because of the impact of various business and environmental factors, there is no such thing as a good or bad renewal rate. Although you may be able to do some limited benchmarking of renewals against associations similar to yours, the purpose of calculating the renewal rate is to help your association focus establishing a better membership retention rate.

Factors Influencing Retention. As a general rule of thumb, associations will see renewal rates vary between 60 percent and 95 percent. This wide variance in typical rates of membership retention is influenced in part by the type of business model in which the association functions and by economic and sociological environmental factors. Common factors that influence renewal rates both positively and negatively include:

• Individual membership organization versus trade association membership. Associations that offer an individual membership as opposed to associations with institutional or company memberships typically will see lower renewal rates. ASAE & The Center reports that the mean renewal rate is 83 percent for an individual membership association and 91 percent for a trade association.[2]

• Consumer-paid dues versus company-reimbursed dues. Associations that serve a market where dues are reimbursed or paid for by an employer will see better renewal rates than dues paid out of pocket by individuals.

• Growing versus declining memberships. Associations with a rapidly growing membership tend to have lower renewal rates than groups with a steady or declining membership. This occurs because growing associations have a larger proportion of first year members and first year members typically renew at a much lower rate than longer term members.

- Incentive-generated members versus full-price members. The stronger the incentive used to get members to join an association, the lower the renewal rate will be when compared to members who joined with no incentive. Members who receive a complimentary membership when they attend the annual meeting, for example, will not renew as well as members who join at full price.

- Transient industry versus stable industry. Associations that serve highly transient markets, where job turnover is high or members are moving out of the industry, will see lower renewal rates than a steady marketplace. A job change for an individual association member or a merger for a trade association member raises the likelihood of not renewing membership.

- Short membership grace period versus longer grace period. Business rules on when a member is considered lapsed vary among associations. Some associations count members as renewing if they receive payment within 90 days of expiration. Other associations lapse a member on expiration and consider a payment 90 days after expiration to be a membership reinstatement.

In addition, ASAE & The Center's study *The Decision to Join* (DTJ) reveals that some membership erosion is unavoidable. DTJ survey "respondents who reported having dropped their membership in an association at any point in their career were asked to give the reason why. Approximately half of them indicate their reasons had more to do with career and other life changes than with the performance of the association. This means that those who worry about their retention rates get a 50 percent discount on their current distress levels."[3]

Because so many variables exist, comparing, or benchmarking, renewal rates from one association to another is a challenge. But when evaluating how members are "voting" for your particular association, these variables are typically held constant and this allows for ongoing monitoring. And, in fact, membership benchmarking is critical to measure improvement. This measurement is accomplished through membership tracking and reporting.

Tracking. Three levels of tracking can be applied when looking at membership renewals. The first level is the macro or big-picture view. This level of tracking helps view the membership as a whole and highlight elements that may be supporting growth or pulling down membership numbers. For example,

---

Calculating Membership Renewal Rates

Renewal Rate measures the number of members kept over a given period of time, usually during a fiscal or calendar year. To calculate the renewal rate, subtract from the current membership the new members who have joined over the past 12 months. (This determines the net renewed members still with the organization.) Then divide this number into the total membership from the same time in the previous year (those eligible to renew). Convert this to a percentage and you have the renewal rate.

The formula is:

- (Total number of members today minus 12 months of new members) / Total number of members in previous year = Renewal Rate

- (105,000 – 15,000)/100,000 = 0.90 (or 90 percent) Renewal Rate

one important area to measure is the renewal rate for first year or "conversion" members. New members tend to renew at lower levels than other membership segments. The macro look at membership shows how much or how little these members are affecting the overall membership.

The macro level of tracking is important because unless you identify where your membership bucket is leaking, it becomes much more challenging to fix it. These key macro measurements will vary from association to association based on what demographics and characteristics have the biggest impact on the organization. However, for most associations the best indicators to track at the macro membership level include:

- Total Membership
  - Current Membership
  - Membership the same month in the previous year
  - Percentage increase or decrease in year-to-year membership

- New Members by Month
  - Current New Members
  - New Members the same month in the previous year

- Membership Conversion (First Year Member Renewals) by Month
  - First year members renew cohort
  - First year members who actually do renew
  - Conversion renewal rates (renewing new members / eligible to renew new members)

- Year Two and Subsequent Renewals (Y2+) by Month
  - Y2+ members renew cohort
  - Y2+ members who actually do renew
  - Y2+ renewal rates (renewing members/members eligible to renew)

- Total Renewals by Month
  - Total members renew cohort
  - Total members who actually do renew
  - Total renewal rates (renewing members/members eligible to renew)

Separate tabs can also be set up for tracking these same key variables by membership type (e.g., student, regular, associate, corporate).

The second level of tracking helps to measure the performance of each step of the membership renewal series. It highlights at what point in the series members are prompted to respond. This is a helpful method to track renewals because members may use the initial mailing form to renew their membership, but they may have been prompted to take action by the third notice. So tracking a code could be misleading. To measure the action that produces the renewal response, renewals can be tracked through a filtering process. Let's say the renewal cohort for a given month starts out at 1,000 members who receive the first renewal notification. If in the next month, the remaining members of the cohort who receive a notice are 750, then it can be inferred that the first notice generated a 25 percent return. This is done through each step of the renewal program. To fully track using this method, you need to run a final "phantom" renewal count to show how many members are left in a renewal cohort after all the renewal activities have been completed.

Finally, the micro level of renewal tracking uses source codes to measure the response of specific head-to-head renewal tests that you are incorporating in the renewal series. As noted earlier, tracking renewal codes has the potential to produce misleading information. So this method is best used when tracking very specific tests or changes to the renewal program.

Micro tracking is accomplished by adding a key code or source code to the renewal form. When the form is returned through the mail, this code is added to the member's record. To capture response on the web and through email, unique URLs can be established that incorporate the source code.

Ultimately, the reason to track is so an association has information available to take concrete actions and use the tools available in the marketing arsenal to address specific renewal challenges. Once a system is in place to monitor the renewal program, a wealth of information will be available on each month's reports. For example, it may become evident that certain membership categories have weaker or stronger renewal rates, or there may be a difference in renewal rates between conversions (new members) and renewing members (longer-term members). Tracking provides the data to make informed marketing decisions.

Communicating Value

With detailed renewal information, you can determine how to use available marketing tools and strategies to more effectively communicate the value and resources provided by the association. To improve your renewal communications, focus on the following elements:

The Copy and Message. The renewal communications you design should have a clear theme or story line running throughout the entire series. Ideally, the story unfolds with each additional notice. The copy and even the signer of each renewal letter tie into the story line that is developed.

For example, the first renewal notice might be a special note from the executive director thanking the member for his participation over the past year and offering an early renewal special. The second notice might be a formal letter from the president saying, "It is time to renew," and highlighting the key achievements of the association over the past year. The third notice might come from the membership manager warning of an interruption in benefits if the renewal is not sent in immediately.

Once the story line has been established, the next step is to ensure that the words used will get the member's attention. Always tell the member thank-you for being a member. Then play up the value of membership:

- List what the association has done for the member over the past year.
- Include what the association intends to do for the member in the coming year.
- Point out how much money members can save or make if they take advantage of their membership.

Graphics and Format. What a renewal series looks like can be even more important than what it says. Just as the copy tells a story with each step of the renewal series, the look of the renewal package needs to support this story. Here are some tips:

- Make the actual renewal notice look like payment is expected. It should look more like an official billing statement and less like a membership application.

- As the renewal series progresses, the graphics need to become brighter and more attention getting.

- Test entirely new package formats for renewals including oversized packages, magazine cover wraps, and reminder postcards.

Be very careful, however, that any design is in keeping with the association's image. If the association has an in-house creative department, get its input about design options. If an outside firm is chosen, make sure to spend time with the designers so they are aware of who the members are and what the association is doing for them now and in the future. But also allow the outside firm to present ideas and concepts that provide a new perspective.

Membership Segmentation. One of the findings that may result from the tracking, research, and analysis done at the start of the renewal review is discovery that all members are not the same. Because of this, it may make sense that renewal communications for special groups should be adjusted to address specific concerns. For instance, since first-year members are generally less likely to renew, a message specific renewal program for this member segment can be developed. Corporate or associate members also have different priorities than do individual members. And members who are also top nondues purchasers might have yet another message.

Technology now supports marketing in providing great flexibility to communicate differently to every member segment and every member if so desired. Computer laser personalization allows for each renewal mail piece to have a specific message targeted to a member. Likewise, text in email and web sites can be driven by a database and present targeted information and messages. The best renewal systems take advantage of these capabilities.

Media. Just getting your renewal notice to rise above the stack of other marketing efforts can be a challenge. To get more attention, consider sending renewals through alternative channels. Some marketing channels now used for renewals include:

- Broadcast fax
- Telemarketing
- Email
- Magazine cover wraps
- Pop-up ads on the association web site

One low-risk opportunity to help determine which of these channels will be most effective is to test them with former members. If one of these tools proves effective in reinstating a member who has left the organization, it is likely to work in renewing current members.

Frequency. Perhaps one of the simplest and often one of the most effective ways to improve renewals is simply to increase the frequency of notices. Increasing the number of notices sent to a member should be considered if tracking reveals that the final notices of the renewal program are generating a strong response or if subsequent reinstatement efforts produce a strong response.

As a rule of thumb, the frequency of renewal notices should be increased until the cost of generating a renewing member through the system equals or exceeds the cost of acquiring a new member. In the rare event that tracking reveals the cost of renewing a member is higher than acquiring a new member, then decreasing the number of renewal notices would be appropriate.

Table 1. Sample Membership Renewal Contact Schedule

Month	Activity
1	Acknowledgment email
2	
3	
4	
5	Change of address/fax/email/phone append
6	
7	
8	Pre-renewal email
9	Mail notice 1
10	Mail notice 2
11	Mail notice 3
12	Expire email or fax renewal
13	Telemarketing
14	Mail notice 4

Methods of Payment. It is not uncommon to find out that members did not renew simply because they did not get around to it. In fact, many associations find that members actually lapse from omission, not commission. They do not make an active decision not to renew; they just forgot about renewing. To overcome this challenge, look at offering different options to actually eliminate the member's renewal decision using payment options like:

• Automatic credit card renewal
• Automatic electronic funds transfer renewal (EFT)
• Multiple year memberships
• Life memberships
• Automatic monthly/quarterly credit card installment billing

These payment options change the renewal dynamic from asking the member to act proactively to continue a membership to requiring the member to act proactively to end a membership. Associations that have members who accept some type of automatic debit or credit card charge can see renewal rates 10 points higher for these members than for typical members.

Conclusion

A lot rests on the effectiveness of an association's renewal system. Well done, it can help membership to climb. Done poorly, it can cause an association to lose members who might have a positive perspective of the association but need the value of their membership reaffirmed. That's why this chapter makes the case that renewals are not an administrative function. They are a marketing function. A renewal program that effectively diagnoses strengths and weaknesses of a membership program with tracking tools and one that responds to these issues by applying the proper messaging, media, frequency, and payment options will help an association maximize its membership potential.

Tony Rossell serves as the senior vice president of Marketing General, Inc., in Alexandria, Virginia. A frequent writer and speaker on association marketing topics, he blogs at http://membershipmarketing.blogspot.com. Email: Tony@marketinggeneral.com.

References

1. Dalton, James and Dignam, Monica. *The Decision to Join: How Individuals Determine Value and Why They Choose to Belong.* (ASAE & The Center for Association Leadership, 2007), p 24.

2. *Policies and Procedures in Association Management: A Benchmarking Guide,* Volume 1 Membership, (ASAE & The Center for Association Leadership, 2006), p. 36.

3. *The Decision to Join,* p 3.

Membership Communications

By Christy Jones, CAE

17

IN THIS CHAPTER
- Understanding your members' world
- Using your association's web site
- Communicating in a global marketplace
- Adapting to trends
- Membership communication models
- Building community
- Segmenting communications

THE ART OF COMMUNICATING reinvents itself as surroundings change. Change is constant, but what is recognized as different today is the rapidity of change. Traditional competition (time, other organizations, and for-profits) combined with technological advances are forcing associations to think beyond simply reviewing how they do business and delve into how they meet the necessities of change on all levels of business. As a membership professional, your challenge is to make sure you are part of this change process because all your communications should enhance the value proposition to both current and future members and customers.

Understanding Your Members' World

If your organization hasn't conducted a recent member survey or poll, see Chapter 3: An Overview of Membership Research, which is devoted to the creation and implementation of this type of primary market research. Include a mix of demographics, lapsed members, and prospective members whenever possible. Understanding your target audience and knowing what messages they want to hear can be accomplished only when the right research has been done.

In addition to—not in place of—conducting regular member research, it is also prudent to conduct periodic 360-degree environmental scans of the industry and to examine secondary market research produced by outside organizations, such as government agencies or academic institutions, to gain insights about positioning your organization, to check trends in your industry as well as in the association community, or to review wider trends that affect all businesses. Members and customers want to know you are thinking ahead, preparing for their potential needs of the future. And such research also may provide insights into how your marketplace is changing, where you may find areas for new potential members, and what new technologies might be useful to reach them.

Excellent resources for associations can be found through ASAE & The Center for Association Leadership (www.asaecenter.org) and your local allied societies. Make sure to sign up to ASAE & The Center for Association Leadership listservers for communication, marketing, and membership or other organizations' listservers (not-for-profits or those in like-minded professions, for example). It is well worth the time to search the Internet for beneficial resources.

To evaluate what is being said about your organization, consider these basic elements[1] of communication:

- Who is educating your audience about your products and services? How is information distributed? An amazing web site or brochure can do little to improve your image if a prospect or member's main contact with your association is with a disgruntled receptionist or membership services representative.

- Identify the individuals in your community who are most likely to share information about your organization. You might be surprised to learn that your biggest advocates are your newest members, not the more senior ones.

- What tools do you provide to make it easier to share information? Blogs aren't just for technology-savvy individuals anymore. There are more than 1 million blogs in the United States alone, and the number is growing daily. Blogs offer insight into what works well and what is broken.

- Study what, when, where, and how opinions are being shared. Listen to the discussions being held between sessions at your next annual meeting. Track the types of calls your organization receives every day for one month. Track the discussions on your listservers. Track your organization's web site page referrals. What information are people sharing? Add a button to every page of your web site that encourages visitors to "tell a friend."

- Listen and respond to supporters, detractors, and neutral members. They all may have more influence than any brochure, web site, or program offered by your organization.

Using Your Association's Web Site

Traditional ways of using the web as a communication tool to enhance member interaction include providing free members-only access to publications or discounted prices on them, Email lists, discussion boards, newsgroups, podcasts, online training and certification programs, online directories, e-commerce, online registrations, and webinars. However, technology's pace is fast and these items, while expected today, are not necessarily what will drive new members or keep members and nonmembers visiting your web site.

The number of people using the web interactively—actually contributing content rather than just using it as a knowledge/information resource—continues to grow daily. The more your members use the Internet interactively, the more they will look to their association's web site to do the same. Make a point to learn about new web sites such as Claim ID (http://claimid.com), del.icio.us (http://del.icio.us), Stumble Upon (www.stumbleupon.com), and other popular social networking sites your members or prospective members may be using to build their sense of community. By exploring these sites, you may find new ways to design your association's online communications strategies to keep pace with change.

Dave Gammel, CAE, maintains, "The new services being developed on the web today now place the customer squarely in the middle of enhancing or even creating the value of the service itself. This new round of innovation has been described as 'web 2.0,' implying that new version of the web is being built by organizations and their members. While content is still important, participation-driven services are the new kings of the web."[2]

New software can be used to enhance communication with members. The complexity and pricing is as varied as the kinds; the key is to choose what is best for your members' needs and expectations. In addition to software, other nontraditional ways use online communication to recruit. The AAUW recently went through an internal struggle about "free" versus "member-only benefit" online offers. What started as a push-pull between departments became a very successful recruitment tool. (See story on page 197.)

Since an organization's web site is a primary communications tool, reaching both members and potential members with ongoing communications, it's essential to examine the quality of the communications offered on your web site:

- Is your web site used by both members and nonmembers, with advantages to both audiences?

- Or is it a public information web site that members would rather see the public attracted to than have as a "member-only" benefit?

- How is your organization's web site primarily used by members? Do members perceive your site as "member-only benefits" locked behind a firewall of sorts? Is it key to member recruitment and retention?

Whether your web site should be for members only, the public, or both depends on the nature of your organization. Is yours a trade association whose members would benefit from giving the public access to information such as safety standards or general industry insights? What are the legal issues of posting member information? Is yours a professional society that doesn't need to reach beyond a potential member base? The key is conducting the necessary research to determine what would be best for your organization, its members, and its customers. Then you can understand how to tailor this important communications tool to best serve your members and attract prospects.

Appendix 1 at the end of this chapter is a sample questionnaire provided by the American Association of University Women (AAUW) webmaster. This survey was sent to all staff, and a slightly modified version was sent to members and a group of nonmember prospects. All audiences were a part of the redesign process. The survey itself was called a great communication "inclusiveness" tool. The real test has been in the ROI of the new web site and its easier-to-navigate design—rave reviews, new members, and improved retention.

Another inclusive tool that can facilitate interactive communications on your web site is a polling function. Inexpensive software products allow you to put questions on your web site so you can get member feedback. Using the web site to ask a "question of the week" and post results is a good way to encourage quick participation while collecting information that may indicate significant member concerns or identify industry trends that can be addressed in publications or educational sessions. With the right tools, you can also tie online surveys into your database.

Using an online survey tool, AAUW conducted a Member-Get-A-Member feasibility survey that concentrated on key questions. Because the database provided demographics of respondents automatically, respondents did not have to take time to fill out the usual demographic information. You also can use your web database for random selection across all categories of membership. The AAUW survey had the highest percentage of respondents to date; the captured information was analyzed quickly in house; and pertinent information was used to help develop the member-to-member campaign. We found visibility and recognition to be key incentives for our members' participation. As a result, we built a member-get-a-member online Hall of Fame to recognize recruiters.

In addition to knowing how current members use (or wish to use) your web site, it is important to constantly scan the web use environment in general. How are people using the web today compared to even one year ago? What was hot then may be considered old tech now, especially with web-savvy potential members who are as varied in age, culture, and professional interest or experience as one can imagine. RSS, podcasts, mobile marketing—which is right for your organization and what is the "buzz" now? Newer forms of wireless or Internet-based communications are vehicles that can help engage your members and attract prospects.

Getting members actively engaged in your organization means you stand a much better chance of having them renew. Knowing how both members and nonmembers are using the web and adapting your web site and digital communications accordingly will help your recruitment and retention efforts.

Communicating in a Global Marketplace

It wasn't so very long ago that *globalization* was a buzz word in the association community; now, it's an integral part of any communications planning process. If nothing else, the Internet, with its ability to provide instant communications and access to information 24/7 worldwide, has forced associations to rethink their approach to communicating in the global marketplace.

Understanding and keeping tabs on global trends is becoming more important to membership recruitment and retention. Numerous web sites provide insights about general global trends and industry trends specific to your organization. Your first stop should be ASAE & The Center's International Section. You will find not only an extensive library of useful articles and archived listserver discussions that might be of great use to your association but also numerous links to other web sites that will provide key insights into doing business globally.

As a membership professional, you should be aware of the markets that are using the association's web site so your communications and membership recruitment efforts can be tailored to them. Who are your international members and customers and how can your communications include them and encourage their participation? Although the answers are different for each association, every association should be asking the questions.

One association realized that although its members were based in the United States, most of its product customers (in particular, publications buyers) were

---

Going Global

Despite the 24/7 convenience of Internet and web site communications, membership communications with global members can still be challenging. If you have not previously considered opportunities for expanding membership into a global arena, you must weigh the advantages and disadvantages. Bonnie Koenig, president of Going Global International, Chicago, Illinois, and a presenter at ASAE's 2000 Annual Meeting, provides factors to consider when going global:

- How do your association leadership, members, and staff feel about moving in a global direction? Are they prepared?
- Who are your champions and skeptics?
- Have you identified the benefits and obstacles?
- Some benefits:
  - Responding to members' needs
  - Growing your membership
  - Building an international reputation or presence
  - Enhancing your association's image
  - Gaining industry intelligence/professional information
- Some obstacles:
  - Leadership, member, or staff concerns
  - Lack of skills (leadership, staff)
  - Cultural diversity
  - Lead times
  - Costs

- Do your homework
  - Conduct needs assessments/market research among key audiences.
    - Will you be fulfilling needs (products)?
    - Meeting expectations (services)?
  - Target prospective markets.
  - Survey your members (their customers and suppliers and other individuals or groups outside the United States that may be part of your association's network).
  - Conduct an environmental scan of potential markets, including culture and customs and economic, political, and technological factors that affect your industry or profession in that market.
  - Research possible competitors and/or partners.
  - Conduct on-site research through study tours, trade missions, or informational visits.
- Uniqueness of global marketing: Why is this different?
  - Targeting the message to your audience (cultural distinctions)
  - Distribution/communication methods
  - Promotional feedback
- Common pitfalls to avoid/hints for success
  - Recognize the lead times involved.
  - Budget realistic expenses. Don't expect to generate new revenue right away.
  - Go slowly. Phase in, evaluate, and monitor.

internationally based. Another organization knew it had a large international attendance at its annual conference but never thought to target this group for other promotions, including membership. Both organizations developed successful international e-membership campaigns to reach these audiences and market their products.

What are the communication expectations of potential international members? The Internet provides instant access to information, and yet delivering the information in American English or without understanding the marketplace of any given country won't help get individuals or companies interested even if what you offer is actually what they want. The "What's in it for me?" mindset of younger generations is also true in the international arena, and international prospects expect you to deliver solutions for their particular needs as well. When developing international recruitment communications, remember that, just like U.S. members, potential international members desire interactivity and relationship building. Your communications must address these concerns and explain how your association—wherever it is based—can provide value to all members, including international members.

However, it is important to realize that moving toward the global marketplace takes considerable planning. Any strategy should reflect your goals. Know what you want to accomplish. Are you seeking to

- Expand your membership?
- Increase visibility for your industry?
- Create clients or distribution networks for your members?
- Become your industry's/professional field's global resource center?

You may need to work with your IT department in adding translation capacities to your web site, discuss with your financial department the option of setting a membership fee in Euros, or get approval to create levels of participation specifically for international members.

Adapting to Trends

In 2005, Scott Steen reported on a survey conducted by ASAE & The Center for Association Leadership[3] that asked thought leaders from both the business world and the association community "to talk about the issues and trends they believe will have the greatest impact on American society and the world over the next five to seven years." Four issues stood out as having significant importance for associations:

- The impact of the post-September 11 era and how we do business globally (increasing outsourcing, fast-growing and increasingly sophisticated economies in Asia, for example)

- The age and ethnic demographic shifts that were much discussed in the 1990s are beginning to have real implications in this decade.

- The growing complexity of 21st century life is driving a need for greater clarity and a quest for a deeper personal sense of meaning not only in private, spiritual arenas but in all aspects of people's lives, including those of work and consumption.

- Consumers increasingly are being given the opportunity to customize the products, services, and experiences they buy to their specific wants and needs, which is driving an expectation for almost universal customization.

Reflecting Current Demographics. Explaining the need to look at new markets for membership growth can take on a whole new meaning after an extensive environmental scan. (The Center for Association Leadership has published a series of environmental scan reports focusing on the future.) Using research showing the changing demographics and aging of the U.S. population became extremely helpful during budget presentations to the board of AAUW. The need to change became more evident with the reading of a quote from a *Washington Post* article ("Immigrant Twist on an American Tradition," Sept 21, 2005), which looked at service clubs' need to adapt to changing demographics. "Once the staples of white, middle-class life, civic groups such as the Lions, Kiwanis, and Rotary have become better known as home of the ROMEO—Really Old Men Eating Out. The average age, some members joke, is deceased."

Given the older age of AAUW's membership, this type of research, combined with an in-depth overview of the four generations in the marketplace, helped show which audience we should target now and which we should target for the future, while helping the board understand the importance of recruitment investment. Of course, in light of four generations, communications to these different age groups should be customized to appeal to different audiences. Determine which member benefits are most appealing to different audiences—small business loans for younger professionals, insurance for older or retiring populations—and be sure your communications address the needs peculiar to the different segments of your membership base.

Implications of Changing U.S. Demographics

What do these changing demographics mean? The ultimate disappearance of the traditional member.

"Organizations may have to change their missions to meet the needs and demands of a whole new membership and service sector. The transformation is a result of dramatic demographic changes in the U.S. population, a force that is altering the profile of U.S. membership associations like never before. The pool of 'traditional' members (i.e., members derived from historic rather than current demographic data) is diminishing quickly as demographics continue to shift." – Michael Faulkner, CAE. Will Demographic Trends Transform Association Membership? *Journal of Association Leadership*, Winter 2005.

Positioning. Market research and environmental scans provide the background knowledge needed to understand where you stand compared to similar organizations. Positioning your organization is the natural next step. Membership communicators know the importance of flexibility, transparency, and inclusion. How do we present ourselves to members, nonmembers, and potential members? Where are we compared to our competitors?

Your association's mission statement should guide the communications and public relations efforts that attempt to define what your organization does and who it represents. You should be able to succinctly articulate these ideas in a couple of sentences, and those statements should guide the appeals you draft to whatever audience segments you address. (See Chapter 2: What is Your Value Proposition?) Whatever vehicles you use to position your organization—whether it's brochures, your web site, your conferences, or your lobbying efforts—they should address the needs of the new audiences as well as your established members.

Membership Communication Models. The following are some of the latest trends in membership communication models that help position your organization.

Integrated Marketing Communication (IMC). Global and association trends are highlighting the breakup of the mass market (demassification), the need for clarity and transparency in customized messaging, and the involvement of members/customers as active participants in the creation of community. Demographics are changing and inclusiveness is a must. If you're responsible for membership recruitment and retention, you must work with everyone on staff who communicates with members and potential members to ensure that your messages are fully integrated.

Jay Schiavo, CAE,[4] describes how "integrated marketing communication," or IMC, "ensures consistent messages, images, sales pitches, ideas, positions, and propositions to all audiences." He maintains that the IMC approach works best when the organization and its stakeholders are committed to making it a successful way of operating. Here are strategies he recommends:

- Do joint marketing-communication plans that include strategies and tactics to serve both marketing and communication objectives, such as lead development, sales, image/brand awareness, public opinion, and audience consensus.

- Find out how your targets like to get news and information and how often. Pay particular attention to shifts in preferences (print ads to web ads, direct mail to email, news releases to search engines, TV to word of mouth).

- Embrace the information age by staying on top of the Internet and expanding media technology.

- Create consistent, coherent messages and images and adapt them for all marketing/communications media channels.

- Engage your audiences in two-way communication to develop dialogues, foster relationships, and build brand loyalty.

- Incorporate the techniques of direct marketing to promote benefits instead of features, create compelling offers, elicit action, and measure responses.

Word of Mouth Marketing. Storytelling is not a lost art; it simply keeps changing and accelerating like everything else. The recipe for a good story remains basically the same, even if the ingredients are different. Is it about a subject of interest to listeners? Is it compelling, newsworthy, or "juicy"? What ingredients would make your organization's story of interest to your prospects? Does your organization stir your members' pride or create community and value? Does how you communicate your association's story match how your members and prospects listen?

All word-of-mouth (WOM) marketing techniques are based on the concepts of customer passion, two-way dialogue, and transparent communications. According to the 2006 Membership and Marketing Conference Handbook (ASAE & The Center, p. 27), the basic elements are:

- Educating people about the exciting aspects of your products and services
- Identifying people most likely to share their opinions
- Providing tools that make it easier to share the enthusiasm
- Studying how, where, and when opinions are being shared
- Listening and responding to supporters, detractors and neutrals

Defined as "the natural act of your constituents' (members, business partners, volunteer leaders, and others) providing information and recommendations to each other," WOM marketing takes it a step further. Marketers are finding they can now harness, amplify, and improve WOM. The ASAE & The Center Membership and Marketing Conference Handbook continues, "Although WOM cannot be directly controlled, WOM can be intentionally fostered, nurtured, amplified, and influenced. Associations can work hard to make people raving fans; they can listen to their members, prospects, experts, and rejecters. They can make it easier for them to pass the word, and they can make certain that experts and other influencers are enthusiastically behind their organizations."

WOM is not simply about using your web site or email to get members talking. According to a study conducted by the Keller Fay Group,[5] 92 percent of WOM conversations occurred offline and almost two thirds of WOM messages feature products in a positive light. Email, blogs, and other online communications comprise only six percent of WOM. The Internet does bring the element of speed to messaging, but even Generation X and Y members have made it clear that, provided associations understand the parameters of how they like to communicate and volunteer, having the chance to meet others in person is still very important.

Associations have long harnessed the value of word-of-mouth communications through member-to-member recruitment campaigns. See Appendix 2 for a case study involving AAUW's WOM member-get-a-member campaign.

Online Research: Member Versus Nonmember Benefit

AAUW's research arm wanted to provide its latest research free online to reach a large audience with crucial information vital to women on college campuses. Membership staff worried about enhanced "members-only benefits," currently perceived as the members' right to receive such information at discount cost. In this case, a compromise worked. Both members and nonmembers were given access to the full report online; however, all users had to leave their names and contact details in order to download the research. Hundreds of names were captured in the first week alone, and compared to other in-house lists, this became one of our top producers in terms of acquiring new members for that time period. The message to members positioned this compromise as a win-win, information important to women was freely disseminated and new members joined the association as a result.

Building Community

Building and maintaining community is challenging if your trade association is affected by mergers, or if your professional society certification programs (your "golden handcuffs" in the past) are no longer required. Even a cause-based philanthropic can begin to lose ground if supporters no longer believe your mission or vision is relevant.

What do your members/customers really want from you, how do they want it delivered, and at what price/exchange? Increased competition for members' loyalty, time, and dollars requires leaders to examine their organizations' structures, benefits, governance, program activities, and strategic positions in the marketplace. According to Karl Albrect,[6] associations vary considerably; however, five key value propositions for members tend to be shared:

- fellowship
- mutual assistance
- learning and growth
- advocacy
- unique products and services

What's often not realized is that not all five have to be of focus of the association. Sometimes only one or two elements are enough to attract and keep members, but it's up to the membership professional to know what those strategic elements are and to communicate them effectively. Conducting market research to find out what members (and prospective members) want in the way of products, services, programs, features, and benefits helps you communicate more effectively and increase the perception of the value of belonging to, participating in, or even of buying products from your association.

Associations are thought to have the corner on the market for community, but few associations are clear about how to successfully implement strategies to build community and how to harness the concept of community as a business model.[7] Face-to-face meetings, grass-roots advocacy, or chapter activities are still valuable if changed to take into account how the new volunteer wants to participate. Studies today are showing even Generation X members will join for a sense of community if the ways they can participate allow for individuals like themselves who have time constraints, are project-oriented, and want to have fun.

Developing participatory online communities, where members communicate freely, is proving to enhance the sense of value to members and nonmembers alike. Allowing them to be creators of their own niche area of interest allows for unlimited opportunities of community. Points to consider when building new online community:

- Make the reason for being in a community compelling, fascinating, interesting, and full of useful information.

- Create as many new groups or areas of interests as you have in your membership. Online communities can be as small or as large as your membership will bear. Special interest communities keep individuals involved.

- Find out what areas are no longer of interest and sunset them. Use data as your guide; don't rely on assumptions.

- Investigate software that would work for your members. Do they like extensive chats? Do they accept nonmembers into their community? Do they simply want information without the fluff?

- What can you put online and what should be kept for face-to-face? One of AAUW's state components said their branches no longer had time for physical meetings. A substitute online community meeting ended up leading to face-to-face meetings, as people got to know each other beyond email. The facilitator used WOM techniques to get important buzz going.

- Some associations are finding blogs useful both for communicating on timely subjects and for starting online communities. Keep blogs diverse, active, and targeted. Use members as facilitators and end those blogs whose purpose has been served.

Segmenting Communications

Demassification, unbundling, and scrimping trends all show the need for market segmentation, the need to successfully communicate by dividing your current or prospective membership base into segments that can be targeted with their specific needs in mind. (See Chapter 2: What is Your Value Proposition?) Total segmentation used to be cost prohibitive; however, online technologies make it possible to reach varied audiences in ways that match their different levels of interest, information or knowledge delivery, and community participation.

Segmentation assigns people to different categories so you can market to them separately, customizing everything from the writing to the photographs to the choice of media, all to ensure your communications with each segment are most effective. According to *Smart Marketing for Associations,* the major elements of segmentation include:[8]

- **Demographics.** Gender, age range, median income, highest degree achieved, marital status, professional title, years as a member, leadership positions held, other characteristics

- **Geographics.** Country, state/region, locale

- **Psychographics.** Attitudes, beliefs, opinions, personality, lifestyle

- **Behaviorals.** Desired benefits/motivations, product/service user status, rate/frequency of product or service use, degree of loyalty, readiness to buy, communication preferences

The speed of change affects the need to constantly update segmentation research—people are moving, aging, changing their jobs, lifestyles, and attitudes. Segmented communication strategies are as varied as the associations that use them. For example, you'll find many articles about the impact of the four generations currently present in the workplace. The majority of the articles will talk about the effects of Baby Boomers as they are poised to retire from their professions in huge numbers. Many segmentation studies focus on Generations X and Y and how to build better communications strategies to reach those populations.

However, AAUW would lose a potentially huge market if it were to focus only on those generations. Baby Boomers themselves are the key next market for AAUW because larger groups of retiring women will have the discretionary income and time to join cause-oriented associations like AAUW. In addition, the demographic of the Boomer generation lends itself to causes, given their history of the 1970s. Even though generational trends are integral to recruitment in all associations, you must find the market that is of particular importance to your association, not just what any given trend suggests.

Another audience that is creating a buzz in the market segmentation world is women. Although often put into the diverse category, women comprise more than half the population. Tom Peters has said that women are the number one economic opportunity for the foreseeable future. In *Marketing to Women*, Martha Barletta[9] points out:

- Seventy-five percent of women 25-54 work outside the home.
- Women make 80 percent of buying decisions.
- Women comprise 58 percent of corporate purchasing agents.
- Women are responsible for 70 percent of small business startups.
- Women bring in 55 percent of total household income.
- Women control 51.3 percent of U.S. personal wealth

Demographics are changing, communications technologies are changing, and members' perceptions of value and community are changing. Association membership professionals must consider all these issues and develop plans to reach members and prospective members with communications tailored to different needs in the marketplace. The best association communications are based on a clear vision of the association's mission and value proposition and are supported by research and member feedback.

Christy Jones, CAE, is director of membership for the American Association of University Women, Washington, DC. She has worked in trade, professional, and now philanthropic associations, focusing on membership and communications. Active in ASAE & The Center, she is a past chair of the International Section Council, was a member of the Membership Section Council, and is currently on the design team for the Summit on Social Responsibility. Email: jonesc@aauw.org.

References

1. Sheri Jacobs, CAE. Giving them something good to talk about. ASAE & The Center for Association Leadership *Membership Developments e-Newsletter*, September 2005.

2. C. David Gammel, CAE. Association 2.0. *Associations Now*. January 2006.

3. Scott Steen. Addressing Long-Term Trends: Leading Associations in a Global, Complex, Diverse, and Customized World. *Journal of Association Leadership*, Summer 2005.

4. Jay Schiavo, CAE. Reaching Today's New Audiences and Segments with Inclusive and Integrated Marketing Communications, *Marketing Insights*, November 2005.

5. Keller Fay Group. Talk Track. Press Release May 15, 2006.

6. Karl Albrecht. Is the Association Model Broken? The Case for Reinvention. *Journal of Association Leadership*, Summer 2005.

7. Diane James, CAE; John Jordan, CAE; and Paul Pomerantz, CAE. Models of Associating. *Journal of Association Leadership*, Winter 2005.

8. M. Michelle Poskaitis. *Smart Marketing for Associations*. (ASAE & The Center for Association Leadership, 2002), p 28.

9. Martha Barletta. *Marketing to Women: How to Understand, Reach, and Increase Your Share of the World's Largest Market Segment*. (Dearborn Trade Publishing, 2003).

AAUW Web Survey

GOALS AND MISSION

1. What are the basic goals of the AAUW website? Does the website currently serve that purpose?

2. What are the basic goals of the redesign project?

3. What is the revenue or cost savings goal or objective, if any?

4. What outcomes will make the redesign project successful?

AUDIENCE

5. Who is the primary target audience and how would you describe them? Include demographics, technical skill and knowledge base details, and other adjectives to develop an audience "persona."

6. Who is the secondary target audience? Other audiences? How would you describe them?

7. What types of visitors are we trying to attract? What are the site goals for each type of visitor?

8. Why would a first-time visitor come to the site? What would make then loyal return visitors?

9. From the homepage, name the five most important tasks visitors should be able to complete (e.g. join AAUW, login to the member area, etc.)?

FORM AND FUNCTION/ LOOK AND FEEL

10. What currently works well on the site? What currently isn't working well on the site? Please provide specific technical, structural, content, or design examples.

11. What new technologies should be implemented on the site and why? How will these technologies enhance the user experience?

12. If the world was your oyster and you could have anything you want, what would the site look like and what would you want it to do? Describe the site experience you want to create.

13. Use three adjectives to describe how the web site should be perceived by the user (i.e. progressive, professional, informative, etc.) Is this different from the current perception of the web site?

14. Who are our biggest "competitors" or others in the same industry? What do you like/dislike about their web sites?

15. Find three high quality sites on the web that relate to our redesign project in terms of mission, audience, design quality and functionality that you feel we should emulate. List the URLs, explain why the sites are appealing and how they relate to our redesign project.

ADDITIONAL COMMENTS

Case Study: AAUW's Member-Get-a-Member Campaign

The AAUW completed a survey testing its members' receptivity to a new Member-Get-a-Member campaign (the first in many years). Statistics revealed that they were interested but didn't want the usual incentive prizes, didn't want to be the one to ask "all by themselves," and believed it was the membership department's responsibility to go after new members. As a philanthropic, the AAUW story is fascinating, interesting, and compelling. But the challenge is how to get past recruitment phobia and provide a communications method that every member would be comfortable using to spread the word.

After reviewing how the different generations of our members liked to communicate, AAUW created numerous tools for the branches to use in group meetings or for the individual to use when talking to their neighbor. AAUW put everything on its web site (including an e-postcard that contained a catchy message that could be sent by any member) and mailed an entire packet to all branches. Along with coordinated brochures, postcards, recognition certificates, and stickers, the packet included a CD with audio of an actual conversation, with testimonials, that test audiences of members helped fine-tune. Short, compelling and easily remembered, the WOM conversation could be played in full at an event, with pictures, or remembered for retelling at the individual's convenience. The CD included lists of former members or nonbranch members in the area for instant targeting as well as communication tips along generational lines.

And what to give as an incentive, since prizes weren't of interest? Recognition! For the year-long campaign, AAUW created four major recognition points, with a culmination at the next annual convention, which was a celebration of the organization's 125th anniversary. A Hall of Fame listing every recruiter was established on the web site, and it spurred competition. Members told others they were now famous, and soon everyone wanted instant fame. This created additional buzz that yielded greater than expected results.

Engagement

By Stuart K. Meyer

18

IN THIS CHAPTER:
- Relevant value and the engagement model
- Segmentation
- Insights
- Resources and services
- Affinity programs
- Communication
- Connection
- Advisory roles
- Community

NEW MEMBERS ARE LIKE newborn infants within your association. To thrive, they require immediate care and nurturing. As their new association home, you must be fully prepared to meet their needs and provide the most relevant opportunities to satisfy their individual interests. Without this proactive level of care, new members will not prosper within your association.

Recruitment is not a destination; rather it is your association's promise to deliver meaningful and relevant value to the new member. Members' expectations are highest immediately after making the decision to join your association. The hope and promise of the membership decision can quickly turn to doubt and even skepticism about whether your association will deliver on your promise and provide a solid return on investment to the new member. Customer service expectations are high and it is not good enough to treat your new member simply as a general member of a profession or trade. Your new members want to feel as though your association knows them. Anticipating and delivering the specific needs of new members through being able to profile their interests and expertise from day one builds a strong foundation for member engagement. The ultimate goal of member engagement is to exceed expectations in creating a familiar and comfortable home for new members.

Relevant Value and the Engagement Model

While a chronological series of engagement concepts will be addressed in this section, the singular measure that member engagement should always revolve around in your association, whether it is welcoming new members or reeling drifting members back into your association, is relevant value.

Figure 1. Member Engagement Model

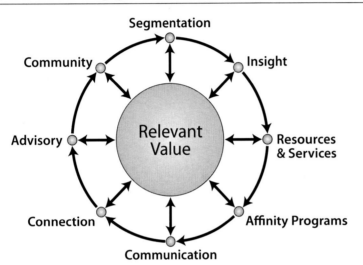

In the diagram above, the process of engagement revolves clockwise, interconnected around the creation of relevant value within and between the areas of engagement. Once the clockwise process has been completed and an engaged community has been established, the segmentation phase may begin again to further focus the level of engagement toward narrower segments. Additionally, if the sense of community begins to stagnate, the process can be applied as a diagnostic approach to revitalization.

While some of the components above have been addressed more extensively in other chapters of this book, it is important to examine how these components combine to facilitate a high degree of member engagement through the creation of relevant value.

Engagement is capturing the attention, affiliation, and loyalty of members by giving them what they need through highly relevant value-building activities.

All members should be viewed, welcomed, and treated as a member of your association family. You want them to have the best of everything and avoid making them feel as though they are lost in the crowd. Because all members are unique, it is vital to understand their needs, interests, and desires so their membership experience can achieve the highest degree of relevancy possible.

A fully engaged member is a valuable asset to your association because it means a strong and meaningful connection has been established, translating into retention and potentially converting a member into a walking testimonial, generating priceless word-of-mouth marketing for your association.

Relevant Value is a level of membership value which is specifically unique to the individual member compared to the basic value presented to the membership as a whole.

It is important to avoid a one-size-fits-all approach to membership. Even in highly specialized associations, there is always room to become more relevant to individual members and/or member groups. Relevant value differentiates itself from the basic value of membership in that it represents a more targeted value proposition geared toward individual members and/or member subgroups. This type of value proposition is about creating the most personalized level of membership possible. In the engagement model displayed above, relevant value is the center that all member engagement activities and efforts should feed into.

As the diagram suggests, relevant value is achieved through the integrated execution of eight components:

- Segmentation
- Insight
- Resources and Services
- Affinity Programs
- Communication
- Connection
- Advisory Roles
- Community

Segmentation

Segmentation means dividing your general membership into more narrowly defined subgroups, which enables your association to provide a higher degree of relevancy at the individual member level. Segmentation can be achieved by several different approaches. Here are two examples:

Segmentation by Specialty/Expertise. Whether your organization addresses all aspects of a profession or focuses specifically on one area or aspect of a larger profession or trade, a deeper level of relevant value can be created through specialty/expertise segmentation. As a matter of fact, the lack of attention and responsiveness to more narrow specialties and areas of expertise often serve as the origin of new specialty associations.

Segmentation by specialty/expertise is, perhaps, the most common form of membership segmentation. Most professions and trades have areas of specialization or specialized skill areas in which generalists develop expertise.

Legal associations are a good example for segmentation because the practice of law consists of a wide array of specialized legal areas. While all attorneys are licensed as generalists, most develop specialized knowledge and expertise in focused areas of practice extending to very narrow niches. Even solo practitioners with generalist practices usually have specific expertise in one or more areas of law. Consider the area of business law:

- Segmentation Level 1: Law
- Segmentation Level 2: Business Law
- Segmentation Level 3: Commercial Financial Services
- Segmentation Level 4: Corporate Aircraft Financing

Note how each level of segmentation is a narrow sub-group of the previous segment.

Professional trade associations, which target companies that serve a particular marketplace, also consist of subspecialties. For instance, a trade association focusing on the broad spectrum of audio visual companies may focus on the following levels of segmentation:

- Segmentation Level 1: AV Companies
- Segmentation Level 2: Sports Venues Specialization
- Segmentation Level 3: Outdoor Stadiums Specialization

Medical associations also pose a good example, especially those generalist areas of medicine that truly require the ability to deal with the full spectrum of medical conditions. Consider the area of nursing:

- Segmentation Level 1: Nursing
- Segmentation Level 2: Emergency Nursing
- Segmentation Level 3: Pediatric Emergency Department Nurses
- Segmentation Level 4: Family and Domestic Violence

Segmentation by Geography. Geographic segmentation applies not only to physical geography but also geographic type. As long as there is a critical mass, be careful not to overlook opportunities to facilitate this level of engagement, since layers of geographic organization can become a vital grassroots network for your association. Examples of localized geographic segmentation include:

- International
- United States
- Regional—national
- State
- Regional—state
- City
- Regional—city

Geographic type segmentation may be organized by:

- Large states
- Mid-sized states
- Small states

or by

- Rural geographic settings
- Urban geographic settings

Segmentation by Career Stage. Each career stage deserves some degree of focused engagement to affirm your association's commitment to all practitioners. Often, unless these groups are treated as defined member segments, they will feel as though they are underserved. A career stage segmentation might look like this:

- Segmentation Level 1: Student/apprentice
- Segmentation Level 2: New/graduate
- Segmentation Level 3: Novice
- Segmentation Level 4: Experienced
- Segmentation Level 5: Seasoned/expert
- Segmentation Level 6: Retired

Primary market research will likely reveal which career stage segment feels most underserved as well as what that segment wants or expects from your association. (See Chapter 3: An Overview of Membership Research.) Often overlooked and underserved career stages tend to be the student/apprentice, new/graduate, and retired member segments. Many associations struggle with the question of how to build meaningful and relevant value for those at the beginning as well as those at the end of their careers. Answers to these questions will be addressed in the connection section later in this chapter.

Segmentation Tools. Segmentation must be formalized and highly visible within your association's structure at all stages and levels of membership. Expose members to the association's available member segment groups upon initial entry into the association and at other points via general member communication vehicles and member service processes. Before you can deliver relevant value, you must have critical mass—enough members—within each member segment area. Here are some tools to consider for adding critical mass to your member segment areas:

- **Member Application.** Include a listing of segmented areas of special interest as part of the standard application process for membership, allowing new members to check their preferences. Your membership database should allow you to capture this information within the individual's membership record for future use.

- **Membership Renewals.** At least once a year, possibly in conjunction with the billing process, actively solicit existing members to select segmented areas of interest.

- **Web Site.** Your web site should enable members to review and select/update their segmented areas of interest at any time. A web form should be visible on your home page. Ideally, this form should be automated and directly linked with your membership database so that the selections are immediately processed.

- **Profiles in Publications.** Use member publications to spotlight segmented areas of interest as well as the benefits, resources, and opportunities of affiliation.

Acquiring segmented areas of interest preferences from members provides a foundation for the development of physical and substantive structure for member engagement. The other areas address such development through the creation of relevant value around member segments.

Insight

Insight is deep analysis of not only membership needs but also motivations, behaviors, emotions, trends, and environmental realities within your members' profession as well as other not-so-obvious factors affecting individual member attitudes toward your association.

The golden rule of engagement is "know thy member." This rule is especially true when building relevant value with member segments. Do you want to know what your members are thinking? If so, ask them. Many associations periodically skim the surface with member satisfaction surveys; however, to deliver the kind of relevant value which will leave members thinking you have read their minds, it is vital to find all possible avenues to continually amass deep insight on an ongoing basis. (See Chapter 3: An Overview of Membership Research for more information about market research.) Here are some ways your association can strengthen engagement through working from the mind-set of your member segments.

Examples of Primary Insights. Primary insights are developed by listening directly to your members. Any number of survey methods can reveal members' opinions about how the association is meeting their needs and providing value.

- **One-on-one interviews.** Never pass up an opportunity to gain insight from members, whether formal or informal, planned or impromptu. On site at a conference, via telephone interviews, or electronic means, always have preset questions to pose to individual members to capture their perspective and a way to record your observations. The more one-on-one interviews you conduct over time, the better the value of insights you will gain.

- **Focus groups.** Focus groups usually consist of a moderated roundtable discussion involving 8–10 members, typically of similar membership segments or demographics. Focus groups should have an established objective, which can range from a very specific discussion about a publication to broad conversation about a substantive area of your association's profession or trade. The key is to develop a discussion guide ahead of time, preparing a set of questions and activities designed to extract true and accurate insights.

- **Shadowing.** Spending time with your members in their professional settings can generate a world of insight ranging from candid perspectives to a deeper understanding of what they go through daily. Looking at the world through the eyes of your members as they move through their workday and listening to their commentary help you better understand how your association can be more responsive to their needs.

- **Single-topic surveys.** You can carefully craft and narrow the focus of your survey research if you build on qualitative insights you have gained via one-on-one interviews, focus groups, and/or shadowing. Web survey tools enable you to quickly ask your membership a question to which you or your leadership is attempting to determine an answer. Technology has provided associations with powerful, cost-effective tools, such as Zoomerang, Survey Monkey, Survey Select, and Zarca, to conduct user-friendly member surveys. Using your membership database, you can survey representative samples of your entire association or focus on individual member segments.

Examples of Secondary Insights. Depending on your association's industry, there may be additional ways to get information about member needs and trends affecting members. Government publications, business publications, and related industry associations may provide additional insights to help create relevant value.

- **Market Intelligence.** The analysis of any and all outside information resources that can provide insight regarding your members' profession or trade as well as the marketplace within which they work. Often, market intelligence provides you with information about approaching new developments which will enable you to be proactively responsive to members' needs. In addition, market intelligence can provide you with information about competitive forces within your marketplace.

- **Trend analysis and predictive modeling.** Sometimes the best insight into your members' mind-set is looking at their actual behavior within your association. Depending on the complexity of your membership database, you should be able to profile members based on any type of membership action or transaction, ranging from purchases to designating member segment areas. The sum of this information can enable you to predict future behavior, allowing you to proactively position highly relevant opportunities and resources with specific member segments.

Over time, as you begin to regularly conduct insight-gaining strategies, you will not only begin to see recurring patterns of behavior but also will be able to detect shifts in behavior. Deep member insight, especially at the specific member segment levels, enables your association to develop and deliver responsive relevant value at all levels of the engagement model.

Resources and Services

Resources and services include substantive publications, information resources, and other opportunities which are available to members as part of membership in your association.

In building a level of engagement deeper than active involvement, you should consider the types of resources and services your association can deliver via both general and specialized formats. In working your way through the insight-gathering phase, you should examine how your association currently delivers or can potentially deliver the most relevant value. At the same time, it is important to understand that association members tend to value quality of resources and services over quantity. Be careful to not equate value to loading members down with mountains of information, especially if such information covers a broad spectrum. To the contrary, members often emphasize that if they receive just one highly relevant article at just the right time, it is more than enough to keep them engaged because relevant value has been established.

Often it is not the physical resource or service itself that creates relevant value; rather, it is your association's ability to use resources and services to engage members and fulfill specific needs and interests.

Table 1 below, Resource Pitfalls and Strategies, examines examples, pitfalls, and strategies pertaining to the development, management, and delivery of resources

continued on page 214

Table 1. Resource Pitfalls and Strategies

Resource Type	Overview	Common Pitfalls	Strategies
Journal	An in-depth scholarly publication which is generally broad by nature and provides detailed analysis of a wide array of timely topics.	Depending on availability of articles, issues can sometimes fail to present a representative series of relevant articles covering key member segment areas. In addition, scholarly articles tend to be written at an advanced level which can alienate members at early career stages.	**Content Strategy:** Ensure each issue contains articles that appeal to your primary member segments to ensure balance and relevancy. Plan for development of content well in advance via an editorial calendar.
Magazine	An easy-to-read periodical publication which provides feature articles and a regular series of departments and columns mirroring a traditional magazine format.	Again, because articles are generally written by volunteer members, it isn't always easy to achieve a consistently well-balanced collection of articles which are relevant to a wide array of member segments in each issue. In addition, a common complaint about magazines is a lack of depth.	**Segment-Focus:** Create regular departments for primary member segments so that each issue contains content which is relevant to key member audiences. **Content Strategy:** Even well-attended conferences may attract only a minority of your membership base. Conference education content can be cross-purposed with little additional effort for articles which will reach a much wider membership audience or simply provide a refresher for those who attended the conference.
Segmented Newsletters	Often driven by member segment groups, segmented newsletters are narrow-topic publications that can be circulated specifically to corresponding member segments in either printed or electronic form. These publications are typically high in relevant value.	It is not uncommon for these types of specialized publications to suffer from content deprivation, as they represent yet another attempt to secure volunteer-written articles, competing against the higher-profile mass publications listed above.	**Content Strategy:** Of all types of association publications, segmented newsletters are ideal for cross-purposing existing content extracted from either stand-alone or conference-based educational programs.
e-Alerts	Often, there are new developments within your association's profession or trade that members will need to know more about quickly. E-Alerts are either general or segmented email broadcasts covering the details of such important developments. These moments are make-or-break opportunities to deliver highly relevant value.	Many associations delay getting the word out to their members regarding important developments, which gives your competition the opportunity to reach your members first. Often, associations fail to respond because they have not had time to prepare an analysis; however, it is more important to get the information to members first and provide in-depth analysis once available.	**Rapid-Response Team:** Have a process for bringing subject-matter experts together to plan to respond rapidly to breaking developments. This group can also be responsible for disseminating additional in-depth analysis when more information is available.

Resource Type	Overview	Common Pitfalls	Strategies
Web Site	Once considered yet another medium to engage your members, web sites will continue to evolve as the resource and service centerpiece for all associations. Your web site is an information resource which can create a high relevant value with member segments if properly structured.	Even today, many associations make the mistake of using their website as a fancy bulletin board geared more toward actively involved membership groups. Further, sites either fail all together or fall short of achieving a segment/topic driven design in which member segments can easily find the relevant information and resource they seek.	**Segment/Topic Driven:** Web site structure should be built around the general association with quick and highly visible access to segment/topic-driven member areas. Segmented and topical information should be organized in a place that is only a short click or two from your home page. Think of your home page as a tool to help member segments find the relevant value.
Audio Cast	An audio cast consists of either live or prerecorded audio which can be posted to your association's web site. Members simply click on the file/format and listen to the programming or download prerecorded content to an audio device for portability.	In some associations, member use of technology may not be keeping pace with advances in technology. Further, file size, format, and streaming speed can present barriers. However, technology will continue to move toward simplification.	**Regularity:** Whether individual topics or an ongoing series, audio casts should follow a listening schedule similar to the structure of local TV listings. **Duration:** 5–10 minutes to keep member's attention. Education programs can be longer. **Segment-Focused:** Similar to format-specific radio stations. Create regular member segment-oriented content channels. **Types of Programs:** Consider leadership addresses, audio versions of articles, product/service-oriented interviews. **Get Started:** Regardless of the level of real or perceived technological skills your members have, start taking advantage of this cost-effective medium today.
Video Cast	A video cast consists of either live or prerecorded video and audio which can be posted to your association's web site. Members simply click on the video file to view on their computer or download to a video-enabled device for portability.	There is some debate about whether the availability of video significantly enhances the value of the standard audio cast. In addition, video production can be expensive compared to the relatively inexpensive equipment needed for audio casts.	Refer to audio cast strategies above
Pod Cast	Considered "push technology," a pod cast is simply an audio or video cast subscribed members receive through automatic downloads to their audio/video-enabled device via a piece of code called an RSS (Real Time Syndication) feed or when connected to the computer.	Requires a moderate amount of technological know-how to subscribe and download content. Eventually, wireless automation will make acquiring pod casts as simple as receiving a cell phone call.	Refer to audio cast strategies above

Continued on next page

Table 1 continued

Resource Type	Overview	Common Pitfalls	Strategies
Active Member Involvement Prospectus	Promoting opportunities to become more actively involved in your association is vital as volunteer leadership and work product contribution is the life blood of your association. An active involvement prospectus provides members with an overview of your association's structure as well as the many areas and capacities in which they can become more involved.	It can be a challenge to cover all available opportunities within a single prospectus. Even more, keeping such a prospectus updated can be a challenge, given that new work groups within your association may emerge at any time.	**Print Version:** Whether a stand-alone publication or as special feature within an existing publication, develop a "teaser" version of the prospectus that drives members to a more comprehensive online version. Doing so saves money. **Online Version:** Create a comprehensive interactive online version of the prospectus which affords your association the opportunity to regularly update structural changes and promote current opportunities via a volunteer job board.
Member Service Concierge	Helping members find what they are looking for amid the ocean of information and resources your association might offer, a member service concierge could prove to be invaluable to your members. A member service concierge provides an interface with members to connect inquiries with your association's resources and services.	Some members may develop a reliance on this service in lieu of performing their own searches or may have unrealistic expectations of what this type of service provides.	**Online Concierge:** Create an FAQ reference page on your web site that serves as a first line response for recurring questions and promotes your association's resources and services. **Member Service Concierge Access:** Create a dedicated phone and/or email address which connects with customer service reps who have a great depth of knowledge regarding your association's resources and services.

continued from page 211

and services. In an organization where a strong emphasis is placed on integrated marketing and communications, the membership professional may have a voice at the table in terms of the creation and modification of member resources and should work closely with the departments responsible for developing member resources and services, such as publications and the web site, to ensure that programs and resources engage members by creating relevant value. In smaller organizations a single staff member who wears multiple hats in terms of marketing, membership, and communications may be responsible for creating, marketing, and administering various membership services and resources, such as those mentioned in the table.

Affinity Programs

Affinity programs can be broadly defined as services, incentives, and/or discounts that may either have a substantive relationship to the profession or even a lifestyle relationship to those who practice within the profession or trade. (See Chapter 2: What is Your Value Proposition?)

In addition to relevant resources and services, most associations offer special types of affinity programs and discounts through a variety of partnerships with third-party organizations. In addition to providing added value to membership, affinity partnerships present associations with the opportunity to generate vital nondues revenue.

In the same way prospective affinity partners are attempting to align themselves with your association in reaching their target consumer audiences, your members likewise will consider these programs value-added benefits only if they are relevant to either their professional and/or personal interests. Thus, the types of affinity programs you provide and promote to members must be just as relevant as the substantive resources and services your association delivers.

Given the volume buying power your association represents, members can often benefit greatly from volume-based rates and discounts as opposed to purchasing products and services, such as professional liability insurance or laptop computers, individually. In many ways, these types of savings can be quantified against the cost of membership and, in the best-case scenario, provide an exclusive benefit that would not be available outside the association membership. These factors can contribute to member engagement and, perhaps most importantly, retention.

The best way to understand the types of programs, products and companies of which your association's members have the strongest interest, you should consider devoting some research time to gathering insight on benefit/lifestyle preferences, patterns and characteristics.

Communication

Depending on the size of your association, you may or may not have primary responsibility for the internal and external communications of your organization. Nevertheless, understanding these principles will help membership professionals leverage collaboration on integrated communications strategies within the association or trade.

Association communications include any and all direct and indirect methods by which your organization conveys information and messages to your membership. Good communication is the glue that unites all components of the engagement model in promoting relevant value. Clearly, you do not want the latest trends, developments, or good-of-the-order work of your association to be the best-kept secret within your marketplace. In its most effective form, communication engages the member by fostering awareness, visibility, trust, loyalty, and understanding on a number of important levels. (See Chapter 17: Membership Communications.)

Relevant communication can be delivered to your association's members via direct internal channels or indirect external channels. Direct communication messages may be your magazine, web site, newsletters, and conferences—any way your association passes information directly to your membership. On the other hand, indirect external channels of communication are used to reach prospective as well as existing members through advancing your association's message, identity, and influence to the media, general public, legislative bodies, and other external stakeholder groups. Members expect not only that their association facilitate communication with them directly on a highly relevant level but also that their association engage key external audiences to strengthen the influence of and represent the interests of their profession or trade.

Of course, engaging internal end external audiences via communication is only half the picture. Effective communication hinges on having engaging and relevant strategic messages to convey. Core association messages do not emerge by mistake; rather they are the result of a deep analysis of the trends, issues, and needs of both members and the profession or trade your association represents. Effective messaging, sometimes referred to as "speaking the party line," depends on discipline, continuity, and repetition. Further strategic messaging must manifest itself within the other components of the engagement model to reinforce relevant value.

As with your association's resources and services, quality of communication is preferable over a large quantity of communication, so choose your messages, channels, and audiences carefully. For a breakdown of the types and levels of association communication, see Appendix 1: Communication and the Engagement of Members and Other Audiences.

Connection

A member's connection is the degree to which he feels an intellectual, social, and/or emotional sense of affiliation to your association. A feeling of connection can result in retention-building loyalty, but a sense of disconnection can create membership-ending alienation. To achieve a maximum level of member engagement, it is important for members to experience a solid, tangible connection while at the same time feeling a strong, intangible connection to your association.

A tangible connection appeals to the intellectual senses and relates to the quantifiable value of membership. The member believes the sum of resources, services, and benefits equals or exceeds the cost of money and time invested in membership.

An intangible connection appeals more to the emotional senses and involves capturing not only the minds but also the hearts of your members. Such a connection can be measured by how well your association is able to make each member feel as though he or she is a vital and recognized part of an organization that reflects and represents their individual interests, beliefs, and needs as a professional and a human being.

Your association has the opportunity to deliver on your relevant value proposition and foster a strong connection with members at a number of defining moments in their experiences:

Student Members. If your association's profession or trade involves a period of formal education prior to entry into the profession or trade, it is vital to capitalize on student memberships. Conventional wisdom suggests the first association to successfully engage a student will most likely win the individual for life. Because training for any career can be overwhelming, with students often wondering whether they will actually prevail in graduating, associations have the opportunity to demonstrate to students that there is not only light at the end of the tunnel but also a community of professionals to welcome and support them.

New Members. The first crucial moment of truth in engaging new members of your association is to connect with them promptly after they join. You want to not only extend a personalized welcome but also begin delivering relevant value immediately. Since it may take a while for the new member's address to hit your circulation list or there might be some time before the next issue of the association's publication, you can bridge the gap by including the most recent issue of the publication(s) in the initial new member welcome mailing.

First Year of Membership. For new association members, the days and weeks which follow the membership decision will be a defining period of time, as they are likely contemplating whether or not they made the right decision to join. During this period, expectations run high and lasting impressions are solidified.

The key to delivering on your association's relevant value proposition is to offer a new member welcome stream, consisting of a series of new member contacts in which your association continues to feed the member relevant resources, reinforce relevant opportunities, and deliver a strong message that membership was the right choice. The goal is to welcome new members and help them settle into their new association home.

Failing to connect with new members during the crucial first year not only risks retention but also may result in disaffection, with a disillusioned member making negative comments about your association to colleagues.

Self-segmenting Members. If a member selects a segmented area of interest on the membership application or at some later point, you should introduce him as soon as possible to the formal subgroups and/or resource channels that focus specifically on the selected segment area. You might send an email with a copy to the leader of the subgroup or ask the subgroup leader to contact the other member personally.

When a Member Reaches Out. It's important that all association staff understand that when a member contacts your office, although it may be one of many member calls of the day, it is always a defining moment for the member who is reaching out. Expectations run high, and often it takes only one negative experience to destroy the reputation of your association.

Customer/member service representatives not only should be trained to provide the highest degree of friendly service but also should be knowledgeable about every aspect of your association and prepared to make additional recommendations of resources, services, or opportunities that might be valuable to the member.

When a Member Pursues More Involvement. When a member seeks involvement, staff and currently active members and leaders must engage, connect, and welcome the member's participation. A process should be in place for orienting members seeking more active participation in the association, whether it involves serving on a committee, writing for the association publication, or becoming a candidate for office. A member may try only once to volunteer, making the attempt a defining moment in developing a deeper connection.

Celebrating Accomplishments. Whether an association accomplishment or an individual member's professional accomplishment, your association should never pass up an opportunity to acknowledge and celebrate. Celebration draws your membership into the organization in an exercise of pride and loyalty.

Retirement. Retired members represent a lifetime of knowledge and a schedule that affords them the opportunity to make a substantive contribution to your organization. Even more, the way younger members see you treat retired members is important as they work through their careers and make the decision to maintain membership throughout their lives.

Advisory Roles

Once you've established a relevant and meaningful connection with members, the next step in the engagement model is to convert them from satisfied members to advocates of your association who will carry the value and mission to others. Giving members an advisory role in the association empowers them with regular opportunities to provide insight and help shape the future of your association.

When a member feels both a tangible and intangible connection to your association, the desire to participate, or give something back, emerges. The degree of participation will vary depending on the nature of the member's personal and/or professional life. This phase of the engagement model represents a tremendous opportunity to turn loyal members into advocates of your organization who engage in word-of-mouth marketing. Personal testimonials can be the most powerful form of marketing because the message is usually coming from a trusted friend or colleague.

One of the easiest places to start is to find ways to place members in the position of trusted advisors whose feedback can make a difference in the association's work. It is one thing for your association to ask a connected member his opinion, but incorporating such opinions into action by creating new programs or benefits gives such members the role of advocate for their member colleagues. Granted, you can not base every association decision on the singular opinions of members, but certain types of decisions can be placed before connected members, achieving a prevailing consensus opinion.

Below are a couple of examples of how your association can create advisory roles for connected members.

Member Advisory Panel. A member advisory panel (MAP) is essentially a built-in "go-to" group of connected members who agree to provide their opinions and advice to the association by responding to periodic electronic association surveys. No further active involvement is necessary. Surveys can cover everything from in-depth membership perspectives to resource/service/product development. If possible, empowering members to influence association decisions can create a strong sense of ownership and loyalty. Here are examples of areas where you might seek the review and input of such panels:

- a new logo design
- a new web design
- a new publication format

- an association position
- new conference-related activities

Beta Test Groups. Contrary to a MAP, a beta test group is a small group of connected or targeted members who are selected to provide a hands-on assessment of an early version of a new resource, service, or product. Feedback from beta test groups

- Enables your association to fine-tune a product/resource concept so necessary modifications can be made to maximize the value of the final product

- Helps you fix potential flaws before a full rollout into your association marketplace

- Increases the likelihood of converting the beta tester to an invested word-of-mouth marketing spokesperson not only for the final product but also for your association

Beta test groups can be used to test web redesign, publications or products, mentoring programs, technology tools, educational programs, networking programs, and leadership development programs

Overall, the advisory component of the engagement model rests on the idea that the best way to create engaged members is to let them help you build the association. Such an investment of time and effort instills a strong sense of ownership in your association that translates into a higher degree of loyalty.

Community

Community is a destination, a supportive structural and substantive network within your association where individual member segments can access specific information, resources, opportunities, and a network of colleagues with a similar professional focus and orientation. Properly executed, all the other components addressed in the engagement model culminate in what every association strives to achieve—a strong sense of community.

One question your association should be asking is whether segmented membership subgroups are achieving their maximum potential in creating a unique home for your members that delivers relevant value and can be uniquely differentiated from your larger association. Your goal is for individual member segments to say, "Yes, this is my place and these are the people who can understand and meet my needs," in the same way a consumer relates to a particular specialty shop within a shopping mall, whether interactions occur in person or online.

Traditionally, the notion of community as well as the focus on individual member segments has been achieved by volunteer-led committees, sections, or interest groups. These entities act like mini-associations within the association, which is both good and bad. Good, because the entity serves as an assembly point for segmented member groups, but bad because they can become political and narrowly focused on only those members who are actively involved.

It is important to keep the interests of all active and passive members within each segmented area in mind when engaging in activities and developing resources.

This reality could be referred to as the 90/10 Rule, meaning that while roughly 10 percent of association members desire a more active hands-on role, 90 percent are more passive by nature when it comes to active involvement but still want to be in the community flow of information and resources pertaining to the latest trends and developments. To build community and engage the full spectrum of members, needs and interests of the often silent 90 percent must be served in developing relevant value at the individual member segment level.

Relevant Value and the Engaged Community

An engaged community is the result of relevant value being achieved by individual members via engagement model components. However, it's important to understand that an engaged association community is really a network of more narrowly specialized member segments that derive a high degree of relevant value in their unique membership experience.

The engagement model can be applied whether your association is just beginning to focus on member engagement or you simply need a starting point for re-engaging with your membership. While engaging members is not a science, it's important for membership professionals to understand the vital relationship between engagement and relevant value as it applies to the individual and collective components of the engagement model.

According to Don Peppers and Martha Rogers, in their book *Return on Customer: Creating Maximum Value from Your Scarcest Resource* (Currency, 2005), "To remain competitive, you must figure out how to keep your customers longer, grow them into bigger customers, make them more profitable, and serve them more effectively. And you want more of them." Getting and keeping members is the life of your association. Providing relevant value and engaging members is the key to keeping them.

Stuart Meyer is marketing, membership, and communications officer for the Emergency Nurses Association (ENA), based in Des Plaines, Illinois. Before joining ENA two years ago, he spent five years with the American Bar Association, where he served as director of marketing and member services for the Law Practice Management Section, associate director of the Section of Business Law, and director of the Section of Labor and Employment Law. He has been a member of ASAE & The Center's Membership Section Council since 2006. Email: smeyer@ena.org.

Communication and the Engagement of Members and Other Audiences

Membership communication includes all direct and indirect methods by which associations convey information and messages to its membership. Communication is the glue which unites all components of the engagement model in promoting relevant value. Clearly, you do not want the good work of your association to be the best kept secret within your marketplace. In its most effective form, communication engages members by fostering awareness, visibility, trust, loyalty, and understanding on a number of important levels.

Thus, communication is both a vehicle and a message. To better understand, examine the following breakdown of the types and levels of association communication as well as some specific strategies as it relates to the engagement model.

Continued on next page

Direct Internal Channels

Direct member communication involves activities geared to and directed specifically toward members.

Type	Overview	Examples	Strategies
Association-to-Member	Direct delivery of your association's information and messages to members via one-way print and electronic communication vehicles.	The president of your association delivers a monthly message to members via an audio cast. Your association announces a special new member benefit in a magazine issue. A news alert covering developments within a specialty area is issued electronically to a specific membership segment. An annual report is issued to all members regarding the financial health and vitality of the association. A personalized letter of thanks is sent to a member who made a notable contribution to your association's profession or trade. Minutes from the latest board meeting are posted to your association's web site.	**Personalization:** Whenever possible, find ways to personalize communications to your membership, whether it be an email broadcast or a mass mailing. Various fields of a communication can be specifically customized to include an array of personalized information. **Appropriate Vehicles:** Choose appropriate vehicles to convey association messages, such as email to convey news alerts or a dues bill to emphasize member benefits. **Segmented Communication:** As with all components of engagement, communication should be targeted toward specific member segments to deliver a maximum level of relevant value. **Transparency:** To every extent possible, your association should be forthcoming and transparent regarding the communication of information about its operations and management to foster member trust.
Member-to-Member	Facilitation of direct internal association communication between members often referred to as "networking"	A committee within your association reports on an important industry development via its quarterly electronic newsletter. Two members discuss an important industry development through a specialty message board or list server geared toward their specific member segment. A member mentor within your association receives an email from a new member who is just starting his career. Special meetings of member segment groups are held at all association meetings and conferences.	**Segmented Communication:** As with all components of engagement, communication should be targeted toward specific member segments to deliver a maximum level of relevant value. **Options:** Members should be given an array of options by which they can identify and contact members with a similar specialty or expertise. Technology offers many choices. **Foster Interaction:** Your association should proactively engage in activities, especially with member segment groups, to promote and foster member-to-member communication. **BLOGs:** Encourage leaders within member segment groups to start web logs (BLOGs) covering specialized topic areas and the shared experiences of professional life.

Indirect External Channels

Indirect member communication includes activities geared toward promoting the identity, awareness, and policies of your association to external audiences, which are witnessed indirectly by existing and prospective members. Ultimately, your association should find ways to communicate these types of activities directly to your membership via internal communication channels.

Type	Overview	Examples	Strategies
Association-to-Media	Pitching key association messages and information, to television, radio, interactive, and print media outlets as a means to increase public awareness and indirectly reach existing and prospective members and demonstrate how your association is promoting and representing their interests.	A media campaign pertaining to a strong association position or industry trends is launched, targeting national mainstream media outlets to raise awareness. An interview with your association's president is secured with a well-known industry trade publication. Local TV network affiliate broadcasts a news story profiling the positive contributions members of your association's profession or trade make within the local area.	**On being left out:** Whenever a media outlet publishes or broadcasts a story about your association's profession or trade in which the reporter did not seek the perspective from your association, always follow up with the reporter to provide additional information, offer interviews with key leaders, and pitch additional stories covering other angles. **Relationships:** As the strategy above suggests, it's vital to build mutually beneficial relationships with any reporter who devotes some or all of her attention to your association's profession or trade. Develop an understanding and respect for the constraints reporters work within and always be willing to provide additional background information and resources even if your association was not asked for a comment or interview. Patience and persistence pays off. **News Angles:** Potential news angles should be taken into consideration whenever your association plans activities. It's important to understand what constitutes newsworthiness and structure the substance and activities accordingly. For example, reporters are always on the lookout for new industry-related data, developments, trends, and fresh angles on widely publicized stories. Put another way, it's always important to have something new to say. **Rapid Response:** The business of information is fast-paced and the shelf life of stories is limited. Your association needs to be highly attuned to emerging issues/developments and be able to respond and advance association-specific positions/messages. **Experts-on-Call:** News stories are more likely to be narrow in scope. Your association needs to be prepared to quickly mobilize subject-matter experts to serve as spokespersons on narrow issues. Reporters are constantly working on tight deadlines and often need response within hours.

Continued on next page

Continued from previous page

Type	Overview	Examples	Strategies
Association-to-Public	Any communication program geared toward either the general public or certain segments of the public which indirectly reaches existing and prospective members in communicating the intrinsic value of your association to the public-at-large and instilling a sense of pride.	A national community safety campaign geared toward building awareness of particular association-related issues affecting the general public is rolled out at the local level. Groups of local members provide free services to individuals whose lives have been struck by tragedy. Easy-to-use online consumer information resources are made available to the general public to assist with complicated purchasing decisions, such as buying a first home.	**Grassroots Efforts:** Always involve groups of members at local levels in developing public outreach efforts. Not only will these activities inspire participating members, but it will also make them more likely to communicate accomplishments with their colleagues who may or may not be members of your association. **Media Outreach:** Public outreach programs should always include a media outreach component so that your association's efforts can be communicated widely in reaching existing and prospective members. **Conference-Related Service Projects:** While association conference schedules are busy, make time to provide organized public service project opportunities that bring members together to perform a few hours of community service. Such projects can be industry-related but certainly don't have to be, as any type of community service is positive.
Association-to-Governmental/ Legislative Bodies	Advocacy-based communication which promotes important legislative or regulatory issues or key positions of relevance to your association. Such advocacy engages members by demonstrating how your association is proactively representing their interests on key legislative and regulatory issues that affect their profession or trade.	A formal legislative briefing conducted by an association to advance its position and polices with lawmakers in support of legislation. Participation in formal legislative hearings conducted by legislative committees or subcommittees. Organized marches and rallies within the U.S. capital and/or state capitals to bring awareness to an association's position and policies in support of legislation. Grassroots lobbying efforts in which key association leaders interface with their elected federal and state officials to advance positions and policies in support of legislation.	**Grassroots Organization:** While powerful capitol lobbyists can be useful in forwarding an association's legislative agenda, the ability to generate an expansive grassroots organization across the state or country to build support through members interfacing with legislators within their districts and supporting their election/re-election campaigns is vital. The term "grassroots" simply means working from the ground level up. **Off-the-Record Agency Meetings:** Some agencies may be willing to meet with leaders from your association for an informal discussion regarding proposed or existing regulations in which communication would benefit both sides. Trusted relationships can make the difference in accessing these types of opportunities. **Political Action Committees:** Some associations have legal political action committees that provide financial and organizational campaign support to particular political candidates who are sympathetic to their legislative agenda. Such activity enables the association to garner the focused attention of the candidate during the campaign and, most importantly, once elected. **Lobbying and Governmental Relations:** Whether it uses high-profile influential members of your association or hired political insiders, your association should spearhead an ongoing lobbying and governmental relations efforts to monitor legislative developments and advance your association's agenda from the inside out in hopes of fostering and/or influencing crucial pieces of legislation.

Now take a closer look at specific types of communication vehicles and how they might be applied to each of the communication relationship levels noted above.

Type	Association-to-Member	Member-to-Member	Association-to-Media	Association-to-Public	Association-to-Governmental/Legislative
Email	Messages and information requiring rapid dissemination	Membership directories provide email addresses to foster easy member-to-member communication.	Media advisories, press releases, and supporting materials can be rapidly disseminated to your association's media contact list.	Association invites public to provide their email address to receive special consumer-level communication relating to your association's profession or trade.	Easy format for both your association and membership to contact legislators and key agency leaders en mass in advancing or defeating legislation or regulations.
Web site	Important association positions, messages, and current news should be highly visible.	Online membership directories should be available in members-only areas to foster member-to-member communication.	Electronic media kit should be available online, including general association information as well as official positions on issues and a backlog of current and archived press releases and news advisories.	Consumer-related information resources should be available either on your association's web site or a special consumer-centric web site.	Position statements and supporting materials should be accessible for legislators and agency staff as well as any other interested party. In addition, during periods of vital pending legislation or regulations, web sites might emphasize specific messaging campaigns.
Publications	All publications can be used to communicate specific messages to members, ranging from leadership-authored columns to important industry news. In addition, informational advertorials in outside industry publications can reach existing and prospective members.	Publications can include contact information for member-authored content for member readers who might be interested in a one-on-one conversation with the member author.	Reporters on your media list should be given complimentary subscriptions to your association's key publication(s) to keep them informed while communicating potential story angles.	In-depth journal articles reporting new industry-related findings affecting consumers can be communicated to the public via media outreach.	Copies of publications devoted to issues surrounding proposed regulations or important pieces of existing or prospective legislation could be shared with legislators and agency staff to communicate your association's position.

Continued on next page

225

Continued from previous page

Type	Association-to-Member	Member-to-Member	Association-to-Media	Association-to-Public	Association-to-Governmental/Legislative
Public/Media Relations	All successful public/media relations outreach yields media content which reach varying levels of existing and prospective members of your association are to inform and reinforce the relevant value of your association.	Potentially facilitates member-to-member communication, especially when particular members of your association are incorporated into media stories, which might lead to other members contacting them.	Communication outreach to media outlets that results in stories/coverage can actually create new story angles with and/or additional coverage from reporters who read, viewed, or listened to the story.	Important industry-related consumer information can reach relevant consumer segments via mass media communication stemming from successful public/media relations efforts.	Important association positions on issues as well as information key points can be communicated to legislators, legislative staff, and agency staff via respected mass media print, TV, and radio channels running stories stemming from successful public/media relations efforts.
Governmental Relations	Association governmental relations channels can utilize all relevant association communication channels to communicate important positions and legislative status updates to members.	Grassroots organizational efforts initiated by your association's governmental relations channels promote member-to-member communication regarding important issues and official association positions.	Formal press conferences and/or briefings conducted by the governmental relations wing of your association can advance your association's official position and recommendations on vital governmental and legislative issues.	Awareness-building communication campaigns can be geared specifically toward industry-related, consumer-affected audiences to build critical mass on vital governmental and legislative issues.	Lobbying and grassroots campaigns are designed to communicate and reinforce your association's position and recommendations on vital regulatory and legislative issues.
List Serves	General and member segment email list serve distribution lists can be used to rapidly communicate timely and relevant information to members.	Email list serve distribution lists offer the capability for member-to-member communication through email replies to the whole list serve or a direct response to the member who made a comment.	General and segmented media email list serve distribution lists can be used to rapidly communicate press media advisories, press releases, and other supporting information to media outlets and reporters.	Your association can invite the public to opt-in to special consumer-level email list serves to receive communication relating to important industry-related consumer news and alerts.	Email list serve distribution lists composed of either general or specific groups of legislators or agency leaders/staff could be created for the rapid and targeted communication of key association positions and recommendations relating to proposed regulations or pending legislation.

Type	Association-to-Member	Member-to-Member	Association-to-Media	Association-to-Public	Association-to-Governmental/Legislative
Message Boards	Can be used to either initiate message threads or respond to message thread postings as a means to communicate and promote official association positions, information, and/or access to member resources, services, and benefits.	Enables members to communicate one-on-one via highly relevant discussion threads by way of replies to individual message board postings.	For internal member communication only	For internal member communication only	For internal member communication only
Web Logs (Blogs)	Leaders of member segment association groups might create a blog to share experiences and perspectives relating to the member segment group and provide a source of interaction between the entity and members.	Your association can review and promote the existence of member blogs covering an array of topics as a means to facilitate one-on-one connection and communication.	Blogs can be useful to media outlets in gaining greater perspective on specific issues; however, it is important that any outside member blog that your association might promote include language that views do not necessarily represent the views of your association.	Blogs can be useful to the general consumer public, especially if such sites help translate industry-related issues affecting consumers into plain terms as well as provide an opportunity for such audiences to submit specific questions.	Exercise caution in the types of Blogs you might promote to legislators or agency staff/leaders, as you will want to be sure such sites reinforce your association's position and messages on key issues.
Chat Rooms	Key association leaders or staff could be made available for regularly scheduled interactive online chats with members to provide yet another medium for dialogue.	A prime opportunity for providing yet another communication medium for real time member-to-member interaction, especially if chat rooms are focused on individual member segments.	For internal member communication only	For internal member communication only	For internal member communication only

Continued on next page

Type	Association-to-Member	Member-to-Member	Association-to-Media	Association-to-Public	Association-to-Governmental/Legislative
Audio/Video/Pod Casting	Key association leaders at general and segmented levels could host regular programs on a host of relevant topics. For live events, technology can provide Q&A capabilities via the posting of instant messages, or simply use a dedicated phone line for questions.	Association promotes the availability of industry-related pod casts as a means to foster increased member-to-member communication.	Audio and/or video from key press conferences or leadership addresses geared toward media can be made available to relevant media outlets on-demand or via pod cast.	Special on-demand audio and/or video casts could be offered to industry-related, consumer-affected public audiences to educate and provide relevant resources.	Online briefings, whether a single topic or a regular series, could be made available to legislators, legislative staff, agency leaders, and/or agency staff. Rather than focus only on times when important legislation or regulations are pending, consider a series of regular informational briefings.
Annual Report	Association transparency has become an important factor with members. An annual report communicates all information related to the health and activities of your association in one concise package.	Association-to-member only	Association-to-member only	Association-to-member only	Association-to-member only
Meetings and Conferences	Meetings and conferences provide your association an opportunity to communicate and reinforce key messages, policy positions and important activities.	Networking is a key motivator in meeting and conference attendance. In addition to formal programs and sessions, it's important to offer informal activities that foster one-on-one member communication.	Meetings and conferences provide opportunities for your association to attract media outlets, building awareness and communicating key messages to external audiences. However, to attract media coverage, your program should include a strong emphasis on key newsworthy developments, providing fresh analysis/insight as well as high-level speakers.	Be sure to consider the delivery of industry-related, consumer-affected issue programs at meetings and conferences to communicate to the public via potential media coverage. Depending on your association's industry, you might even consider offering a public education session to the general public.	Ideally, if your association has close ties to either legislators or governmental agencies, you might consider hosting key leaders at your meeting or conference to participate in an interactive roundtable discussion or special keynote address with a comprehensive Q&A period.

Type	Association-to-Member	Member-to-Member	Association-to-Media	Association-to-Public	Association-to-Governmental/Legislative
Conference Calls/Teleconferences	An inexpensive, easy-to-access communication medium by which your association can conduct informational briefing or value-added education sessions pertaining to important association issues.	N/A	Key media contacts can be invited to listen to particular conference calls or teleconferences in which your association is disseminating its official association position on particular issues.	Whether by teleconference or a special consumer hotline, your association can communicate with your industry-related, consumer-affected public via telephone.	N/A
Billing	Regular communications to members should not be overlooked, as they provide opportunities to deliver specific association or benefit-specific communication. The use of buck slips or a special letter in invoices is a common means of communicating to members.	Association-to-member only	Association-to-member only	Association-to-member only	Association-to-member only
Robocalls	A quick and efficient way to communicate brief yet important messages to your association's membership.	N/A	N/A	N/A	N/A

As the tables above suggest, there are a variety of ways in which your association can directly and indirectly engage existing and prospective members via communication channels to convey relevant value. With so many options to choose from, it's important to focus on how integrated communication strategies can be used to advance key messages. Integrated communication involves combining all relevant communication channels and vehicles to maximize the dissemination of association communication.

Finally, as with your association's resources and services, quality of communication is preferable over a large quantity of communication. Therefore, choose your messages, channels, and audiences carefully.

Member-to-Member Recruitment

Lori A. Ropa, CAE

19

IN THIS CHAPTER
- The logic of member-to-member recruitment
- Understand your members
- Set goals and objectives
- Design program features and tactics
- Provide tools for success
- Develop rewards and recognition
- Measure your success and move forward

WHAT IS MEMBER-TO-MEMBER RECRUITMENT? In today's language, it's a form of "word-of-mouth marketing," and it's been around as long as people have talked to each other. Member-to-member recruitment can be the most effective and least expensive way to bring members into an association. Unfortunately, many membership professionals believe that word-of-mouth marketing should happen spontaneously as a result of member commitment and perhaps be motivated by a logo-laden flashlight or other promotional product given as a reward. The truth is effective member-to-member recruitment takes meticulous planning, a good deal of work, and some budget commitment.

The Logic of Member-to-Member Recruitment

Incorporating member-to-member recruitment as one component of growth strategy makes sense because:
- It's effective.
- It's relatively inexpensive.
- It results in improved retention rates.

- It allows association-wide participation.
- It engages members.

Effectiveness. No argument is more convincing than the one that comes directly from someone with experience:

- "The National Association of Fiddle Faddle is the best investment I've made in furthering my career. You should join!"

- "The networking opportunities are great. I got my last job because I knew someone else in the association who could get me hooked up with the right people."

- "The information I have access to as a member is invaluable. I couldn't do my job efficiently without the American Society of Hipsniffle."

Each prospect weighs the potential benefits of joining versus the expense and makes a value judgment based on that information. There is tremendous power in person-to-person value communication. Though your membership brochure may be excellent, it cannot convey the value of membership as clearly and directly as someone's personal story. If a prospect knows a member personally, and that member conveys the value of membership in the association, the prospect will likely agree.

Cost. Membership recruitment is an investment, and it's often one that associations are reluctant to make. Membership professionals are frequently faced with ever-shrinking budgets and increasing membership growth goals. Oftentimes those decisions are made by board members who believe so strongly in the mission that they know that, as in the movie *Field of Dreams,* "If you build it, they will come." Unfortunately, those days are long gone, and so the investment in membership has become even more critical.

Member-to-member recruitment is relatively inexpensive and has an excellent ROI. It requires far less of an investment than direct mail, trade show participation, or other media and is easily scalable to associations of any size and type.

Improved Retention Rates. Although no formal studies have been done to confirm improved retention rates, individual association data suggest that members brought into associations by other members are more likely to be satisfied and, therefore, stay longer. Increased member retention translates to greater growth, assuming that recruitment continues at the current rate.

Association-wide Participation. Membership staff traditionally has been responsible for recruitment. In that model, the Membership Department, which could have only a single staff person, carries a tremendous burden. If membership growth is a part of the association's strategic plan, it's to everyone's benefit to have a formal way for members to assist in achieving that goal. More people focused on recruitment and communicating the value of membership will result in more members being recruited. The membership staff designs the framework within which membership recruitment operates.

Member Engagement. Members who choose to get involved in some way tend to be long-term supporters of the association. Engagement comes in all forms, ranging from committee involvement to board participation, from manuscript review to giving presentations at conferences. However, such activities require a more intense time commitment than members can make. Member-to-member recruitment provides members a task-oriented, quick option for getting involved in the association in a meaningful way. If these members are rewarded appropriately, they will get satisfaction from their efforts and will continue to recruit new members to grow the association.

Understand Your Members

The first step in creating a successful member-to-member recruitment program is to understand your members. To create a program with impact, you must appreciate your members' perceptions and experiences and know what motivates them.

Perceptions and Experiences. Conducting interviews with members will give you personal insight into their reasons for joining the association. Their individual stories won't provide you with a statistically validated data source, but they will give you some great qualitative data. You'll be able to understand not only their decision process for joining but also their thoughts and feelings. Be sure to check your archives for the following:

- New member survey results
- Member satisfaction studies
- Focus group notes

These data will tell you in an aggregated and objective way why people joined the association and why they stay.

Find out how your members and their peers interact with one another. Spend some time with them and observe, or simply ask them questions. Are their experiences face-to-face? Do they participate in other work-related activities together? Are they extremely social or more reserved? Are they competitive with one another? Learning about your members' perceptions and experiences will give you the information you need to create tools to help your recruiters be successful.

Motivation. Most members choose to bring others into their association because they believe in the organization's mission and find value in its activities. If they don't hold these beliefs, no amount of recognition or gifts will motivate them to put their personal reputations on the line by convincing friends and colleagues to join.

Some members will recruit simply to evangelize. They need no other reward than the satisfaction of having a colleague join. Others require recognition and/or rewards to keep recruitment at the top of their minds. These members, who are by far the majority, are the members you have to work to keep engaged in word-of-mouth marketing; creating a relevant reward and recognition program is the best way to do that.

Set Goals and Objectives

No program can be successful without clearly defined goals and objectives. Your member-to-member recruitment program objectives must be measurable and designed to support the association's overall membership goals. Let's say that you've set a membership goal to "increase organization memberships by two percent." To support that goal, you should set at least one campaign objective around it. For example,

- Member-to-Member Campaign Objective 1: Increase the number of member recruiters who actively pursue organizations as members to 10 percent.

- Member-Member Campaign Objective 2: Each recruiter contacts at least three organizations about association membership.

Design Program Features and Tactics

Once you have defined goals, drafting your program will be easier than you imagined. Always keep in mind that your recruitment program should be designed to encourage recruiters to pursue new members in a way that supports your overall membership goals through your campaign objectives. If we use the example started above, a possible series could look like this:

- Association Membership Goal 1: Increase organization members by net two percent.

- Member-to-Member Campaign Objective 1: Increase the number of recruiters who actively pursue organizations as member to 10 percent.

- Program Feature: Increase recognition and rewards to members who bring in organizations.

If your members are particularly competitive, you also could build a high-profile competition feature into your program to support this objective. Members could compete to achieve the highest number of organizations or individuals recruited.

The program features will be incorporated into your tactics. To determine what those tactics should be, ask yourself, "How?" after reading the objectives. Your answers will likely serve as the tactical portion of your plan.

"How will I increase the number of recruiters who actively pursue organization members by 10 percent?" In the example shown in Table 1, we've chosen to use direct mail, provide increased recognition, collateral materials, and greater incentives for recruiters.

Provide Tools for Success

If members are going to be successful recruiters, they will need tools to help them. Membership professionals must design campaign support materials to ensure that recruiters can do the job you are asking them to do. Consider what you learned about your members early in this process. If you have information about what

Table 1. Association Membership Goal 1:
Increase organization members by net two percent.

Campaign Objectives	Tactics
1. Increase the number of recruiters who actively pursue organization members by 10 percent	• Conduct direct mail effort to past recruiters to encourage them to recruit organizations. • Provide expanded, high-profile recognition to recruiters who bring in organization members.* • Provide members with tools to convince organization members to join, including membership brochures, a FAQ sheet, and an organization benefits list. • Create greater incentives for members to recruit organizations.*
2. Each recruiter contacts at least three organizations about association membership	• Provide interested recruiters with a lead sheet of organizations in their area, including all contact information. • Organize chapter presidents to visit along with recruiters to increase the recruiters' comfort level in contacting the companies.

Tactics with an asterisk (*) directly support the feature described in the example.

members value, why they join, and how they stay satisfied, you can incorporate that into useful tools for recruiters. Useful tools you might provide include:

- Survey data summaries
- FAQ sheets
- Targeted membership brochures for the audience you wish to recruit
- Information sheets with membership benefits detailed and the value of those benefits defined
- Calling scripts
- Letters of introduction
- Easy-to-navigate membership web pages
- Copies of your latest periodical
- Leads
- Form letters
- Tips and tricks from other recruiters
- Rebuttals
- Forward to a friend email feature
- Mentor recruiters
- Membership training

The better-informed your recruiters are, the more likely they will be to approach prospects confidently and comfortably.

Develop Rewards and Recognition

Promotional products bearing the association logo may not be the best recruitment rewards. In fact, it is unlikely that there is any single best reward at all. Most people are motivated by a combination of factors. Create a system that combines recognition and rewards and reflects your membership's personality, interests, and values.

Recognition. People like to be recognized for their accomplishments, especially when those accomplishments benefit someone else. When the association benefits from an individual's effort, it is imperative that recognition be provided. This recognition should be appropriate to the level of achievement and take into account the general psychographics of the membership. Some ideas for member-recruiter recognition are:

- Regular web site updates with the top recruiters listed
- Newsletter feature spotlighting the "Recruiter of the Month"
- Awards programs
- Recognition at events
- Thank-you letters
- Letter recognizing the achievement to the recruiter's boss (with permission, of course)

Relevant, Tangible Rewards. The key to tangible rewards is relevance. Though generalizing is never 100 percent accurate, knowing your members' demographics and psychographics will be valuable as you decide what rewards your member recruiters might like to receive. Would your group of engineers like a stuffed animal with an association t-shirt on it, or would a uniquely designed calculator be more appropriate? What about cash or a choice of goods from a catalog? Airline tickets won't mean much to an association of pilots but they might be a terrific incentive for restaurateurs who want to travel to try new foods. The better you know your members, the more likely you will be to be able to select items that are truly valued and motivating.

Charitable Contributions. Some members are motivated by the promise of the association to support a charity or cause they believe in. This could mean a donation for each new member to your own association's scholarship fund or foundation or to a related or adopted charity.

Measure Your Success and Move Forward

No campaign is ever complete until you've measured results. Since you set goals and objectives and defined tactics, measuring your success will be easy. Here are a few simple steps for measuring your success.

1. Review your original plan.
2. Run the appropriate reports to determine whether you achieved your objectives through your tactics.
3. Survey recruiters about the program and learn how they felt about it.
4. Make any changes to get ready for next year.

Member-to-member recruitment programs can be excellent investments in your association's growth. By putting time and effort in to a comprehensive plan, you will see results.

Lori A. Ropa, CAE, is director of affiliate operations at the National Foundation of Dentistry for the Handicapped in Denver. Lori has more than 18 years of nonprofit management experience and served as the lead subject matter expert for ASAE & The Center's Membership Boot Camp Course. Email: lropa@nfdh.org

CD-ROM Contents

THE CONTENTS OF THE accompanying CD-ROM are intended to provide users a sampling of documents, spreadsheets, and other tools that some organizations are using in creating and executing membership strategy, calculating membership budgets, recruiting and retaining members, hiring membership professionals, and more. The files could be used as starting points or to generate ideas for creating your own documents and tools. The files should not be considered as legal guidance, and users should evaluate the applicability of any recommendations in light of their particular situation. Because each organization and situation is unique, users should seek legal review and guidance for any areas that pose legal dangers or might increase their liability.

In addition, while the organizations have given ASAE the right to reproduce the documents for this CD-ROM, unless otherwise noted in the document, the organizations have not given users permission to use the graphics and artwork in the documents, or to copy the text of the documents.

List of Forms

1. ABA Drop and Renew Member Email (PDF)
2. Affinity Agreement Application (PDF)
3. Affinity Agreement Template (PDF)
4. AMS Functional Checklist (PDF)
5. Expired Dues Notice (PDF)
6. First Renewal Email (PDF)
7. General Membership Brochure (PDF)
8. IADD Member Drop Survey (PDF)
9. IADD Membership Recruitment Plan (PDF)
10. IADD Renewal6-07 (PDF)
11. IDS Dues by Payroll and Grants (PDF)
12. InfoComm Membership Dues by Membership Type (PDF)
13. List Rental Sample Policy and Sample Order Form (PDF)
14. Mailing List Rental Agreement (PDF)
15. Marketing Brief Form (PDF)
16. Member Get a Member Letter (PDF)
17. Member Prospect Inquiry (PDF)
18. Member Recruitment Budget Spreadsheet (PDF)
19. Member Relations Director Job Description (PDF)
20. Membership Application (PDF)
21. Membership Director Job Description (PDF)
22. New Member Call Sheet (PDF)
23. New Member Welcome Letter (PDF)
24. Membership Renewal Strategy (PDF)
25. NJSCPA Renewal Phone Call Scripts (PDF)
26. Renewal Email with Contest Incentive (PDF)
27. Renewal Notice Schedule (MS Excel)
28. Renewed Membership Budget Calculation Spreadsheet (MS Excel)
29. RFP for Association Management System (PDF)
30. Sample Renewal Campaign Pieces (PDF)
31. Six Month Contact Letter
32. Thank You for Renewing Email (PDF)
33. Trade Dues by Unit Manufactured (MS Excel)

Index

A

Acquisition metrics, 157–161, 168
Active member involvement prospectus, 214
Administrative staff, 66, 68
Advertising, 178
Affinity programs, 21–22, 47–48, 215
Assessments, 90
Asset audit, 14, 15
Association management systems/ customer relationship management (AMS/CRM), 97–106, 124
Asynchronous technologies, 19–20

B

Benefit(s), 10, 11 13, 16–18, 77, 87, 176
Beta test groups, 219
Bias, types of, 39

C

Certification, 3, 17
Chapters, 18, 75, 76
Charitable contributions, 3, 5, 236
Chat rooms, 20, 227
Communication(s), 47, 67, 189–200
  audience, knowledge of, 189–190
  channels, internal and external, 222–224
  direct mail, 158, 159–160, 168, 178
  in a global marketplace, 192–194
  integrated marketing communication (IMC), 196
  member access, ensuring, 142–144
  in member recruitment and engagement, 46, 215–216, 221
  in membership renewal, 141, 185–188
  member-to-member, 222
  models, 196
  positioning, 195–196
  segmenting, 199–200
  trends, adapting to, 194–198
  vehicles, types of, 19, 20, 67–68, 197, 212–214, 225–229
Community, 18–21, 198–199, 219–220
Conference calls/teleconferences, 20, 51, 229
Confidentiality, 112
Core purpose and motivation, 2, 5–6
Cross-selling, 69–70
Customers, 34, 55, 58–59

D

Data. *See also* Membership data
  audits, 110
  entry and processing, 47, 102, 103–104, 116
  integrity, 114
  inventory, 109

key terminology, 127
  mining, 36, 127
  overload, avoiding, 112
  privacy laws affecting, 112
  security, 109, 112, 115
Direct mail, 158, 159–160, 168, 178
Dues
  billing and remittance of, 79–80, 229
  first-year discounts, 173–174
  increases, 85–87
  installment payment options, 175
  linking to member benefits, 77, 87
  membership terms, 80–81
  preparation and transparency, need for, 88
  pricing structures, 74, 76–79, 83–85
  reporting revenues from, 82
  restructuring, 87–89, 92–95
  uncollected, 147

E

Engagement, 46, 205–220
  advisory roles, 218–219
  affinity programs, 215
  communication, 215–216, 221
  community, 219–220
  connection, 216–217
  insight, 210–211
  member-to-member recruitment, 232–233
  organizing web sites for, 131–133
  relevant value and, 206–207, 220
  resources and services, 211–214
  segmentation, 207–209

F

Federations, 3, 75
Feedback, 69, 70
Finance department, 67
Financial management and budgeting, 145–153
  accounting methods, overview of, 145–148
  cash flow, 150–151
  internal controls, 147–148
  invoicing and collections, 148–149
  projecting revenues, 149–151
  revenue mix, 151–153
  training budgets, 52–53
  uncollected dues, 147
Focus groups, 36–37, 210
Foundations, 3, 5

G

Gap analysis, 14, 16
Geographic scope, 4
Globalization, 192–194
Golden handcuffs, 17

"Good of the order," concern for, 4, 6, 215
Governmental relations, 224, 226

I

Individual membership organization (IMO), 74–75
Initiation/application fees, 90
Integrated marketing communication (IMC), 196
Interest groups, 18
Internal Revenue Code [Section 501(c)(3), Section 501(c)(6)], 5

L

Lapsed members, 148
Lifetime value (LTV), 128–129, 161–163
Listservs, 19, 226
Lobbying, 3, 5

M

Mailing lists, 19, 48, 61–62
Market identification, 30–31
Marketing, 17, 54. *See also* Direct mail
  media, compared, 177, 178
  membership data and, 117–118, 127–129
  for membership renewal, 185–188
  for new member acquisition, 117–118, 160–161
  promotional tactics, 176–177
  for recruitment, 47, 175–176
  word of mouth, 178, 196–197
Market intelligence, 211
Market penetration, 128
Market share, calculating, 125
Meetings, conferences, and trade shows, 66, 228
Member advisory panel, 218–219
Member-Get-a-Member programs, 178, 203
Member participation, 14, 25, 53–54, 59
Member satisfaction, 129
Member service concierge, 214
Member service, providing, 46, 55–60, 163–164
Membership cards, 142
Membership categories, 17, 74–76, 78, 79, 90
Membership data
  access to, 115
  best members, identification of, 122
  CEO's perspective on, 121–129
  collecting, reasons for, 107–108
  evaluating and maintaining, 110–111, 113
  management of, 109–110, 114–115
  marketing and, 117–118

matching priority products and
    services to members, 123
programming languages, 115
recruitment and, 118–119
reporting, 116–117, 127
sample record types and uses, 111
tracking, 119
updating and validating, 113
value of, 119–120, 122
what to collect, 111–113
Membership department, v, 48–50, 65,
    66–71
Membership directories, 9, 135–138
Membership professional, duties of, 6,
    7, 45–48
Membership renewal. *See also* Retention
    anniversary vs. calendar cycle, 80–81,
        141, 154
    calculations, 155, 156, 164–166
    grace period, 141–142
    invoices, 141
    methods of payment, 187–188
    notices, frequency of, 186–187
    online, 148–149
    rates, 166, 183
    sample contact schedule, 187
    sample timetable for, 80
    segmentation and, 186, 209
    slippage, 81
    tracking, 183–185
Membership research, 25–43
    areas of inquiry for, 30–34
    association performance assessment,
        32–33
    competing influence assessment, 33–34
    defined, 26
    establishing a strategy for, 27–30
    importance of, 26–27
    market identification, 30–31
    market research, types of, 35–36
    membership environment assessment,
        31–32
    methodologies for, 35–38
    optimal research infrastructure,
        creating, 42
    outcomes, identification of, 26, 27
    research audit questions, 43
    research consultant, using, 41–42
    researcher, responsibilities of, 40–41
    results, analyzing and presenting,
        39–41
    survey deployment and analysis, 38–42
    tools used for, 36–38
Membership segmentation, 17, 66–67,
    117–118, 186, 207–209
Membership staff, 16, 45–46, 48–50, 54,
    62, 63–64, 65, 68–69
Merger and acquisition fees, 90
Mission, v, 9, 11, 56, 59

N
Networking events, 9, 12
New member(s), 29, 46, 67, 139–140,
    168, 173–175, 217

O
Organization types, 3, 74–76
Orientation programs, 46
Outsourcing, 70–71

P
Peer-to-peer connections, 4, 18
Porter's Five Forces, 33–34
Predictive modeling, 211
Professional development and training,
    3, 4, 51–53, 135
Publications, 67–68, 209, 212, 225
Public/media relations, 223–224, 226

Q
Quality standards, 2, 4, 114

R
Recency/frequency/monetary value
    (RFM) analysis, 117
Recognition and rewards, 46, 142, 218,
    236
Record management, 47
Recruitment, 46, 171–180
    ideal member, 118
    incentives and special offers, 173–174
    marketing strategy for, 47, 175–176
    membership package, 173
    member-to-member, 231–237
    promotional tactics, 176–177
    target market, determining, 171–172
    testing and tracking, 177–180
    using membership data for, 118–119,
        127–129
Relevant value, 206–207, 220
Retention, 58, 181–188. *See also*
    Membership renewal
    benchmarking, 182–185
    communicating value, 185–188
    factors influencing, 46, 182–183
    membership steady state, calculating,
        181
    and member-to-member recruitment,
        232
    rate of, 29, 81, 169
    schedules, 109
    using membership data for, 127–128
Return on investment (ROI), 6, 12–13,
    17–18, 160, 177
Revenue, 149. *See also* Dues
    mix, 151–153
    nondues sources, 54, 73–74, 90, 151
    projecting, 149–151

S
Sales, 48, 53–55, 178
Sections, 75, 76
Self-segmenting members, 217
Shadowing, 210
Silo mentality, 68–69
Surveys, 14, 202
    bias, 39
    deployment and analysis, 38–42
    membership department, role of, 47
    salary, 9
    single-topic, 210
    target audience, 38
    types of, 37–38
Sweepstakes, 174
Synchronous technologies, 20

T
Tax-exempt status, 3, 5, 21
Trade association, 3, 75
Training. *See* Professional development
    and training

U
Unrelated business income tax (UBIT),
    22, 151
U.S. Chamber of Commerce, Survey
    on the Future of the Competitive
    Association, 121

V
Value, new definitions of, 10
Value proposition, 7–23
    auditing your programs and identifying
        gaps, 13–16
    creating and segmenting new benefits,
        16–18
    defining mission-critical benefits, 8, 13
    determining what you want to be to
        members, 8–9
    determining who you are to members,
        7
    evaluating affinity programs, 21–22
    fostering communities with
        technology, 18–21
    quantifying value and members' ROI,
        12–13
    understanding and articulating, 9–11
Vendors, 34, 66

W
Web sites, 202, 213, 225
    member self-service, 48, 98, 105, 134,
        144
    target audiences, 132–133
    uses of, 131–133, 135, 190–192, 209